THE TRIAL
WAR ROOM
HANDBOOK

G. Christopher Ritter

Amie J. Bailey

Michael Skrzypek

**Defending Liberty
Pursuing Justice**

TORT TRIAL & INSURANCE PRACTICE SECTION

Cover design by The Focal Point LLC/ABA Publishing.

Page layout by Quadrum Solutions.

Library of Congress Cataloging-in-Publication Data

Ritter, G. Christopher.
    The Trial War Room Handbook: Effective Strategies From the Trenches by G. Christopher Ritter, Amie J. Bailey, Michael Skrzypek.
        p. cm.
    Includes bibliographical references and index.
    ISBN 978-1-61438-421-2 (alk. paper)
    1. Trial practice—United States. 2. Law offices—United States. 3. Trial practice—United States—Psychological aspects. 4. Lawyers—Job stress—United States. 5. Lawyers—United States—Handbooks, manuals, etc. I. Bailey, Amie J. II. Skrzypek, Michael. III. Title.
    KF8915.R58 2011
    347.73'7—dc23
                                    2012014347

www.ShopABA.org

16 15 14 13 12   5 4 3 2 1

Contents

Dedications

To Jill Stevenson Ritter for her love, patience, and support.

–G. Christopher Ritter

To my friends and family, of whom I am merely a reflection of the love and support I receive from them each and every day. And to anyone who has ever written even part of a book. You have my empathy.

–Amie J. Bailey

To my wife, Meredith, and daughter, Alice, for whom I do what I do, and for my mother, Danuta, without whom I could not have done anything.

–Michael Skrzypek

Acknowledgements

It may seem to those that have never written a book that the process only involves one or two people, usually an author and an editor. We are here to tell you that it takes a host of people to bring a book to fruition, and we have many to thank for helping with The Trial War Room Handbook.

First and foremost, we thank the American Bar Association for seeing the need for a book of this type, and agreeing to publish it. Additionally, without Rick Paszkiet, Sandra Johnson, and their editorial team, it would not be as good as (we think) it is. We would also like to thank the team at Quadrum Solutions for their expert typesetting, and working with us to create a truly great looking book.

Lillian Koponen is solely responsible for all of the illustrations included in this book, along with the cover design. Lillian has lent her considerable talents to The Focal Point for over 20 years at the time of this publication, and working with her is always an absolute joy. You can see the clarity of her design sense in every graphic she works on, and we are very proud to feature her work here.

Without Susan Davis, who worked tirelessly with us to solidify themes, create outlines, and give us the jumping off point for the text, we would never have gotten off the ground. Her talents are always welcome, and her efforts are endlessly appreciated.

Jill Kustner would be a welcome addition to any editorial team, and we are extremely fortunate to have her on ours. A style and grammar expert with a powerful red pen, Jill's contribution to this book is inestimable. She makes us look great, and somehow makes the editorial process enjoyable. That alone proves that she is worth her weight in gold.

Without the tireless efforts of Sarah Tolai, we would not have had the time needed to make sure that the book was ever written. Her deft scheduling allowed us to focus on the work, her skillful negotiations with others needing our time created space for everyone to excel, and her tireless support got us to the finish line without injury.

We would be remiss in not thanking each and every person who works at the Focal Point. Their dedication to great storytelling, commitment to excellence, and general camaraderie are what brings us to work every day. Here's to you: Yousif Abdelaziz, Brian Bakale, Richard Cho, Joel de Berry, Michelle Z. Diago, Dennis Duong, Katie Gabriel, Kathryn Golden, Chris Grimm, Guy Grogan, Scott Hilton, Ina Lim, Malcom Lowe, Jason Lundy, Hem Ching Mai, Dan Martin, Kate McEntee, Maureen McGraw, Paul Roberts, Chris Sizemore, Andrew Spingler, Linda Spingler, Aaron Stienstra, Carolyn Webster, Shelley Woo, and Jeremy Young.

Lastly, we want to thank our clients for making us a part of their teams, day in and day out, for over 1500 trials. Their commitment to the law and to their clients is admirable, and we are privileged to have been a part of some of the most ground-breaking litigation of our time in a wide range of venues across the nation. Every chance to work alongside them is a new opportunity to learn, improve, teach, and work for the common good, all rolled into one.

CHAPTER 1

Overview

If you have picked up this book, we can predict five things about you:

1. It is highly probable that you are facing a major adversarial event of some kind. Most likely it is a trial. But based on how legal practices are evolving, it might also be something else, such as an arbitration or a Markman hearing in a patent case.[1]

2. If you are a lawyer, you know (or at least strongly suspect) that preparing and organizing for trial will require expertise beyond what you learned in law school. Of course, you will use all of the persuasion skills associated with writing briefs, researching the law, and presenting the evidence. Yet given the nature of any trial, you will also need a level of practical advice and organizational ability beyond what you use in your everyday practice.

3. You suspect that a "war room"—which is basically a place specifically set up to prepare and support your efforts in court—will improve your chances of things going smoothly and, one hopes, successfully.

---

1. Whatever your particular adversarial event, for purposes of this book we will refer to it as a "trial." Likewise, we will refer to the place where this event takes place as "court" or the "courtroom." Unless we expressly state otherwise, the principles outlined in this book are equally applicable, regardless of the type of adversarial event, the subject matter of the dispute, or the location where that event takes place.

4.   You have a lot of pressing questions about how you (or someone on your team) should set up and run this war room.

5.   You do **not** have the time to wade through a lot of text searching for answers to your questions or to learn the best ways to proceed with very real, very practical, and very immediate problems.

Who We Are

We can predict one more thing: you probably are asking yourself, "Who are these people, and can they really give me the advice I need?" The answer is "Yes." Collectively, the three of us have been to trial several hundred times. We are very experienced trial participants and war room managers. Moreover, because of our different types of expertise and experience, we can provide you with the diverse perspectives and know-how needed for creating and running war rooms.

For the first 20 years of his legal career, **Chris Ritter** tried cases and taught trial practice in law school. For the past 10 years, he has been a partner at The Focal Point LLC, where he has worked with many of the country's best trial lawyers developing trial strategies and graphics for hundreds of high-profile cases. He also is the author of two of the American Bar Association's best-selling books on these subjects, *Creating Winning Trial Strategies and Graphics* and *Powerful Deliberations: Putting It All Together for the Jury.*

Michael Skrzypek (pronounced sha-PECK) is The Focal Point's Trial Presentation Department manager. In that role, he (or one of his team members) sets up and runs the equipment that trial teams need to be successful in war rooms and courtrooms throughout the United States. He and his team

also develop databases that allow lawyers to show the exact document, video deposition clip, or demonstrative they need at precisely the right time. In addition, he has spent countless sleepless nights in war rooms alongside tired (dare we say sleep-deprived and sometimes irritable?) lawyers and witnesses, making sure that practice sessions are productive and that the trial presentation goes off without a hitch.

Amie Bailey is The Focal Point's production supervisor. She is an organizer and coordinator extraordinaire. At any one time, she can be working on up to six different trials in six different venues. She makes sure that what needs to be at the war room and in the courtroom is there before anyone even has to ask. Then, while the trial team is drinking (either in celebration or in commiseration) after a verdict, Amie is making sure that everything and everyone gets back to where it/he/she is supposed to be. She is widely known for somehow making the impossible possible.

What We Have Learned

Over the years, when it comes to organizing, setting up, and running war rooms, we have done lots of things right and, admittedly, some things wrong. In response, we have systematized the good processes and learned from those that went awry. The systems outlined here are effective whether we are working on a civil or a criminal case, on a straightforward dispute or a highly complex series of cases, and with a two-attorney trial team or one blessed with 20 support staff.

We hope Mr. Tolstoy will forgive us for comparing a war room to his opening line in *Anna Karenina*: "Happy families are all alike; every unhappy family is unhappy in its own way." But the comparison is apt: all successful war rooms are successful in similar ways, while an unhappy or stressful war room is difficult in its own special way.

Happy and unhappy war rooms alike, however, are bound by one universal law: something will inevitably go wrong. Your laptop battery will die. Your projector suddenly will not work. Moments before trial starts, the judge will uphold the opposition's objection to your opening graphics. Or a key member of your war room team will get food poisoning. (Yes, this actually happened in one of our war rooms and explains why to this day we jokingly [only partially] advise our fellow staff members, "No 'fresh' seafood unless it is really fresh.")

We cannot tell you how to handle every kind of crisis, but we can teach you the basic principles that will help prepare you for these inevitable disruptions skillfully and effectively. Equally important, we will give you tips on how to set up and create a war room that keeps the unavoidable turmoil to a minimum, sustains rather than depletes your team members, and works toward the result you want: a win in court.

Why We Wrote This Book

Most lawyers go to trial once every couple of years, which makes it hard for them to accumulate the experience it takes to put together and run a war room successfully. Here at The Focal Point, we are more or less constantly in trial. As a result, we get hundreds of questions every year about how to get things set up for trial and how to make things run smoothly in the courtroom itself.

We believe these questions have right answers and wrong answers. We also believe that, depending on how you answer these questions, your life will be either a lot easier or a lot harder. We wrote this book to teach you about the former and help you avoid the latter.

What You Will *Not* Find in This Book

This is not a scientific analysis of war room methodologies, complete with excessive citations and footnotes. In fact, we are not even sure that such a thing exists, and if it did, we question whether it would be that helpful. Instead, we have chosen to create an informal, easy-to-read, quick-reference guide for readers who either are in the planning stages of their trial strategy or need answers **now**.

What You Will Find in This Book And on Our Website

We know that many attorneys get so busy preparing for trial in a strategic sense that they think they do not have time to prepare for trial in a logistical sense. We wrote this book to help you avoid, or at least minimize, the problems associated with this quandary.

To that end, *The Trial War Room Handbook* includes four different types of resources:

1. Answers to two key questions:

What is a war room?

A war room could be anything from a suite of rooms to a desk in your office. It is the place where you and your trial team (colleagues, witnesses, and consultants) can go any time of day to focus and get things done for trial.

How do I set up and run a successful war room?

The balance of this book addresses a variety of questions— some very serious and others less so—that deal with the who, when, where, how, and why of setting up and running a successful war room. For example:

- Who should staff your war room?
- When should you start planning your war room?
- Where should you set up your war room?
- How should you configure your war room?
- Why is a bag of peanut M&M's your team's best friend at 2 A.M.?

We have divided the main text this way so you can scan the table of contents, find a section that deals with a particular question you may have, and then get a succinct (or relatively succinct) answer.

2. Numerous sidebars and topical asides

Throughout the book you will find quick-hit sidebars that address the good, the bad, and the really ugly of what works and does not work when you have a team of people working around the clock on a high-pressure trial for days on end.

3. Quick-reference appendices

Obviously, we hope you will read this entire book. Nevertheless, we are very familiar with handling complex issues when, as we like to say, "your hair is on fire." To be clear: we do not favor constantly operating in such a stressful environment, but we do know that trials often force you to do so. Consequently, we have tried to condense as much of this book as possible into quick-reference appendices organized by Chapter that you can consult quickly when you have no time to do anything more.

The appendices include the basics of what you need to know, whether it is what equipment to bring to your war room, what materials you need to load into your database, or just what the person in charge needs to keep in her back pocket.

4. *The Trial War Room Handbook* website

As a supplement to this book, we have developed a website devoted specifically to war rooms at www. thetrialwarroomhandbook.com. We hope that you will visit the site to read blog posts about war rooms, learn about emerging trial technologies, utilize the many resources we have created and made available for your use, and join the conversation with the best and the brightest in the industry.

Visit us at www.thetrialwarroomhandbook.com for an ongoing conversation about war rooms, as well as additional tips and tools for trial preparation.

Who Can Use This Book

Anyone involved in your trial can use this book: lead attorneys, paralegals, associates, secretaries, those who have never been to trial, and those who have been to trial scores of times. That being said, the primary person who can use this book is the one who will be running the war room (who we later refer to as the "Sergeant Major"). This individual needs to understand both the "big picture" of war rooms and the myriad details of their setup and management. All of that is included in the following pages.

A Couple of Things We Hope You Notice About This Book

First, in addition to talking about many of the technical aspects of running a war room, we spend considerable time talking about attitude. That is because running a war room effectively is as much about an attitude of preparation as it is about the nuts and bolts of implementation. In other words, how people work together and how they communicate is a key component of how effective your war room will be.

Second, our book features a certain lightness of tone and respectful humor. Trust us, we take trials and the activities associated with them very seriously. Some of the most challenging periods of our professional lives, in fact, have been spent either trying cases or helping others do so. At the same time, we have consistently found that the best war rooms—meaning those with the most successful results, both in and out of the courtroom—facilitate teamwork, reward respectful behavior, and spontaneously burst into laughter on occasion. We sincerely hope that this book will help turn your war room into one that is as effective and smooth-running as these.

CHAPTER 2:
War Room Basics—Asking the Right Questions

When a client walks into our offices at The Focal Point and asks "Do I need a war room?" our response often surprises them. Since we routinely help set up and staff war rooms throughout the country, potential clients seem to assume we will say, "Why, of course!" Instead, we inevitably (but politely) shrug our collective shoulders and say, "It depends." Then we pepper them with a series of questions, such as "What do **you** mean by a 'war room'?" "Who is going to be working on the case prior to and during trial?" "Who's going to be in charge?" and "What do you need to do when you get to court?"

We ask these questions for three reasons. The first is obvious, the second more subtle, and the third is for an entirely ulterior motive.

The first, most obvious reason: Every trial is different. There is no stock answer as to whether someone needs a "war room" or even what the term means. Asking these questions helps us determine what is needed for a particular case.

The second and more subtle reason we ask these questions is because the answers tell us a lot about the person or trial team responding. There are no "right" or "wrong" responses to our questions. However, the answers do let us know how well prepared the trial team is and how much experience it has. Both factors are important to consider.

There is nothing nefarious about the third reason we ask these questions, but we admit to having an ulterior motive in doing so. Specifically, we want to force our clients to step back and plan their

9

logistics for trial. In some instances, this is the first time they do so in any kind of meaningful way.

This Chapter focuses on questions—the questions you need to ask yourself and your team whenever you start assembling a war room. Obviously, we cannot answer every question you may raise as part of this inquiry. Instead, we want this Chapter to serve two broad purposes: (1) to give you some basic information so that you can at least start a dialogue (both internally and with your team) about your logistics needs; and (2) to direct you to places in this handbook where you can begin to find some answers.

Strategy Versus Logistics

In order to win, you (or others on your team) need to plan both your trial **strategy** and your trial **logistics.** These crucial elements of every case are different. **Strategy** is your line of attack. It is what they teach you and test you on in law school during trial practice classes (e.g., "What is the case theme?" "What is the story?" "Which witnesses will you call?" "In what order will they testify?").

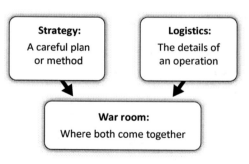

Logistics are rarely taught in any formal setting, much less in law school. Logistics have to do with how you are going to implement your trial strategy: creating trial graphics, presenting video clips, preparing witnesses, and making sure your entire team is well fed throughout trial. You often only learn these crucial skills in the heat of the moment during trial—and then what you really learn is what **not** to do next time (e.g., allocate less than an hour to fix a graphic to which opposing counsel objected; send your trial tech into court without breakfast; send your key paralegal home before a verdict is announced). This is unfortunate, because you will rarely get the verdict or other result you want without having fully developed both your trial strategy and your trial logistics.

Most trial teams decide they need a war room when they step back and acknowledge an important truth: "If it is going to work in the courtroom, it has to first happen in the war room!" No matter how brilliant your argument or how extensive your evidence, if you fail to practice your opening statement or create a space for witness prep, at some point you will undermine your own best efforts.

Some of our clients do not bother with a war room because they believe that their case probably will settle, so they view these efforts as a waste of time. Statistically, that is hard to argue with, as the vast majority of cases never get to the courtroom. Nevertheless, we have seen considerable harm result when trial teams delay planning the necessary logistics for trial. Let's face it: some cases that should or could go away do not. In such instances, the resulting delay means that an enormous amount of work must be done to get ready in a hurry. Consequently, both the costs and the chances that something will go wrong increase substantially.

We rarely see a downside in planning ahead, even if you are relatively sure your case will settle. French mathematician Blaise Pascal summed up the wisdom of such an approach when he explained to his atheist colleagues why he went to church each Sunday. Pascal admitted he did not know what would happen when he died. If there was no heaven, he reasoned, going to church had done no harm. But if there *was* a heaven, he "gained all." While we leave religious arguments to others, we see considerable merit in applying Pascal's approach to war rooms. That is, it does not hurt to plan ahead, even if there is no trial. And if there is one, you will experience considerable gain.

Pascal's wager:	Trial happens	Trial does not happen
I prepare	Potential favorable verdict	Minor cost in time & planning
I do not prepare	Probable defeat	Negligible savings in time & planning

First Key Question: What Is a War Room?

In our view, a war room is a space that you set aside to prepare for a major legal event. Most war rooms are set up in anticipation of a milestone in a case. Typically this is a trial, but it can be an arbitration or a major hearing, such as a Markman in a patent case, a preliminary injunction hearing in a trade secret case, or a significant summary judgment hearing.

Often these milestones require attorneys to stand up in court, present actual evidence, and speak knowledgeably and persuasively—all of which requires intense, focused preparation. War rooms provide a place to do this work, no matter what event you are facing.

More specifically, a war room is the place where you can

concentrate and plan. It is far away (psychologically, if not always physically) from the day-to-day distractions of home and office. We call this, with apologies to Virginia Woolf, "A War Room of One's Own." War rooms also are places for entire teams to gather to work out key case themes, theories, and critical next steps. They are inner sanctums, if you will, where teams craft case strategies and make major decisions both before and during the heat of trial.

At the outset, we want to make it clear that when we talk about a war room, we are **not** talking about some specific layout or space plan. You can set up your war room in a series of hotel suites near the courtroom or on a table in the corner of your office. The point is, a war room is a specific place (regardless of actual size or proximity to court) that you *consciously set aside* and *conscientiously maintain* as the location to which you go in order to do what needs to be done for trial.

The size of the event notwithstanding, more often than not it behooves you to at least consider whether you need a war room. Ask yourself if you need a place where you can get away from distractions, where you can store all of your materials, where you can reflect, and where you can confer privately with others on your team. And ask yourself if you need a place that is specifically designed for one project only: getting ready for trial.

A war room is not just a place to get away *from* it all. It also is a place to *go to* so you have everything that is essential to your case. It is a place (regardless of budget) where you and your team (regardless of number) organize and store what you need for trial—from staplers, pens, and snacks, to copiers, trial exhibits, and deposition transcripts. It is the one place you know you can go any time of the day to focus, because everything you need is there.

You set up and use a war room to accomplish something very specific. It is a special time and place to concentrate, collaborate, and execute your legal strategies. It is a place to get, and stay, on point.

Clearly, having such a space is helpful not only for practical reasons but for psychological ones as well. A war room is a place where you and your colleagues work collectively as a team and form the personal bonds necessary to endure the tribulations of trial. Psychologically, it is the place you go each morning just before court to put on your "game face." Equally important, it is the place where you can take *off* your game face when you return from court and are ready to focus on what is needed for the next day.

Second Key Question: How Do I Set Up and Run a Successful War Room?

If, upon reading the prior section, you are left thinking "Yes, I *do* need a war room," your next question should be "How do I set up and run a successful one?"

Unfortunately, this is not as simple a question as it may first appear. Instead, it leads to a series of other questions. Lest that seem complicated, let us assure you that just asking yourself these questions serves a crucial function: it increases your chances of operating a successful war room because you are forced to consider (and reconsider) all of the possible contingencies and to anticipate all of your possible needs.

For example, thinking about how many workstations you need may remind you that you have not yet hired someone to synchronize your video depositions. Asking questions about how war room personnel might best help the lawyer present her case may convince your team to use a projector and screen to display graphics, instead of a flipchart or whiteboard. Or thinking about where to house everyone during trial can remind you to advise a key witness of the new trial date and when he may be needed.

In the broadest sense, these additional questions fall into five categories: Who, When, Where, and How?

"Who" questions

Your war room is nothing without the right staff—in both the courtroom and the war room. Simply assessing the number of people who will be working on the case is not enough, though. You must also consider:

- "What is each of these people likely to need in order to do his or her job, in terms of both support and supplies?"
- "Who is my intended audience?" because that determines what to do and bring to the war room.

For a more detailed analysis of how these and similar issues affect your war room, turn to Chapters 3, 4, and 8.

"When" questions

The big "when" question—one of the first we ask any potential client—is "When is the trial?" Heading to trial next week will have profound effects on the viability and scope of your war room. We are not saying it cannot be done, but there are limits (physical and often budgetary). If your event is four weeks, six weeks, or, better yet, eight weeks away, you can do a lot more, and at a more comfortable pace. Other "when" questions include "When should I set up my war room?" and "When do I need to set up my equipment in the courtroom?" You can find answers to these questions in Chapters 5 and 9.

"Where" questions

Location is key to figuring out what kind of war room to set up and how best to run it. The "where" questions include "Where is the trial being held?" (i.e., "Will I need hotel rooms for my staff?" and "Where will I set up the war room?") plus "Where is my staff located?" (e.g., "How will they get there?"and "How long do they need to stay?"). We discuss location, location, location in Chapter 6.

"How" questions

Of all the questions we are asked about war rooms, we probably field more "how" questions than any other. These range from very general inquiries, such as "How do I determine what size exhibit boards I should use in court?" to highly technical and specialized ones, such as "How do I change a lightbulb on my state-of-the-art projector?" or, even more seriously, "How do I create a trial presentation database?" While many of the more specialized and individualized questions are beyond the scope of this general handbook, we do cover some of the biggest and most common ones, including:

- "How do I set up my war room?"
- "How do I run and manage the war room?"
- "How much is this going to cost?"
- "How do I make one of those databases that organizes all the materials I want to show in the courtroom?"
- "How do I set up in the courtroom?"

We discuss these and other "How" questions in Chapters 7 through 11.

CHAPTER 3:

Who Is Your Audience?

As we discussed in Chapter 2, this book draws a (sometimes artificial) distinction between two different yet intensely connected groups:

- The *strategic* team—those people who focus primarily on making the record in the courtroom at trial; and
- The *logistics* team—those people who work behind the scenes and in the war room to make sure that the strategic team has what it needs to accomplish its goals in court.

While these teams may perform different functions, and sometimes have different immediate areas of focus, it should not surprise you that one of the first questions each team must consider is: "Who is our audience?"

When members on the strategic team answer this question, they most often focus on the ultimate decision makers. Typically, these could be:

- A judge sitting as the sole "finder of fact" during a bench trial
- A judge presiding over jurors who are charged to reach a final verdict
- One or more arbitrators in a binding arbitration.

Obviously, "the decider" is an important audience. But as we will see, while the strategic team may focus almost exclusively on these ultimate decision makers, the logistics team also must focus on a second and very important audience—the court's support personnel. Employed by the judicial system, these crucial people do the necessary and often difficult work of making sure that court proceedings run smoothly and effectively.

Both audiences are important. In fact, we would go so far as to say your entire team can damage your case—and certainly make trial life more difficult—if anyone on your team (whether strategist or logistician) ignores either crucial audience.

Your First Audience: The Ultimate Decision Makers

The answer to the question "Who is deciding my case?" will have a subtle but important effect on your logistics and activities in the war room. As a general rule, the presence of a jury (as opposed to a judge or panel of arbitrators) often complicates matters, and not just because it means your strategic team has more people to convince.

For example, you may need to produce 12 copies of material for evidence binders (one for each juror), as opposed to a single copy for the judge. Likewise, judges who might be willing to be a bit lax in applying rules of evidence when they are the sole finders of fact may be far stricter when a lay jury needs to make similar decisions. This often results in an accelerated exchange date for graphics, advanced designation of video deposition testimony, and other restrictions or requirements that necessitate additional forethought and personnel in the war room.

Knowing who the final decision maker is also can affect how you present your material during the proceeding, which in turn affects who needs to be part of the war room team and what equipment you may need to bring. Again, the presence of a jury tends to complicate what needs to be done both in and out of court. For instance, if you decide to display your exhibits and demonstratives electronically, presenting to a jury often requires more equipment and prior preparation. What might be a single monitor for a bench trial could suddenly become a dozen, with one for every two jurors, plus one for the judge, the witness, opposing counsel, your team, your tech, their tech . . . as you can imagine, this makes things more complex.

Jury trials are not the only venues that present challenges. For example, arbitrations tend to be held in conference rooms, which are not usually designed for adversarial or "court-like" proceedings. These rooms are long and narrow and rarely offer an appropriate place for a witness stand or a podium for counsel.

Arbitrators often encourage the parties to forgo opening statements, relying instead on written pre-trial briefs to learn about the dispute. Some arbitrators will not permit any direct examination of witnesses, and will rely instead on written reports or written declarations for this form of testimony. In such instances, the only live testimony may be cross-examination, which may include a disproportionate amount of impeachment, using either printed or videotaped deposition testimony. In this example, you will need to consider how the team will help the lawyer display this material, in a constantly changing environment that requires the lawyer to respond dynamically.

Arbitrations can seem to go on for forever, with arbitrators starting and stopping proceedings to accommodate the different schedules of each arbitrator. Even once the evidence is submitted, the arbitrators may wait weeks before scheduling closing arguments or ordering the parties to make final arguments by way of written submissions. As a result, your logistics team needs to figure out, for example, how it will create a portable war room that can be set up and taken down repeatedly, or left dormant for extended periods of time.

The immediate point of this Chapter is not to provide solutions for each of these challenges; instead, much of what you need to know is covered in subsequent sections of this book. At this point, we merely want to get you thinking about how the ultimate decision maker in your case may affect the logistics team and its efforts in the war room.

Your Second Audience: Courtroom Support Personnel

Your second audience is made up of the people who staff the courtroom, who are also very important to your case. All members of your team, be they strategic or logistic, need to understand who these people are, what roles they play, and how best to approach them. That's because no matter how good your evidence, how tight your strategy, how perfect your graphics and video clips, if one of your team members offends, say, a court deputy, your entire case can get a lot harder.

Who's Who in the Courtroom

While the number, type, and responsibilities of key courtroom personnel will vary, they often include:[2]

The judge's courtroom deputy

This staff person oversees virtually everything that happens in the courtroom, both when the trial is in session and when it is not. Best described as the "stage manager," the courtroom deputy makes sure that courtroom business happens in a timely and efficient manner. While exact responsibilities will vary, most courtroom deputies do the following:

- Perform crucial administrative tasks such as courtroom calendaring and scheduling
- Maintain the case file which, if necessary, will eventually be the core of the record on appeal
- Prepare minutes of the trial proceedings
- Process orders
- File important documents
- Coordinate courtroom setup (e.g., determining where your audiovisual equipment can be placed and when you can do so)

---

2. See the "Career Profiles" page of the U.S. Courts website (http://www.uscourts.gov/Careers/CareerProfiles.aspx) to learn more about the important role of courtroom support personnel. While the information focuses on federal courts, it is an excellent introduction for most courts.

- Organize and keep track of exhibits, including making the crucial record of whether something has or has not been formally admitted into evidence

- Keep the judge informed, including (informally) how your logistics team members are behaving or not behaving in the courtroom

- Support the judge during jury selection (e.g., making sure that questionnaires are distributed and collected)

- Schedule when other court personnel (e.g., court reporters and IT specialists) and court equipment (e.g., projectors, screens, or monitors) are available during trial

- Maintain contact with the lawyers and the logistics staff throughout the trial, including during emergencies and during that final, nerve-wracking period when the jury is deliberating

The staff attorney and the judge's law clerks

These staff members often sit in the courtroom throughout the trial and assist the judge by:

- Conducting legal research and analysis for the judge

- Initially deciding whether an issue warrants immediate and extraordinary legal attention by the judge or can wait to be heard in the ordinary course

- Providing initial (and sometimes the only detailed) analysis of filings on behalf of the court

- Drafting legal memoranda and proposed opinions and orders for the judge

- Initially deciding which jury instructions may be used

As you can infer from the above descriptions, the staff attorney and law clerks inevitably have legal training. In fact, staff attorneys often are experienced lawyers who have made a career of working for the court. Many have considerable experience in the private sector. Law clerks often are recent law school graduates who have decided to gain additional experience for a year or two prior to going into private practice or academia.

MIND YOUR PS AND QS

A lot of debate surrounds the etymology of the phrase "Mind your Ps and Qs!" (Is it a reminder for drinkers to tally up their "pints and quarts" at the local tavern or a reminder for typesetters to double-check their set?). But one thing is for sure—it's really good advice in the courtroom. Forgive the Ann Landers routine, but it's worth saying that good manners are important in all situations, and even more so when you are in front of the judge and jury. If you are not used to courtrooms, or if some team members are novices, make sure everyone knows the following:

R.E.S.P.E.C.T.: Find out what this means to the judge before you get to the courtroom. Check the court's website for local rules and talk to colleagues who have appeared before her about the judge's pet peeves.

Tempus Fugit: Time does fly when you are speeding toward a critical deadline, but we cannot stress this enough: Be. On. Time. Or better yet—be early.

Total turnoff: We know many are tempted to just leave their cell phones on "silent" when in court so they can check their emails or calendars. Just make sure you know how to truly silence your phone, as some have alarm functions that can override silent mode, and some vibrate so powerfully that others can hear it. The safest move is to power down rather than risk the judge's ire or have the jury find out your ringtone is Kiss's "Rock and Roll All Nite."

Lookin' sharp!: In these times of varying dress codes and "business casual" at the office, it can be easy to forget that a courtroom is a very formal place. In fact, it's one of the last truly formal public places. Pay it the respect it requires. Dress in formal business attire and make sure that everyone on your team does the same.

> *Scents and sensibility:* We have all been overpowered by someone's perfume or cologne. Remember that your job is to sway jurors with your sense, not your scents.
>
> *When in doubt, do not.* If you are unsure as to whether it is okay to do something in court, just do not do it. Unless it's an emergency, wait for a break to ask team members a question or resolve an issue.

The strategy team will have more contact with the staff attorneys and law clerks than people based in the war room. Unlike the courtroom deputy, who is constantly in the courtroom, staff attorneys and law clerks are in and out. Unfortunately, because of this, some logistics teams forget about these pivotal staff people and do things that easily could be seen as being rude.

For example, many times we have seen logistics people set up the courtroom in a way that inconveniences the staff attorneys or law clerks by, say, putting equipment in the clerk's work space or making it impossible for him to see what is going on during trial. Likewise, we have repeatedly watched logistics teams (clearly on the other side, never ours) fail to bring enough copies of important material from the war room to the courtroom so that the staff attorneys and clerks have their own copies of key documents. Such silly mistakes can be remedied easily, provided the logistics team remembers and respects the courtroom personnel.

The court reporter

As far as we are concerned, the court reporter must be some kind of magician. He sits quietly in court absorbing everything that is taking place and somehow create a verbatim record of the courtroom proceedings, capturing everything that is said (sometimes simultaneously) by the judge, the witnesses, and the lawyers. Traditionally, reporters did this using either shorthand or stenotype, which typically requires that the court reporter record up to 250 words per minute. Certain jurisdictions, however, are exploring other methods of obtaining accurate records, such as sophisticated recording devices and speech recognition systems.

Most commonly, the war room team will deal with the court reporter on such important topics as:

- Obtaining real-time or expedited unofficial transcripts produced immediately during the proceedings (check to see if your court will accommodate or offer this service and how you can access it).

- Obtaining official transcripts on an expedited basis, usually for special occasions or emergency legal proceedings. For example, an attorney may need an accurate copy of what was said by a witness during trial for purposes of impeachment or as part of the attorney's closing argument. Less frequently, the war room team will need to get certified (official) copies of the record for emergency filings with courts of appeal.

Prior to the start of trial, someone from the war room should introduce himself to the court reporter and determine the procedures that the reporter likes to follow.

The IT/AV specialist

As courtrooms build in various forms of trial technology or gain access to equipment that rotates among courtrooms as needed for particular cases, these specialists, who are in charge of courtroom trial technology, are becoming more common. Whether you decide to use the court's equipment or bring your own, you will likely need to coordinate your logistical effort with the court's IT/AV (information technology or audio-visual) specialist. By the way, these folks can be your best friend in court, especially if a court-owned piece of equipment malfunctions or, worse, breaks.

Just as the level of sophistication of court-owned equipment will vary, the level of experience of the IT/AV specialist will vary from venue to venue. Some courts, primarily in the federal jurisdiction, employ such specialists full-time. Others have someone who is available either part-time or on an as-needed basis. Still others rely on outside contractors or other court personnel (often the courtroom deputy) to handle this aspect of trials.

Whatever level IT specialist your court may have, the war room team needs to be willing to lend all necessary assistance to make sure that your particular trial runs smoothly. Once you know exactly where your trial will occur, schedule a call with whomever is responsible for courtroom technology. Such scheduling is often done through the courtroom deputy in her role as overall manager of the courtroom.

During that initial discussion, ascertain what equipment is available, determine if you need to bring additional equipment, and solicit whatever assistance the IT/AV specialist may provide to your team. Then, if possible, have a knowledgeable member of your team test the courtroom's equipment to make sure it is of sufficient quality; Is the projector bright enough? Is the screen big enough? Does the Elmo project in color or only black and white? If you cannot test the equipment, then try to get the model numbers of the equipment and look up the specifications online. Finally, if you need to reserve equipment through the court, do so as early as possible and reconfirm that you have what you need well before you show up for the first day of trial. (For additional information, see Chapter 9.)

Other key personnel

Other staff members with whom the logistics team may have contact:

- *The jury administrator,* whose job is to recruit, qualify, and make available a large enough pool of potential jurors so that a jury can be seated at the conclusion of voir dire. If your team administers a "jury questionnaire" as part of voir dire, you may need to coordinate with the jury administrator.
- *The case administrator,* whose job is to maintain the official case file from the time the plaintiff files his complaint up to the case being assigned to a particular judge for trial (at which point the file is often transferred

to the courtroom deputy), and then once again after the trial is complete and appeal is pending.

Some special observations about courtroom deputies

While everyone deserves respect, the courtroom deputy often deserves a double dose. As one of Chris's early mentors explained to him when he first started trying cases, "See that person over there? That is the courtroom deputy; she is definitely **not** someone you ever want to piss off." Another of Chris's mentors told him that he would know he was in trouble when the courtroom deputy shot him "that look—you know the one . . . and if you do not, you will, the instant you first see it."

The courtroom deputy is nearly always a career position, and many deputies serve with the same judge for years. As such, most deputies are incredibly loyal to "their judge" and have a powerful incentive to make sure that everything is done smoothly and consistently in "their courtroom."

The feeling, by the way, is mutual. Many judges will freely tell you that they would be entirely lost without their courtroom deputy. As such, most judges are very loyal to their deputies and will almost always support whatever decision he or she reaches. You would do well to respect this relationship.

It is fair to say that if you have questions, the courtroom deputy will know the answer or can tell you who will know. Whatever logistical issue you may have, the courtroom deputy, who has overseen scores of trials in your specific courtroom before your particular judge, will have faced that issue before. That means she will have a suggested solution or a tried-and-true way of doing things. She also will know what the judge prefers, so you need to ask politely and listen very carefully to her suggested solution.

When dealing with the courtroom deputy, we recommend the following:

- **Be respectful.** Assume you are dealing with the judge whenever you deal with the courtroom deputy. You may be tempted to be less formal or more flippant; do not be.

- **Ask, do not tell.** Approaching the courtroom deputy (or anyone, for that matter) in an entitled frame of mind rarely gets you anywhere. We all know that asking for something rather than demanding something is a far better way to get what you need. Remember, the courtroom deputy does not work for you, and you are on her home turf.

- **Be careful.** While it is not the job of the courtroom deputy to be a tattletale, assume that the judge will hear about any major screw-up or disrespectful action by either trial team. Of course, news of war room teams that go out of their way to be respectful and adhere to the court's preferences will also reach the judge's ears.

- **Remember (and this is very important):** The courtroom deputy is your conduit to the judge. In many jurisdictions it is considered improper for anyone associated with a trial to approach the judge directly. During trials, lawyers often are required (even when the judge is only a few feet away) to hand documents to the courtroom deputy, who quickly reviews them and then hands them to the judge. The war room team needs to respect this general rule, too. If you need to deliver something to the judge, give it to the courtroom deputy. There is a practical reason for this, by the way—often the courtroom deputy is required to stamp or otherwise do something with the document before the judge can see it. There also is a potential ethical reason for doing so. One of the courtroom deputy's roles is to help protect or insulate the judge from improper *ex parte* (private one-on-one) contact with someone working with one of the parties. Respect this. Even if you are delivering something as simple as a routine list of equipment that needs judicial approval before being brought into the courtroom, you need to go through the courtroom deputy. No one will fault you for doing so, but not respecting the judge by approaching her directly can get you into lots of trouble.[3]

- **Be professional.** Some courtroom deputies are friendlier and less formal than others. It is not unusual for members of the logistics team to develop close and long-standing professional relationships with certain deputies—relationships that extend past any particular trial and allow these team members to seek advice informally between trials or in advance of your next appearance before a particular judge. To the extent that you can do so properly, work to develop such a relationship. Deputies are a fount of knowledge. Nevertheless, always remember that this is a professional relationship and needs to be maintained as such.

- **Avoid making special requests.** The courtroom deputy's job is to remain neutral toward all parties. If you need to make a special request, even a minor one, try to get the other side to agree with it first and then have representatives from both trial teams approach the courtroom deputy together. This process will increase your chances of getting what you want. It also will eliminate any fear the courtroom deputy may have of not being fair to all parties.

- **Be prepared.** The courtroom deputy may refuse your request. You have to be ready to accept that response gracefully. Courtroom deputies will often refer to the place where the trial takes place as "my courtroom"— and it is. If you are in doubt, ask permission or make a suggestion, but be ready to accept whatever answer you get. If you truly believe that the answer you get is wrong

---

3.   Let us be clear: we are not suggesting that judges are ogres. The majority are very friendly and, when court is not in session, informal. The point is, unless and until the judge expressly indicates that it is okay to deliver material directly to him or to directly ask him questions, deal with his deputy.

(for example, you justifiably believe that a flat-screen monitor is better placed in a different part of the room), **and** you truly believe that this issue matters, proceed with caution and a great deal of deference.

- **Work it out.** Try to get the parties to solve their problems before seeking assistance from the courtroom deputy. It is not her job to play referee (or, worse yet, traffic cop) between competing logistics teams. Inevitably, the way your team wants to do something may differ from what the other side wants to do. Do your best to get those involved to come to an agreement before seeking aid from the courtroom deputy.

- **But still ask for help when you need it.** Because most courtroom deputies have considerable experience, they have likely seen your issue before. They know what has and has not worked in the past and, perhaps even more important, they know what the *judge* believes has worked or not worked in the past.

- **Do not be a pest.** Make your questions count. Keep a list of ongoing questions so you can ask them all at once or at the appropriate time. This minimizes the perception that you are bugging the poor courtroom deputy every few minutes.

DEALING WITH JURORS

*Handle jurors with polite caution. Treat them with civility, but as if they were strangers. Obviously, you do not want to do anything stupid in front of them, like talk about the case or make disparaging comments about the other side. Less obvious, it is best not to have **any** conversations in front of them. Your charming story to a colleague about your darling 3-year old may be entirely innocent, but if overheard by jurors, it could be mistaken as some form of less-than-subtle pandering. In fact, for this reason judges*

*frown on anyone (including staff in the war room) having
what may even **look** like routine verbal exchanges with
jurors, including wishing them "Good morning." Your
safest course of action is to say nothing to them and,
without appearing rude, curtail all discussions in front of
them.*

*How do you avoid appearing rude? Follow basic
manners. For example, if a group of people, including a
juror, is walking toward a door and you would ordinarily
open the door for them, go ahead and open the door. If that
same group is walking toward the elevator and you would
ordinarily push the "open" button to let them board, do that
as well. Just avoid any contact until the case is over.*

*If, after the verdict is read, you see a juror, avoid
approaching him. If he wants to approach you, that's fine;
some jurors are completely happy to talk with you about
the verdict. Others do not want to have anything more to
do with the case and want to get home. Respect this. For
goodness sake, do not in any way disparage the jurors who
did not see the case your way. Whether you like the result or
not, these people fulfill a very important role in our delicate
judicial system and should be treated with the utmost
respect.*

- **Work together.** The longer and more complex your trial,
  the more likely two things will happen: (1) you will need
  to rely on the courtroom deputy's expertise; and (2) you
  will risk the wrath of the deputy for doing something
  wrong. At the outset of the case, schedule a meeting
  where a representative from each side's war room team
  can meet with the courtroom deputy to iron out as many
  issues as possible. This does not have to be a formal or
  long meeting. But ask such fundamental questions as:
  When is the courtroom open? Where is the best place is
  to store boxes of documents that need to be kept handy

but may not be needed for trial immediately? And how many extra copies of material does each side need to bring for filing or distributing to the judge and other court personnel?

- **Designate.** If you have multiple law firms representing numerous parties, assign a single person to be the contact person for that side. Make it that person's job to communicate with the courtroom deputy.

- **Maintain your credibility.** As we will repeat throughout this book, all of your trial team is connected in the court's eyes. A screw-up or example of disrespectful behavior by one member (whether that person is part of the strategy or logistics team) will reflect negatively on the whole team. Likewise, positive actions by individual members will inure to the entire group's benefit. If you promise to deliver something at a particular time, do it. Without fail.

- **Do not forget to ask about emergencies.** Inevitably something unexpected happens during trial. Unfortunately, sometimes these events are genuine emergencies (e.g., the testifying witness or questioning lawyer becomes seriously ill). The courtroom deputy is likely to be your contact if you need to advise the judge of such events. Find out in advance what the judge and deputy expect you to do in such an instance.

- **Be cooperative.** Do everything you can to make the courtroom deputy's life easier. One of the most important things you can do is to find out how she likes to handle exhibits. Many have preferred methods to designate which exhibit is being sponsored by which party (e.g., all of the plaintiff's exhibits are numbered starting at 0001 and all of the defendant's start at 1000). Some courts require that courtroom deputies physically mark such exhibits a certain way. Often someone on your team can do this work in advance, which not only makes the trial move faster but also makes the courtroom deputy's life a little easier.

Is it possible to inadvertently upset courtroom personnel? It is, and it does happen. But by understanding the roles of each staff person and respecting their experience and power, all members of your team are more likely to keep your case—and your client—in a favorable light during trial.

CHAPTER 4:
Who Should Be There?

Your most valuable assets walk into the war room every morning and walk out of it (not too late, we hope) every night.

Obviously, we are referring to everyone on your trial team.

But an important question for any war room is "Who should be there?" It is essential that you accurately answer this question if you are going to come up with the **right numbers** for your war room (e.g., "How many hotel rooms do we need?" "How many chairs?" "How many breakfasts/lunches/dinners?"), as well as the **right mix** (e.g., "Do we need more paralegals?" "Do we need a trial tech or a graphic artist?" "What's our most effective combination of support staff?"). Picking the right number and mix of people to staff your war room can mean the difference between it running like a well-oiled machine and it squeaking to the finish line like the Tin Man after a rainstorm.

Who Is Going to Be in the Courtroom?

When we ask "Who should be there?" the word "there" refers to two locations: (1) the courtroom and (2) the war room. While the focus of this book is on the war room, in order to get the **right numbers** and **right mix,** you need to begin your analysis by examining who is going to be in the courtroom and what each of these people will likely need or want by way of support.

The principal characters in the courtroom will be:

- The client or client representative

- The lawyers
- The percipient witnesses
- The expert witnesses

Obviously, other members of your team—the paralegals, the trial tech, even your messenger—will be in court on occasion, but let us hold off discussing them for now.

We separate out the client, the lawyers, and the witnesses for special consideration because they are likely to take more out of the war room than they will give back. We do not mean this in a negative way. Instead, we are merely acknowledging what should be obvious: much of what the logistics team does in the war room is done to support those who are in the courtroom. The trial tech, for example, may be working to create impeachment video clips to give to the lawyers to take into court for a particular cross-examination. Similarly, the graphics consultant may be creating a series of demonstratives that the expert witness can use to educate the jury about an important technical issue.

COMMUNICATIONS BETWEEN THE WAR ROOM AND THE COURTROOM

While the lead attorneys are in the courtroom trying their case, the war room team will be in the war room, working on the case. The teams will need to communicate, which is not always easy. Before we offer suggestions, remember the cardinal rule: Do nothing that violates court rules or in any way disrupts court proceedings.

Here are some options for when you really need to get in touch:

1) Email text, or IM from the courtroom: If you really need something from the war room, and your courtroom has wireless Internet access, you can ask your trial tech to send an email, text message, or instant message. Make sure the laptop

> screen is private, the sound on the computer is
> turned off, and that you log off when you're done.
>
> 2)   Cell phone: No, you cannot make calls from the
>   courtroom, and you should not even be texting.
>   But during breaks you can step out of the
>   courtroom and call your war room team.
>
> 3)   Pass a note: This is a time-honored tradition in the
>   courtroom. Give a handwritten note to a member
>   of your team in the gallery. Just make sure you do
>   not create any kind of disturbance!
>
> 4)   Transcript: If you want to update the war room
>   team on what is going on during the trial, ask for
>   a live-feed transcript to the war room (you will
>   need to find a vendor to provide this).

Figuring Out the Needs of the Strategic Team

Merely tallying the numbers and names of the people who are going to be in court is not enough. Do not forget that each person's needs will be different because of:

- His personal preferences
- His particular role in court
- What he can reasonably be expected to contribute outside of court hours in the war room (this varies depending on his experience, seniority, and available time)

For example, the needs of a senior partner (in this scenario: 55 years old, courtroom-savvy, technologically challenged) will likely differ from those of a junior associate (25 years old, never been to court before, and a technological whiz). Correspondingly, the junior associate will be expected to provide considerable assistance in the war room, while the senior partner who is trying the case will provide little war room assistance.

Likewise, not all witnesses require the same amount of attention. Therefore, you need to adjust your analysis accordingly. While both percipient and expert witnesses may need your help securing hotel rooms and transportation, percipient witnesses tend to need much less support in the war room than do expert witnesses. The latter, for example, may have an elaborate set of demonstratives that the graphics consultants will create in the war room and the trial tech will display in the courtroom.

Our point is that it is not enough to just count the number of people who will be working on the case; you must also consider what each individual is likely to need in order to get her job done. To determine this, you need to corral key participants (people you *know* will be going onsite with you, whether it is just you and your paralegal, or your three partners and a team of support folks) well in advance of trial. And you need to push them to think (often for the first time) about what they will need in the war room.

We use the word "corral" for two reasons. First, it can be hard to get some of these people to sit down and meet for any extended period.[4] Second, some of these people may find it difficult to think so far in advance of trial, or they may not be willing to commit to what they need in time for you to make a meaningful assessment. Nevertheless, you need to help them see that the time they spend discussing these matters with you is time very well spent.

Interviewing the Strategic Team

Once you have your strategic players together, get ready to ask a lot of questions and be politely persistent in getting the answers you need. The kinds of things you should be asking them include the following:

---

4.   Some people refer to the difficult task of bringing busy people together to focus on one thing as "herding cats." Chris sometimes refers to that same task as "herding trial lawyers."

- *What are they expecting by way of support?* Bear in mind that whatever estimates you get can be wildly inaccurate. While every lawyer is different, we have found that most lawyers tend to underestimate how much time and help they need. This is probably an indirect compliment to the lawyer's staff, which may insulate her from needing to know how things actually happen. But it is also further evidence (as we discuss below) that, when in doubt and you can afford to do so, err on the side of providing more resources, not fewer.

- *Whom do they see as being vital to the trial efforts?* Ironically, the very same lawyers who can instantly zero in on and dissect a crucial strategic point well in advance of trial will often stare at you blankly when you ask them this question. To help them answer accurately, you should be ready with three follow-up questions:

  o Is there any specific person (by name) that they feel needs to be there?

  o Is there any type of person (by category, e.g., trial technician) that they feel should be there?

  o Is there any special project (e.g., cross-examination by video clips) that they think needs to be done for trial?

- *What did they do/need in prior trials?* To the extent that the past can help predict the future, take advantage of this information, with two important caveats:

  o First, remember that every trial is different, and what was done earlier may differ substantially from what you need to prepare for now.

  o Second, find some of the people who actually worked in prior war rooms with these team members to confirm that what you were told is accurate. This is important. It is amazing how different recollections can be. The lawyer who tells you that there were no problems at the trial he did a year ago with only one paralegal may not know about the 36 hours during which no one slept because the team was under-staffed.

- *What services do they typically rely on in the home office?* We are creatures of habit. When someone works in a war room, he will likely look for and want the same kind of services he has at his offices when he is not in trial. If he normally has access to and takes advantage of a pool of administrative assistants that are available 24 hours a day, he will likely need similar support at the war room. While it is not always possible to duplicate these services away from the office, knowing this information will give you an idea of what the strategic team might need and expect.

- *What are their typical work hours?* Do they work well into the early morning hours or do they religiously get all of their work done early enough to get a solid eight hours of sleep each night? The answer to this question helps you confirm that you have the right number of support people available and at the appropriate times, consistent with when presenting attorneys will need them.

- *When will they need support?* Stand-up comedians and war room planners both know that timing is everything. As you assess who needs to be part of the war room team, do not forget to ask, "When will you need these people?" Just knowing when the trial starts is not enough information. Trials have a natural ebb and flow. While you never know for certain, you can often predict when you will most likely be busy and need additional staff (e.g., a few days prior to opening statement, during your case in chief, just before a key cross-examination, and at closing) and when you will not. Ideally, you will be able to adjust the number and mix of people so that you have a little more help exactly when you need it.

Take the time to talk to each person's normal support network at his regular office. Again, be ready to ask questions:

- *When the lawyer or witness is not in trial, what resources does he routinely use to get his work done?* Does he operate autonomously, with very little formal assistance? Or does he work as part of a team where each person only performs a special function? Each style is likely to generate different needs at trial.

- *Whom does the person regularly rely on?* It is helpful to find out if the person relies on an assistant, a secretary, and/or a senior paralegal. Often—but not always—these people will be part of the war room team. Regardless, talk to them and find out how the person you'll be supporting operates and what kinds of help he or she may need. Not surprisingly, the in-office support team will know a lot more about the lawyer's needs than the lawyer may know or appreciate.

Based on the answer to these questions, you can start to extrapolate who (mix) and how many (number) you may need to do this work.

The War Room Crew

Those who go to court can rarely do their jobs well without the support of a war room crew, which is likely to include paralegals, secretaries, trial technicians, graphics consultants, jury consultants, IT personnel, and potentially a number of other crucial team members.

The size of your war room team

One school of thought says that war room teams should **always** stay as lean as possible. According to this way of thinking, having fewer people on the team keeps individual responsibilities and lines of communication clear and avoids having unproductive (and low-billing) personnel sitting around or bugging others for work. We do not doubt that such problems arise, especially in exceedingly overstaffed teams. At the same time, we know from considerable experience that going with a small staff increases the chances of your team imploding, especially as things get more intense at trial and the temperature in the war room rises.

Ideally, the size of your war room staff will be like Baby Bear's bed in Goldilocks: "Just right!" In such an instance, everyone will be happy; you will have exactly the right number of people, and your client will feel that she is getting the absolute maximum benefit from each billable body. But remember that we live in the real world, and it is sometimes hard to know in advance exactly what you will eventually need, particularly in a place as volatile and unpredictable as the courtroom. Just as it is always better to underpromise and overdeliver, it is also better to be slightly overstaffed in a war room than understaffed.[5]

INNOCENT BYSTANDERS

One strategy you can employ to keep costs down without putting your war room at risk is putting people on standby, rather than billing your client for them around the clock simply for being onsite.

What does "standby" mean? In general, it means that these people are available for work at any time and remain within an hour's travel time of the war room. You can choose to have them either be completely off the clock (and therefore free to do whatever they wish as long as they are prepared to return to the war room at a moment's notice), or you could have them work remotely with the home office on other projects until work on the case you are trying materializes for them.

---

5.   Amie, who is also a professional pastry chef in her "spare" time, suggests that the philosophy she applies to staffing a war room is similar to how she prepares for a dinner party. No one eating at Amie's ever goes away hungry, and she would consider it a major *faux pas* to actually run out of food. So, Amie always prepares extra of everything on the chance that someone may drop by. She suggests that the guest list for your war room is rarely fixed and is more likely to expand than contract. Plan accordingly.

> *With today's technology, many of us can work whenever from wherever. But make sure these folks are properly set up to do so with wireless Internet access, laptops, and reliable access to your networks.*
>
> *Also recognize that keeping someone on standby may have costs. While we leave the details to you, it's often reasonable for such workers to charge for a guaranteed minimum number of hours or a retainer. Work this out well in advance.*

As a result, our philosophy is that staffing a war room team is like building a wheel. You start at the center with the hub, which holds everything together. The hub consists of the lead attorney(s), associate(s), and senior paralegal(s), all of whom know the case inside and out. These are the people who are required to be at every trial. To slightly distort a basic economic concept, these are your "fixed costs"—they have to be there, no matter what. But the size of the tire surrounding the hub can vary considerably, depending on the terrain you need to cover. So, do you need a wheel for a tricycle or a monster truck? If you do not exactly know, then go one size bigger than you think you might need.

Clients may ask if all the people in the war room truly are needed. This is an entirely reasonable question, and we suggest that you respect their concerns. Erring on the side of slightly overstaffing does not relieve you of the serious responsibility of trying to get it "just right." But you can assure your client of the following:

- **You are sympathetic to his concerns.** That is why you have gone through a systematic review of what is needed and have settled on what you honestly believe to be the appropriate staffing needs.
- **You have experience.** You know that far more war rooms suffer (and often suffer very badly) from having too few support people than having too many.

- **You can always send someone home if you are overstaffed**. This is far easier and much less disruptive to the overall team effort than bringing someone into the war room in the middle of the trial who did not expect to be there. Showing up at the war room after others have already been there for a while often leaves the new addition playing a constant game of "catch-up." This is both unpleasant and inefficient. Rarely are people upset when you tell them they get to go home early; rarely are they happy when you force them to show up at the last minute at a place they never intended—and may be unprepared—to be.

Do Not Cut People Loose Too Soon

At one of our war rooms, our client flew its IT person home after he had set up the network and local server. Everything was working fine, and there was nothing for him to do, so it seemed to make sense. You can probably guess what happened: the very next night the network went down, and the team could not access their exhibits until the next day, when he flew back and fixed the problem in under half an hour. Needless to say, they kept him around for a few days after that, just in case.

An Overview of Who Is Typically in the War Room

In addition to the in-courtroom folks we discussed above, you typically find five groups of people in a war room:

- **Logistics support:** These people include what we call the "Sergeant Major," who oversees what is going on in the war room, as well as the paralegals and the administrative support.

- **Tech support:** This group includes the IT personnel and your presentation technology specialist (or "trial tech").

- **Strategic support:** Increasingly, war rooms are relying on jury consultants and trial graphics consultants to help with strategic decisions regarding persuasion, messaging, and graphic presentation.

- **Remote support:** Improved technology (web conferencing, smartphones, ubiquitous Internet connectivity, etc.) has made it increasingly possible to rely on key people who are not physically present in the war room. Often these people are at the home office, where they can marshal and focus the support located there.

- **Vendor support:** Outside vendors are often an effective and efficient way to supply assistance to the war room. These individuals, who tend to have a very specialized focus and assist at discrete moments in the case, include messengers, process servers, and printing and copying specialists.

Logistics support

The "Sergeant Major"

The legal team almost always includes a lead attorney, upon whose shoulders falls whatever happens (good or bad) in the courtroom. The war room needs a similar leader, who we, with great deference, call the Sergeant Major.

In the army, the Sergeant Major is the senior enlisted advisor to the commanding officer. The Sergeant Major's job responsibilities include directing, monitoring, and advocating on behalf of the enlisted personnel. While we do not encourage you to enforce a strict military hierarchy in the war room, we do believe that you need someone who is ultimately responsible for directing, monitoring, and speaking on behalf of those on the logistics team—and upon whose shoulders falls whatever happens in the war room (good or bad).

The Sergeant Major can be a lawyer (provided that he is not overwhelmed by what is going on in court) or a non-lawyer. As a practical matter, a non-lawyer usually fills the position. No offense to lawyers, but in our experience, few lawyers have the logistical talents and technological abilities required to be great Sergeant Majors,[6] and those lawyers who do have such experience are too busy with what is going on in the courtroom to be of much help directing the war room.

The Sergeant Major should be at the center of all war room information. She should be the person through whom all logistics questions pass—from travel and lodging to equipment rental, from vendors to court deadlines. The Sergeant Major does not need to know the answer to every question, but she should know who does.

There Is No Such Thing as a Stupid Question

It's crucial that the members of your war room team feel they can ask questions, even ones that may seem obvious. Why? Because sometimes in the heat and the rush of the moment, people make nonsensical requests. For instance, Chris once asked a paralegal to hole-punch 1,000 pages on the right-hand side. The paralegal dutifully punched the holes on the wrong side and gave them to Chris, who immediately realized his error. She said she thought that the request seemed wrong the whole time, but when Chris asked her why she hadn't said anything, she replied, "But you seemed so sure!"

Michael says: It's also important that the war room is staffed with people who aren't afraid to ask questions.

---

6.   This is an opinion that even Chris, who himself was a trial lawyer for more than 20 years, fully endorses.

Knowing Chris, I'm sure he did nothing to intimidate the paralegal. What's more likely is that she was blindly following orders, which is not a good trait for someone in a war room.

Amie says: I agree with Michael, but it is also important that requestors are clear about what they need. Before you ask someone for something, make sure you understand what you need so that you can give concise and accurate direction.

The Sergeant Major does not have to do everything—and in fact it is often a disaster when she tries to do so. Instead, she needs to know how to delegate tasks effectively, keep track of delegated tasks, know the results of the delegation, and be able to provide meaningful feedback. If it sounds like this role requires an extraordinary amount of work by a highly efficient person, that is because it does. (See Chapter 7.)

The paralegals

Just as there is no single definition for who formally qualifies as a paralegal, there is no single list defining what practical assistance paralegals can provide in the war room. At a minimum, you will need people to perform the following tasks:

- Draft basic filings for court
- Attend the trial to take notes and observe how jurors and others are responding to testimony
- Assist with keeping jurors and challenges straight during voir dire
- Prepare and serve trial subpoenas
- Prepare or supervise the preparation of adversarial graphics
- Organize exhibits, depositions, and the mountains of documents that fill most war rooms

- Mark and keep track of what has or has not been admitted
- Prepare witness binders
- Transport documents and files to and from the courtroom
- Coordinate witness preparation and travel logistics
- Make and distribute copies of documents
- Summarize testimony
- Do about a million other things, usually on an expedited basis

Many of the war rooms we have seen are lawyer-rich but paralegal-poor. Having enough lawyers for the work in court is, of course, crucial. But for purposes of staffing a war room, lawyers tend to be less effective than paralegals because they are often considerably well-qualified in some areas (the law) and under-qualified in those that are actually needed (logistics and technology). Moreover, if your lawyers are doing things like retrieving depositions, cites, or exhibits; creating binders; ordering supplies; making copies; dealing with the hotel; and ordering staff meals, they will be less effective in their lawyerly duties.

One note: Unless your trial is a small one, you should not push everything onto one paralegal. It is unfair to the paralegal and, ultimately, unfair to the client as well. If fairness alone is not a sufficient reason for you to carefully consider the number of paralegals you have in the war room, consider this: not having enough paralegals to perform the crucial nuts-and-bolts duties of the war room will inevitably have a negative effect on how well you do in the courtroom.

So, what are you looking for when you select the paralegals to staff your war room? Obviously, there are no scientific answers to this question. Nor are there any hard and fast rules or requirements. Nevertheless, your ideal paralegal has:

- **Experience with the case, especially the discovery or investigation.** The bulk of pre-trial time is spent figuring out exactly what happened leading up to the matter on trial. The bulk of trial time is spent marshaling this information and figuring out how to present it. Most of this information is developed either through discovery or other forms of investigation. Ideally, the paralegals you take to the war room will have participated in this crucial portion of the case and will have gained experience by doing such things as:

o   summarizing various discovery responses, such as interrogatories or requests for admission;

o   organizing documents obtained during discovery;

o   summarizing various deposition transcripts; and

o   summarizing key records.

Participating in some or all of these activities usually gives the paralegal two important bits of information: (1) what happened, and (2) where he can find important facts and documents related to the case.

- **Experience with the key lawyers.** Just as no two trials are identical, no two lawyers do things the same way. If they are honest, trial lawyers will admit that they can be an idiosyncratic and opinionated bunch. The pressures associated with trial often sharpen these traits. This is not a criticism; we mention it only because the less time the paralegal (or for that matter any member of the logistics team) has to spend learning what makes a particular lawyer tick, the more time can be spent working on the task at hand.

- **A good working relationship with the client.** Many logistics teams only see one thing when they look at a client or client representative—someone they need to keep happy. While you do need to keep the client satisfied, do not forget the client is often a very important source of information at trial. In some instances, the client is a key witness, who can answer, based on first-hand information, what happened leading up to the dispute. In other instances, the client is your conduit back to his home office or other location, where vital information is stored or potential witnesses reside. While they may not like to admit it, during trial many lawyers are too busy to spend much time interacting with the client. Find someone who is capable of doing this job. Ideally, this paralegal:

o   Will have already developed a good working relationship with the client.

o   Will have a basic understanding of the client's relevant particulars. That is, if the client mentions the "home office" or describes a crucial aspect of its products, the paralegal will genuinely understand what he is talking about.

o   Will be able, particularly in tragic cases, to empathize with the client. While we do not want to characterize lawyers as an insensitive lot, even the most compassionate ones may not have the time to provide a shoulder for the client to cry on during trial. Hopefully someone on the logistics team can provide this important assistance to the client whenever it is needed.

•   **Experience in other war rooms.** Often the logistics team is left to its own devices to figure out what needs to be done and how certain tasks are best accomplished, such as having a demonstrative edited, adding new arrivals onto the computer network, etc. Even the most experienced trial lawyers (or should we say, especially the most experienced trial lawyers) have little experience working out the exact logistics of these tasks—that is not their job. There is no substitute for experience; it is best to have paralegals who have done these kinds of tasks before.

•   **Knowledge of the fundamental issues, theory, and themes in your case.** One of the most basic lessons that lawyers are taught in law school about trying cases is "Know your theory/themes and never do anything inconsistent with them." Most basically, a theory is the story line of what happened. The themes are widely accepted principles that allow you to add moral authority to your theory. The last thing you want is for someone to do anything that runs contrary to your theory or theme. While this principle is most often tested in the courtroom, the people in the war room also need to understand that as they gather their documents and construct graphics, they must do so in ways that are consistent with the case theory and themes. Ignoring this rule will, at best, waste time by creating work product that the trial team cannot use and, at worst, actively undermine the case. Ideally, the strategists will have developed the case theory and themes long before trial, and you will be able to bring paralegals who are familiar with the theory and themes, and who also understand not to stray from these important elements of your case.

- **Knowledge of key technical issues.** Not surprisingly, an increasing number of cases that actually go to trial involve highly sophisticated technical issues, particularly in patent cases, where the dispute may be over a minute piece of hardware or a difficult and proprietary process. Often the stakes in such cases are so high that settlement is difficult or impossible. In such instances, the people you bring to the war room need to understand these technical issues. It is not unusual to see war rooms include people with special technical training (such as attorneys with multiple advanced degrees). If you need such people, make sure to identify and reserve them early.

- **Patience and endurance.** For obvious reasons, all but the smallest trials require patience and endurance. Find paralegals with plenty of both.

SHORTER TRIALS CAN BE TOUGHER

The duration of a trial does not always correlate to the amount of war room staff you will need. Counter-intuitively, sometimes shorter trials are the most difficult, in the same way that it is harder to write a short story than a novel. That is, when time is compressed, you have room for only what is essential, which means you need to know what to cut and how to get to the point quickly. This leaves little room for error, because you do not have time to course-correct. Additionally, in short trials, delays are even more costly than in long ones, because they represent a bigger percentage of your time lost.

We recently worked on a patent trial in the rocket docket of Tyler, Texas. The trial lasted only one week. But the war room consisted of more than ten attorneys, three paralegals, one full-time IT person. We also had four people from our office: a graphics case manager, a graphic designer, and two presentation technology consultants, or "trial techs": one to run the in-court presentation, the other to stay up late to prep material for the next day. All told, eighteen people worked onsite in two conference rooms, and even with that large of a staff many people still worked around the clock. And it paid off: our side won a jury verdict with damages well in excess of the amount offered in settlement talks.

*The lesson here is that your determination of who to include in the war room needs to be based on how much work there is, **not** how long the trial is scheduled to last.*

Administrative support

Unfortunately, war rooms often lack adequate administrative support. This is probably due to the fact that increasing numbers of people do much of what traditionally was seen as "secretarial duties" (including typing, data entry, filing, placing phone calls, and getting coffee) on their own. While this degree of self-reliance is admirable, war room pressures often make this form of independence impractical. To the extent possible, find someone who, among other things, can type, keep track of calendars, copy documents, and make a run to the local coffee shop when needed.

Additionally, look for someone who:

- **Has a good working relationship with the Sergeant Major.** Inevitably the Sergeant Major and the person providing administrative support work closely together. Find someone who will assist, not hinder, the war room leader.

- **Has as many basic skills in as many areas as possible.** The wider the variety of skills, the more valuable he is likely to be. A person who can confidently navigate Word, PowerPoint, and Excel—as well as safely drive people to court on a moment's notice—will be far more effective than someone who can only do one of these things. As you assemble your team, realistically assess which of these and other skills are needed in your war room and make sure you have at least one person capable of doing them.

- **Has the ability to multitask.** Rare is the war room where the staff is so large that each member need only concentrate on one task at a time. Common is the war room where every member is simultaneously balancing at least three or four tasks. Administrative staff (who take direction from many people at once) usually balance an even heavier load. Find someone who can handle such multitasking challenges with aplomb.

Technical Support

Every single member of the strategic and logistic teams will need IT support. Additionally, the lawyers and witnesses probably will need help from a presentation technology specialist, who sets up the trial database and runs the display equipment in the court. These professionals routinely supply services and often have skills far beyond the scope of what could be expected of us mere mortals. And, while we acknowledge their considerable talents, for the purposes of this book we will refer to them simply as the "tech folks."

IT specialist

The IT specialist is responsible for setting up your computer, network, and Internet systems; preventing problems before they arise; and fixing these problems when they do occur. Many companies now specialize in supplying equipment to traveling teams and some even specialize in trial war rooms. **Do not assume you can just take your in-house IT person to the war room.**

We cannot name a single law firm that does not have at least one IT specialist on staff, or in the case of the sole-attorney operation, a steady relationship with a freelance "IT guy." Sometimes war room teams are tempted to press-gang this poor in-house person, transport him 500 miles to the war room, and make him an official member of the war room team for six weeks. Think long and hard before you do this, for three primary reasons:

- **First, the IT needs of the war room are almost always different and more complicated than those of the home office.** This is not to suggest that managing IT needs at the home office is easy. But unless your war room is in your existing office space, the person setting up, maintaining, and troubleshooting the war room IT system is usually in an unfamiliar space and often far from the resources to which he is accustomed. Make sure he has the expertise to do this work.

- **Second, your war room IT person will need sufficient people skills to work smoothly with a group of people he is unlikely to have met or worked with before.** For example, if you set up your war room in a hotel suite, he is going to have to coordinate with hotel employees, who will have varying degrees of IT sophistication. We are not saying that your in-house person cannot do this; most rise admirably to the occasion. Our point is that you need to check with him to see if he honestly feels capable of doing this work.

- **Finally, while taking your in-house person away to trial may be great for the war room, it could spell disaster for the home office.** The needs of the home office will not automatically stop because you and others from the office are off in trial. As you select your IT person, make sure you do not leave your other colleagues in the lurch. While some firms have the resources to send their in-house personnel onsite, it is not the norm, and we encourage you to be thoughtful while making this decision.

IT staffing requirements in the war room

Assuming you have found the right person to provide your IT needs at trial, the most common question is: "How long should the IT specialist stick around the war room?" Answering this question would be easy if you could predict exactly when something might go wrong with your IT system and equipment. Since you cannot, we suggest three possible answers to this question.

- **Best staffing solution:** If your trial, your staff, and your budget are large enough, we recommend having someone who is fully capable of undertaking all of the IT tasks onsite for the **entire** trial. In fact, as discussed in Chapters 5 and 6, we think you need to get your IT specialist to the war room several days before trial starts in order to get everything set up and make sure all equipment is working properly. It is almost always faster and more beneficial to have an IT person available onsite to solve your problems than for you or a valuable team member to spend hours on the phone trying to explain the situation to someone 500 miles away. If you need immediate proof of this, remember back to the last time you tried to reconfigure your cable service or talk to a tech-support person about a problem you were having with your home computer.

- **Next-best staffing solution:** If it is not feasible to have an IT person at the war room for the entire trial, do your best to have him set up the war room and then stay at least through opening statements. Hopefully, he can prevent problems by properly setting up and configuring your equipment—and then correct any problems, which most likely (but not always) will develop within the first few days. Then make sure you have someone you can call 24/7 to help you handle subsequent problems.

- **Minimum staffing solution:** At the very least, have a knowledgeable IT person talk to someone at your venue well before you set up the war room. Make sure he determines the quality, speed, and reliability of your Internet connection, including how to get a better one installed if necessary. Also, have him tell someone in the war room the best way to set up, configure, and maintain your equipment. Make sure that you continue to have someone available by phone at all times to answer technical questions and fix problems. Ideally, this will be someone from your office whom you know and have worked with before. But even having someone you have never met before, but is available locally is far better than having no one. We can guarantee that you will have technical questions and problems, and they very likely will arise at 11 P.M., not 11 A.M.

Presentation technology support

We divide technology into two categories: electric and acoustic. What we call acoustic technology works without having to be plugged into an electric socket. These tools include printed foam-core boards, flip charts, whiteboards, models, handouts, other tangible technology. As the name implies, electric technology plugs into the wall. These tools include (in roughly increasing degree of sophistication) overhead projectors, Elmos, document cameras, PowerPoint presentations, trial presentation databases, and Flash presentations that show images and video through a projector and/or on monitors located throughout the courtroom.

Attorneys are increasingly digitizing their material—including demonstratives, exhibits, and witness testimony—to electronically display it at trial (see Chapters 9 and 10). Gone are the days when lawyers feared that the jury might be biased against the side using such high-tech evidence displays. This is because of the following factors:

- **The cost of using such equipment has decreased.** Granted, a full set of equipment (for courtrooms that have none), plus the presence of a professional trial tech to run it, is not cheap (and if it is, you should be worried). But display equipment is now within the reach of many parties, both plaintiffs and defendants, and thus more common during trial.

- **Increasingly, courts provide this equipment for all parties.** As new courtrooms are being built, and as civic budgets allow, more and more courtrooms feature their own electronic display equipment, which is made available to all parties. The type and sophistication of this equipment vary from jurisdiction to jurisdiction, and the courts rarely provide much assistance as to how to use the equipment during trial. Nevertheless, it is no longer true that only aggressive, well-financed defendants have access to these tools.

- **Jurors expect such displays.** High-tech displays (in and out of court) are the norm, not the exception. If you have any doubt of this, look at how most people learn and gather information these days—they do so through television, computers, and other electronic devices. For most of today's jury pool, learning about a case in court through electronic technology seems commonplace. Even Chris's parents (who are in their 80s) are no longer surprised or impressed when they see information displayed electronically. In fact, they expect it. At the same time, Chris's children (in their 20s) would be more alarmed if they did *not* see you using such technology. Neither Chris's parents nor his children (who collectively represent both ends of your likely jury pool) are unique in this regard.

- **Jurors see it as saving them time.** Jurors do not want you to waste their time in court. While it is possible to use electronic technology badly and alienate jurors, careful planning and judicious use of this equipment will move your case forward at a pace appreciated by the jurors and the judge. In other words, the jurors will perceive your effective use of such technology as *helping* them, as opposed to some kind of high-end parlor trick.

Given this shift in expectations and attitudes, if your trial requires showing more than a handful of exhibits or demonstratives, using display technology may provide a critical advantage in getting your point across. If you do go this route, find someone for your war room team who can: advise you on what equipment you need, set these tools up in court, troubleshoot problems when (not if!) something goes wrong, and be in court to run the equipment. All of this is in the province of the trial presentation specialist, commonly referred to as a trial technician, or "trial tech."

A trial tech needs to be experienced enough to fully understand the pressures of being in trial. Ideally, the person you select should have no responsibilities beyond getting your material ready to be displayed in court, practicing in the war room with the lawyers and witnesses (to make sure things run smoothly during testimony), and actually being in court to run the presentation as planned.

Our clients will sometimes say, "We'll just have the paralegal pull up the exhibits." This is usually not realistic because few paralegals have in-depth knowledge of trial presentation software, and most have not had experience with the pressure and stress of presenting material in court. Plus they already have dozens of other crucial tasks to perform. In other words, if you are going to use this sophisticated equipment, get a professional to run it. This is not a part-time job for someone who has never done it before.

In fact, the whole topic of using specialists reminds us of an old joke one of our partners tells: A person who recently had surgery is looking at her hospital bill and is amazed at how much she was charged for the anesthesiologist. She calls the hospital and says, "Why'd I pay all this money just to be knocked out?!" The person at the hospital replies, "You didn't—you paid all that money to make sure you woke up." For trials, you are not spending all that money to put data into the computer; you are spending it to be able to get it out of the computer, exactly when you need it. Get someone who can do just that!

Hiring a trial tech

If your firm has an experienced trial tech on staff, the question of who should do this work may be easy to answer. If not, then you need to find the right person to add to your team. Finding a candidate should not be difficult, as more and more companies are providing such services. What is difficult is determining who will do a good job at your war room and in the courtroom. Consider these questions when making such a choice:

- **Has your prospective trial tech worked in trials and on complex cases?**
  - Trial time—the more, the better. Frankly, the only way to get good at this kind of work is to do it, and to do it in the pressure cooker of the courtroom. Do not be afraid to ask your potential trial tech how many actual trials she has worked, rather than merely worked *on* in the pre-trial phase.
  - Complex cases—the more, the better. If your case is *long* and complex, this is an absolute requirement. Nevertheless, even if your case is not complex, you are better off with someone who is used to larger cases. Try to find someone who has at least a few decent-sized civil or criminal cases under her belt. Do not be afraid to ask about what type of cases she has worked on and the size of each (and by size, we mean how many exhibits, video depositions, and witnesses were involved).

- **Does your prospective trial teach plan on using software specifically designed for trial presentation?**
  - This is crucial. Some of the names you want to hear include TrialDirector and Sanction.
  - Some larger trial-tech shops use their own *proprietary* software. They claim it is superior to TrialDirector or Sanction. We leave that for others to argue. What we can explain is the potential disadvantage in using such programs. Whether intentional or not, proprietary software makes it harder for you to share this material with other parties who are relying on more commonly used software. It also makes it harder to change vendors, because if the new vendor uses other software, he may have to re-create your database for you. Give careful thought to whether this is worth it. It very well may be; our point is merely that you should be aware of this issue.
  - What you do **not** want is a trial tech who relies primarily or exclusively on programs that, while they might be good for limited or other purposes, are not specifically designed to display sophisticated graphics in court (e.g., PowerPoint or Adobe Acrobat). These programs have their place, and your trial tech should be familiar with them, but not as a primary means of trial presentation.
- **Does your prospective trial tech know not only how to work with the equipment, but also how the equipment itself works?**
  - Your trial tech does not need to be an electrical engineer. But he should be able to troubleshoot basic problems when things go wrong—e.g., something gets unplugged, gear gets moved and has to be put back, a projector bulb turns out.
  - You are hiring the functional equivalent of both a driver and a mechanic. More complex problems will

inevitably arise during trial. A person who does not know how to fix these problems is of only limited use to you in the courtroom.

- **Can your prospective trial tech go into a courtroom and immediately figure out how to set it up in a way that makes it useful for everyone?** "Everyone" includes the judge, the court personnel, opposing counsel, the jury, and spectators. "Making it useful" includes identifying the best configuration for a projector, screen, monitors, speakers, switcher, easels, microphones, and other tools. (See Chapter 9.)

- **Is your prospective trial tech familiar with your specific court and particular judge?** If not, is he willing to do the necessary preliminary legwork to get this basic information well before trial? The best trial techs will do reconnaissance on the courtroom and judge. They will visit the courtroom, take measurements, and talk to the clerk. The very best will do this before they even give you an estimate of what it will cost.

- **Will your prospective trial tech be fully dedicated to your case?** During trial you want him to be able to work full-time and around-the-clock without complaining (at least to you).

- **Does your prospective trial tech communicate well? Is he proactive?**
  - Good techs do not just wait for instructions; they suggest a time line of tasks that need to get done and also give you advice on how best to work with them and to provide them what they need.
  - When there is a problem, the good techs can explain it to you in simple everyday language, not technical jargon.

- **Does your prospective trial tech have a broad range of technical skills?** While he does not need to be a full-fledged IT specialist, a good trial tech will have intermediate-level skills in digital video and audio editing, Microsoft Office, Adobe Acrobat, and scanning software, as well as a general knowledge of litigation software used for things other than trial presentation.

- **Is your prospective trial tech calm under pressure?** The one trait all good techs have is that they know how to stay calm. Do not be afraid to call and check with your trial tech's references, and when you do, ask how he reacts under pressure. Find this out before you hire him.

Strategic support

Larger or "bet the company" cases increasingly rely on two key specialists: jury consultants, who help select the most favorable jury possible, and trial graphics consultants, who help use visual images to make complex issues simpler and easier for judges and jurors to understand.

Often these individuals are present only during key portions of the case. For example, most jury consultants work intensely through the completion of voir dire and then leave the day-to-day operations to the war room. The trial graphics specialists occasionally work in the war room throughout the entire case. More often they are present just before and during certain portions, such as opening statement, key witness testimony, and closing argument.

The jury consultant

While the jury consultant may play a variety of roles in the life of the case (e.g., organizing mock trials or other research exercises), her primary role at trial is to provide strategic insight and jury selection support. For the most part, jury consultants work on their own. While they probably will need space at the war room and access to some of the logistics team's resources (copiers, computers, Internet service, etc.), most jury consultants need only minimal support from other members of the war room team.

Trial graphics consultants

It is a fact of the modern age that almost every trial relies on a visual presentation of some sort or another. If you are using graphics consultants, plan to bring them onsite with you as part of your team, rather than as an afterthought. As noted earlier, these days jurors not only *expect* a visual explanation of your case, they practically *demand* it; you will need specialists on hand to support your efforts. Book them early (even these types of consultants can conflict out of your case), and integrate them into your team as soon as possible.

Remote support

Technology increasingly makes working remotely an option for certain members of your war room team, whether your war room is a few blocks or several thousand miles from your main office. As you assess who needs to be there, remember to ask yourself what role people back at the home office might play to supplement your staffing and ensure that your needs are met. We have seen a team of lawyers, paralegals, secretaries, and administrative staff whip up briefs from thousands of miles away as fast, if not faster, than the team at the war room itself.

When possible, take advantage of time zones. If your office is on the East Coast and your war room is on the West, remote staff can start three hours earlier than war room staff can. If the opposite is the case, i.e., your offices are on Pacific Time and your war room is running on Eastern, take advantage of the fact that people on the West Coast can work long after those in the war room have called it a night.

Other vendors

Your team cannot do everything, nor should it be required to. In most venues you can find excellent vendors that offer such services as:

- Deliveries
- Process serving
- Photocopying and assembling of documents

- Transportation
- Food services

In many instances, the local services will do a superior job to what you might be able to do. For example, do you really want someone from the war room who is not from the area to serve as a messenger when something has to be delivered before a specific (and thrillingly close) deadline? Likewise, do you really want one of your key war room personnel attempting to serve a trial subpoena on a reluctant witness?

For purposes of staffing your war room, you need to take four steps to find vendors:

- Determine if such services are available in the local area. Generally, unless you are in some extremely remote location, they exist.
- Find out who is good and who is not. This is a matter of reference checking and testing.
- Choose one person in your war room to supervise and keep track of what vendors are doing.
- If you cannot locate a trusted vendor to perform a certain task near the war room, add a staff person to your team to do this work.

Some Final Thoughts

As you determine who needs to be in your war room, keep in mind the following additional factors:

- **The particular needs of a trial may break up the existing home team.** Do not assume that the same people the lawyer works with in the office will also be at the war room. Certainly, many will, particularly paralegals and others who have lived with the case for a long period of time. But the skills that are needed in the war room may be different from those needed in the office. Consequently, it may be advisable to leave certain home office people at home. Additionally, it is sometimes impossible, even for the most dedicated support person, to leave the office (or home) to work in a war room for several weeks. It is important for the lawyer and the war room planner to appreciate and respect these limitations. It is equally important for the war room planner to have a candid conversation with existing team members to really assess if they are the right people to staff the war room.

- **Encourage the in-court team members to get as much done in advance as possible, using your in-office support personnel.** We suspect that we are preaching to the choir on this point. Inevitably, things are easier to do at the home office before you go off to trial than at the war room while you are in trial. Encourage everyone to take advantage of this fact and get done what needs to be done early on, thereby leaving more time at the war room to take care of the unexpected.

CHAPTER 5:
When Is Trial?

When we first meet with clients, there is always a crucial moment when, if you listen very carefully, you will hear that we have temporarily stopped breathing. This is the moment when we turn our heads and ask, "So, when is trial?" Then we close our eyes and hold our breath in anticipation of the answer.

Why is this question so important to us? Because the more time you have to plan, the more comprehensive and effective your logistics will be. That being said, we are realists. We know that a lot of unexpected variables can affect timing, including random court orders that shift dates, settlements that fall apart, and last-minute trial counsel substitutions.

Because time frames can vary so dramatically, we have divided this Chapter into two sections. The first section outlines what you should consider doing **when you have plenty of time** and, thus, the luxury of proceeding in a more or less orderly and systematic manner. The second section deals with what you should do **when your lead time is short** and, as Amie (who is not only an expert in war rooms but also a chef) describes it, you need to create a "short order" war room. Rest assured, if you plan properly, you can create highly functional and effective logistical support for your trial, whatever the timing.

When You Have Time

Let us assume that, well in advance of trial, your lead attorney has informed you of the need for a war room. You should consider a number of timing issues to make sure that your war room runs smoothly and your logistics team is properly staffed. As you review these suggestions, please keep a couple of points in mind:

- This list is merely a framework. We have listed tasks here that may **not** apply to your particular trial. Likewise, undoubtedly you will have tasks for your specific case that are not listed in this Chapter.

- None of these timing suggestions is absolute. If you can complete some of these tasks in an effective manner **earlier** than suggested here, more power to you; go ahead and do them. Likewise, if you miss a suggested deadline, do not panic. Just complete the task as efficiently as possible when you can.

Tasks That Are Never Too Early to Start

Notify everyone of the trial date and keep them advised of changes

One of the silliest mistakes people make is also one of the most easily preventable: they forget to keep everyone involved in the case (internal team, vendors, percipient and expert witnesses) aware of the trial date. Rarely does a case run from pleadings through voir dire with only one immutable trial date. More often, dates shift either as a result of a decision made by the court alone or in response to a motion by one or both parties.

How do you solve this? Assign one person on your war room team to:

- Communicate the original date to the entire team as soon as it is known

- Immediately notify everyone of subsequent date changes

- Make the necessary adjustments with vendors whose contracts require advance notice of any changes or cancellations (i.e., hotels, airlines, and other vendors who will charge you fees for last-minute changes)

This person also should be responsible for informing everyone if the case ultimately settles. Vendors who keep working after your case has settled because no one told them it was over are justified in expecting to be paid. And clients who have to pay for this post-settlement work are justified in being upset if this happens.

Witnesses (both percipient and expert) usually are the last group to find out about trial date changes. We suspect this is because they often are not in constant contact with other members of the war room team. Since it is hard to have a trial without these people, make sure they know when they are supposed to show up—and give them enough notice so that they can clear their calendars or let you know of an unavoidable conflict early enough that you can advise the court of scheduling problems.

Start the "Golden Binder"

In the war room, as in all areas of life, few things are more frustrating than redoing something you have already done or losing key pieces of information that you have carefully assembled. As such, it is never too early to begin systematically collecting and organizing all of the information that you and others will be gathering for the war room.

We strongly advise developing what we call "The Golden Binder." This is **the** place for information related to the war room. "Back in the day" (as Amie's niece refers to anything prior to 2005), we actually kept this information in a bright yellow binder—hence its name. The binder resided in a predetermined place and could not, except under penalty of death, be removed from that location. One designated person had sole responsibility for updating the Golden Binder; all changes had to be funneled through that person. If a dispute arose as to what information was correct or most recent, everyone knew that what was in the Golden Binder was right.

It is never too early to start assembling and maintaining this resource. These days, you have a choice: you can keep this material in a physical binder or electronically in a predetermined location either on your network or on a secure online repository. (Note: It should *not* live solely on one person's computer.) Whatever the format, remember that while anyone on the team can submit proposed changes or information to the Golden Binder, only one person should have the actual ability to make changes to it.

What goes in the "Golden Binder"?

We have all seen them: the master binders that all great assistants keep at their desks as reference material. They contain birthdays, preferences, contacts, and all sorts of other helpful information. You, or your Sergeant Major, should have one of these too. (See Appendix B for a sample Golden Binder.)

The Golden Binder should contain answers to basic questions for anyone who may be serving in the war room, not just your Sergeant Major. Examples of those answers include the following:

- Contact information for all vendors
  - IT
  - Messenger service
  - Equipment rental
- Contact information for all the war room team members
- Flight, hotel, and rental car logistics
- Contact information and schedules for witnesses
- Instructions for getting an exhibit board made
- Directions for changing toner cartridges in the printer (and what to do with the empties)
- Hotel contact names and numbers for catering or other services
- Relevant account numbers
- Maps of the local area

The mere act of putting the binder together can both bring up and address a lot of logistical questions you may have, and the more you can do before your war room is in place, the less you will have to keep track of while you are there, which means you can focus on the more important matters at hand.

DISASTER! (INFORMATION WE HOPE YOU NEVER USE)

We know it's hard to imagine, but sometimes bad things happen that are not in your control. This can be distressing, but you can prepare yourself for disaster before you depart by gathering some basic information for your team to reference should the worst happen. We recommend that you keep the following information in your war room Golden Binder:

- *Emergency contacts for all traveling team members*
- *A map and driving directions to the hospital nearest the war room*
- *The customer service number for your firm's health insurance provider*
- *Location and directions to the nearest shelter for extreme weather*
- *Driving directions to local police and fire stations*

Also, do not forget to review safety information in your initial daily meeting so that people know where to go and for whom to look in case of a disaster that requires people to evacuate the building.

Create, publicize, and regularly maintain a master calendar

As soon as possible, create a master calendar and make sure that all important dates (both those issued by the court and those you have agreed on internally) are on it. Assign someone to maintain this calendar and store it in a place readily accessible to members of your team (e.g., in the Golden Binder). Whoever is in charge of maintaining the master calendar should circulate it regularly so that everyone is aware of what needs to be done and when.

Things to Do as Soon as You Know Which Judge Will Preside Over Your Case

Various jurisdictions differ as to when they let you know which judge will be presiding over your case. Some assign a judge as soon as the complaint is filed, which can be a year or more in advance of trial. In those cases, the judge oversees everything related to the dispute, including resolving motions and eventually presiding at the trial. Other courts do not assign a specific trial judge until a few days before trial starts. Whichever procedure your jurisdiction follows, your war room personnel need to do several things as soon as they know who the trial judge will be.

Know your court's rules, and follow them

A complex set of rules will govern much of what you do in the war room. At the risk of stating the obvious, you need to know about and be ready to implement these rules. Failing to do so will, at best, ruffle the court staff's feathers, and at worst, leave you or your attorneys facing sanctions. Believe us, when you're sent off to prison for contempt, the last thing you want is this conversation with your cellmate: "Me? I'm here because I failed to comply with certain court rules at trial, thanks for asking. How about you—what are you in for?"

To avoid this embarrassing scenario, find these rules and:

- Carefully review them
- Make sure that everyone on your war room team knows them
- Make sure that everyone on your war room team follows them

Granted, merely finding all the relevant rules is sometimes easier said than done. Typically, courts operate at the intersection of four sets of rules. To understand this point, we need to step back and explain a bit about courtroom hierarchy and the concepts of "jurisdictional-level rules," "venue-level rules," "courtroom-level rules," and "common custom."

Jurisdictional-level rules

These rules apply to every court at a particular level of the judicial system, regardless of its location. For example, trial courts in the federal system are referred to as "United States District Courts." The trial courts in California are referred to as "Superior Courts."[7] Each jurisdiction (whether the federal government or the individual states) has adopted jurisdictional-level rules that apply to all cases pending in the trial courts of that jurisdiction. So, for example, every case (and by extension every associated war room) in any United States District Court, regardless of location, has to follow the *Federal Code of Civil Procedure* or the *Federal Code of Criminal Procedure*. Likewise, in California, all cases (and their supporting war rooms) in Superior Court are bound by, among other things, the *California Rules of Court*, the *California Code of Civil Procedure*, and the *California Code of Criminal Procedure*.

Venue-level rules

These rules apply to a particular geographic division within a jurisdiction. The United Stated District Court, for instance, includes various venues based on geographic location, such as the United States District Court for the Northern District of California (based in San Francisco) or the United States District Court for the Southern District of New York (based in Manhattan).

State courts also have venues. The Superior Court of California system, for instance, contains venues fixed by county boundaries, such as the Superior Court for the County of Alameda (based in Oakland) or the Superior Court for the County of Los Angeles (obviously, based in Los Angeles).

---

7. While all states have trial-level courts, there is no uniform name for them. For example, in Illinois, trial courts are Circuit Courts. In New York, they are referred to as Supreme Courts. And in North Dakota, these courts are called District Courts.

Each of these venues can (and often does) have its own set of venue-level rules. For example, the *Local Rules of the United States District Court* for the Northern District of California fill a medium-sized notebook. Likewise, the rules for Alameda County Superior Court fill an only slightly smaller binder. Someone in the war room needs to collect, digest, and communicate the applicable venue-level rules for the case at hand—including what can be stringent deadlines for submitting material, plus detailed directions on how you should do so.

Courtroom-level rules

In addition to jurisdictional and venue rules, each judge and courtroom deputy has preferences as to how things should be done in their specific courtrooms. These rules are rarely the same for any two courts, even those that are right next to each other. While you generally can get the jurisdictional-level and venue-level rules well in advance of trial, you will not be able to get the courtroom-level rules for your trial before you know who your trial judge is. Yet these courtroom-level rules can be highly specific (e.g., setting court hours, outlining exchange dates for exhibits, and explaining how the deputy clerk wants the war room staff to pre-mark potential exhibits). These rules will have a profound effect on how the war room operates. In fact, by the time you get to trial, these rules may have the greatest impact on what you are doing in your war room.

Common custom

To further complicate matters, over the years various courts have developed certain ways of doing things. These common customs are rarely formally adopted or even written down, yet everyone who has been in the courtroom—or prepared material to be used there—seems to know what these customs are. War room staffers are unlikely to get formally sanctioned for violating these customs. But not understanding the expectations can make you, your attorneys, or your witnesses look pretty stupid, so knowing and complying with these customs is important.

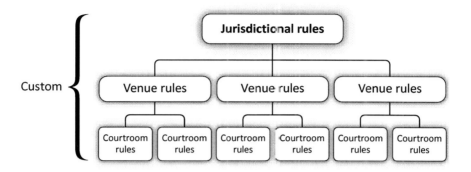

If this hierarchy sounds confusing, it can be. You may have to do some digging to figure out which rules apply. Our suggestions:

- **If you are not an attorney, first check with the lawyers on the case.** Often they are familiar with the courtroom and know which rules apply. But (and this is an important "but") war room staff also should independently investigate the rules, particularly those at the venue and courtroom levels.

- **If your war room is not in your home venue, check with any contacts your firm has in the trial venue.** Often clients have local counsel in those locations. Do not be afraid to check with them. Making the out-of-towners aware of what to do and how to act is one of local counsel's important functions and one reason out-of-towners hire these firms.

- **Contact the court clerk and ask about any courtroom-specific rules.** It is amazing how many times we have seen the courtroom deputy happily reach into a desk drawer and produce a preprinted sheet setting forth exactly what we need to know by way of courtroom-level rules.

However, just getting a copy of these rules and filing it away is not enough. Once you have them, someone on your war room team needs to review and summarize the relevant portions for the rest of the team. Specifically look for various rules concerning the following:

- Exchange dates for exhibits and other demonstratives
- Guidelines for pre-marking exhibits
- Exchange dates for deposition transcript designations
- Length of advance notice you must give before calling a witness
- Procedures for getting equipment and other material into the courtroom
- Special rules for providing for jurors (e.g., some jurisdictions require that you "post" or deposit special fees to pay for jurors' per diem compensation; if you forget to send a check to court, you could lose the right to have your case decided by a jury and end up with only a judge)
- Anything particular to the judge or courtroom (e.g., certain courts require that counsel jointly provide snacks and soft drinks for the jurors during trial and deliberations)

Make a list of these requirements and circulate them to your team. Post a "cheat sheet" or summary of the most important rules in a prominent place in the war room (as well as in your Golden Binder, of course) and regularly consult it.

Get background information about the courtroom, the judge, and the courtroom staff

In addition to getting the rules, get whatever background you can on the judge, the courtroom, and the courtroom staff. If possible, visit the courtroom so you know its layout. What kind of display equipment is available? How does the clerk handle admitting exhibits or displaying video clips? Does the courtroom have sufficient room to store material and equipment, or does the trial tech need to break down everything and take it to the war room each night?

In the old days, war room teams had no systematic way to get information about the judge, his style, and his preferences. You merely consulted people you trusted who had worked on recent trials in front of that judge and asked questions. Today, you can find an increasing number of electronic databases that claim to provide this information. Local bar associations operate some of them; national organizations operate others.

We have to admit that, as of this book's publication, none of the more general websites has impressed us very much. Instead, we prefer sites maintained by state or local bar associations, as they tend to be more complete. Even so, we recommend taking this information with a grain of salt. Half of the lawyers posting on these sites win and the other half lose; neither group is above letting the outcome of a case influence what they say about the judge. Frankly, this may be one instance where technology has not improved upon the old-fashioned way of doing things: asking knowledgeable, trustworthy people for their opinions about a judge based on years of personal knowledge or recent court appearances.

At Least 90 Days Before Trial

Much of the work for the war room should begin at least 90 days before the trial. First, catch up: do any of the items listed above that you have not done already.

Organize your internal support team

Make sure that everyone knows and clears the appropriate dates for staffing the war room. As you will see below, often this means confirming that participants can start working onsite (i.e., in the war room) for extended hours at least a week before trial is scheduled to start and then remain available several days after proceedings end. If the case is not close to your office, confirm that each of the potential team members is willing and able to be away from home for this extended period. This last point is particularly important, as many potential participants in the war room also will have family commitments that need to be balanced with the substantial burden of a lengthy out-of-town trial.

Conduct periodic meetings with key members of your internal support team. You can start with meetings every week and then make them more frequent as the trial date gets closer. These meetings help everyone keep track of what needs to be done and how things are progressing. They also help to open lines of communication among key members of your team.

Coordinate with the in-court team

Usually by this point you will know who is on the strategic team. Most likely that team will include the lead trial lawyer, a second chair, and various associates and paralegals to provide backup. Get a list of these people and start figuring out what kind of resources and support they will need. Undoubtedly these needs will change over the next several weeks, so keep all of this information updated in your Golden Binder. Often these teams meet periodically to update each other on what is going on in the case. Work with the team to ensure that a portion of each meeting is set aside for logistical concerns (the first or last 15 to 30 minutes). There may or may not be anything to discuss, but it is important to block out the time. We like to use the last portion of the meeting for logistics, but if there is nothing to discuss, we do not refer to it as wasted time; we consider it as having given the team "the gift of time."

Retain your external support team

Determine what external support you will need and line it up. Do you need trial presentation support? Retain that as soon as you can. What about a graphics firm for demonstratives? Line up that assistance immediately as well. The best external trial support teams have to be retained very early on so you are not left with a "second string" team due to conflicts.

Start your list of to-do's and determine who is responsible

Organizational psychologists have determined that teams are more likely to get tasks done (and done well) when specific people are assigned to do them. At this point in your preparation, you should have an idea of what types of tasks will need to be completed prior to and during the time you formally establish your war room. Make this list and begin to assign people responsible for the tasks on it. Obviously, you will not be able to immediately fill every spot; fortunately, you will not need to do so. Nevertheless, having such a comprehensive list will not only help you keep track of where you are in the process but will also help you determine whom you eventually will need, based on what is left to accomplish when you start working in earnest in your war room.

Reserve hotel rooms

You do not need hotel rooms just for out-of-town war rooms. In many instances, you also need hotel rooms for war rooms in your home town. Witnesses, trial techs, jury consultants, graphics people, and other staff involved in war rooms will need hotel space if they are traveling from out of town, and local people may need a place to stay near the war room for those evenings where they work until 2 A.M. and have to be back four hours later.

Reserving hotel space involves a lot of variables, but working with a hotel sales representative will greatly ease the process. For example, you may want to set up your work space very close to where people are staying, or even in the same complex. The sales manager can help you create a contract that includes all services as well as rooms. By setting this up early, you can ensure that your team remains together in the same location, avoid scrambling for last-minute accommodation, and not worry about room-cancellation fees when witness arrival is delayed by court-mandated changes to the trial schedule. (See Chapter 8.)

If you need additional incentive to start lining up rooms early, remember that many cities feature only a limited number of places where you can stay near the courthouse, and these places can vary greatly in quality. In some venues, for instance, you may find only one hotel that is very nice, while the rest are rather, let us say, "basic." The war room coordinator who locks in the nice hotel has very likely secured a distinct advantage for the team. In fact, getting the best possible hotel space is sufficiently important that you should consider touring the facilities before booking rooms.

Locate potential work space

Regardless of where your trial is in relationship to your usual office, you will need work space for the war room. Even if you do all of the work in your office, you probably will need to find at least a spare conference room or two where you can concentrate on getting ready for trial. If you are going out of town, you will need to find a spot where your team can all work together, such as a conference room or a suite of rooms at a hotel, at another law firm, or in rented office space.

Do not forget to check with the court to see what kind of space may be available there, at least during court hours. Some courts let you reserve small conference rooms in the courthouse near the courtroom. Check with the clerk to see whether you can have exclusive use of this space (ideal) or you will have to share it with other lawyers trying cases in that courtroom (less than ideal but common). Again, inspecting these rooms ahead of trial is well worth your time and effort. These "breakout" rooms cannot function as your war room (too small, limited hours of access), but they can be helpful during court hours as a hub for your team. (See Chapter 6.)

Stake a claim on extra space at your office

See if you can get some extra space at your office to serve as your temporary staging area. This is where you can start assembling the documents, the deposition transcripts, the equipment, all of the different things you will need for trial. It is easier to keep track of this material if you have a place where you can put it during the time leading up to trial, and it will help simplify the packing process when it is time to move the war room if you are going onsite for trial.

At Least 60 Days Before Trial

Get a hard fix on who is going to be part of the war room

By this point, you should have a solid working list of who is going to be part of the overall trial team, including the lawyers, the client(s), the witnesses, the in-court support team, the war room team, outside vendors, and anyone else who will be needing or providing support. This information will determine your needs for work space, hotel rooms, supplies, and other resources. At this point, you should know exactly who each of these people will be; if you do not, you should address it immediately. As a rule of thumb, it is better to be overinclusive at this point. It is much easier to cut someone loose from the team than try to draft someone at the last minute.

Sign contracts for work spaces

As we will discuss later, hotels have various policies concerning deposits and guarantees. Make sure you understand what is and is not refundable, when payments are due, and other contractual concerns. To the extent possible, retain as much flexibility as you can. For example, hotels have varying lead times for confirmation of the number of rooms you will need, catering contracts, etc.

Assemble your preliminary list of equipment

Based on this list, determine what equipment you have available and what you will need to buy, rent, or borrow for the war room; what the court may have; and what is available at your hotel business center. Also make sure that whatever equipment the court or business center offers actually meets your needs. If it does not, make arrangements to bring in equipment that does. (See Chapter 9.)

Start assembling your database of potential exhibits and video depositions

If you are going to electronically display documents, demonstratives, or video deposition testimony at trial, start doing whatever you or your vendors need to do to assemble this material. This often involves assigning someone to make sure that everything that potentially could be shown is in the correct digital format for use in court. (See Chapter 10.)

PLAN FOR REASONABLE PRODUCTION TIME FOR YOUR PRESENTATION MATERIALS

Time both speeds up and slows down in a war room. Deadlines are tight, events change constantly, and exchange deadlines may be mandated, necessitating updates to your presentation materials. But when you are waiting for a graphic to be completed or a brief to be written, it feels like time is crawling by. When does it need to be done? Yesterday! So why is it taking so long?

*Under these circumstances, it may seem like production time for things like graphics, video deposition clips, PowerPoint slides, and boards should be able to speed up. But this is difficult to do without sacrificing quality and accuracy. A good way to plan for quick turnaround times is to complete as much as you can **before** trial. That way, you can make changes rather than start from scratch.*

Just because your presentation material is created with the latest technology doesn't mean it will necessarily be quick. Any type of demonstrative, but especially 3D models, Flash, animations or PowerPoint can be time intensive even for small revisions. Try to get time-to-complete estimates so you're not caught by surprise, and you know what's possible. And whatever you do, when you're in the war room, do not hover over the person doing the work. Deadlines can be powerful incentives to hurry, but being scrutinized often makes people self-conscious and slows them down. State a realistic deadline; then leave and let your people work.

30 Days Before Trial

Finalize your hotel rooms

This means giving the hotel specific numbers for rooms and dates, plus confirming what services you will need the hotel to provide. Remember, it is far better to be overly inclusive here (even at the prospect of a room going empty for a night or two) than to have to scramble to find lodging for a surprise witness or team member.

Finalize vendor contracts

As discussed above, it often makes sense to hire or contract with established vendors to provide key support activities. For example, copy services can produce five sets of exhibit binders faster than you can, especially at 4 A.M. Likewise, caterers can deliver food to your work space more efficiently than a staff member can pick up food from a restaurant. By this point in your planning, you should be finalizing contracts with any outside support vendors.

Order or rent your equipment

Work with your internal IT department (if you have one) to make sure that you are not spending money needlessly and that what you order and/or rent is compatible with your current setup. If you are not tech-savvy, assign this responsibility to someone who is, or you will run the risk of a late-night data emergency.

Finalize transportation

How are you going to get everything and everyone to the war room? Equally important, once trial is over, how are you going to get all of this stuff back to your offices? Are you going to move it yourself, are you going to hire someone to move it, or are you going to use common-carrier vendors, like UPS or Federal Express? Answer these questions as soon as possible, and line up whatever support you need. (See Chapter 8.)

Visit the venue

If you have not done so already, now is the time to visit the courtroom, your work space, and your hotel. There is no substitute for going to a place in advance and confirming that, based on your prior planning, you have lined up what you will need. If you are using local vendors, meet with them and confirm that they have everything they need from you in advance so that there are no last-minute surprises when you try to establish an account, figure out their file format requirements, or discover that they are, in fact, not a 24-hour operation. Walk the neighborhood where the work space is located to see what restaurants are available, if there is a 24-hour copy center nearby, and just how safe it will be if staff members have to travel between the war room and the hotel late at night.

POWER TO YOUR PEOPLE

Copiers and printers require a lot of power. Ask the hotel to confirm that your war room can handle all your equipment. You also can ask them to install faster Internet connections or ask permission to have your vendor install them. Be sure to confirm prices before going forward with this type of work as it can be expensive.

Lay out the anticipated schedule through the conclusion of trial

Figure out who needs to be where and when (i.e., when you will meet with clients, prep witnesses, practice opening statements, and file paperwork with the courts), as well as when your team should start arriving onsite. If it is going to be a long trial and you expect that you will be rotating staff (i.e., certain people will leave at various times during the trial and be replaced by others), make sure that this schedule is finalized so that everyone has time to plan and to know what is expected.

14 Days Before Trial

Confirm your equipment and office-supply deliveries

If there has been a misunderstanding about what you want and when you want it, you do not want to find out after you have arrived onsite. Contact whomever is providing your equipment and supplies and reconfirm that exactly what you need is arriving when you need it. While you do not want to be a pest, your vendors should understand (and most do) your concern that everything go smoothly for everyone, including them.

Make preliminary travel arrangements

Fourteen-day advance purchase often allows you to get a cheaper fare than booking at the last minute. You should be able to get these kinds of tickets because by now you should have a good idea of exactly who is going and when. This way you also avoid change fees that might result from booking when plans are less certain.

Finalize your database of potential exhibits and video depositions

If you are planning on using technology to display these materials at trial, everything that is available should be organized in a trial presentation database (e.g., TrialDirector or Sanction). Your trial exhibits in the database should be labeled by their trial exhibit numbers, not Bates numbers. This enables quick call-up at trial. (See Chapter 10). Also, the exhibits in the database should be the exact same version that you give the court and that you exchanged with the other side.

Lay out your war room

Grab some paper and sketch out the general shape and size of the war room. It is helpful if you can do so in approximate scale, but it is not necessary. This exercise will do the following:

- Give you a rough approximation of who is going to be working where. This requires you to think about such things as placement: "Putting the copy machine in the meeting/rehearsal room is probably not such a good idea . . . maybe we should put it over here, next to the shelves with the deposition transcripts."

- Confirm that you have enough tables, chairs, shelves, and other pieces of equipment. This requires you to visualize: "We can put one chair here, one here, one here . . . I need to order a couple more chairs."

GETTING TESTY

Test your equipment before sending it; that way you will not arrive on the scene with equipment that does not work. Then test everything once you receive it, just to make sure nothing got banged, shaken, or cursed on its way to the war room. We recommend you have all staff members test their workstations the night they arrive to avoid emergencies that invariably occur before major deadlines.

7 Days Before Trial Begins

Send out your Sergeant Major and a small advance team of logistics staff, including IT, to set up the work space. Among other things, this group needs to:

- Confirm that the Internet and other technology are functioning smoothly

- Coordinate the deliveries of equipment and supplies, which need to be up and running prior to the arrival of the rest of the war room team members

- Unpack boxes and organize their contents

- Physically set up the war room
- Problem-solve for any issues prior to the rest of the team's arrival

Pack It Up, Pack It In . . .

Getting everything to one place in one piece begins with one of the most tedious parts of the process: packing. While your personal suitcase is your own business—you may be an Amie, with an orderly list and a plan of action, or you may be a Chris, who figures if it is not in the bag when he arrives, he can get it there (which has led to some interesting neckties which we know his wife would never have purchased for him)—we do have some recommendations for getting your equipment and supplies to your destination in working order.

A word on boxes: *Because we work in war rooms all the time, we have specially made hard cases for our equipment and supplies. This not only ensures that our stuff arrives safe, but we get the added bonus of appearing to be a rock band upon arrival. While you may not choose to invest so heavily in shipping boxes, this is not a place to be pennywise. Buy solid cardboard boxes in a variety of sizes. Even if you do not ship small boxes, you will need them to protect items that get packed in a larger box.*

Bubble wrap is for more than stress relief: *The two things we use most in packing are bubble wrap and newspaper. It's reusable, easy to get if you run out, and it is easier to manage and clean up than packing peanuts. The stress-relieving properties associated with popping the bubbles are simply a bonus.*

Technological concerns: *It is important for you to be thoughtful about what electronics you ship. Monitors, keyboards, and other sturdy items are fine to ship, as long as* *you protect them (in factory boxes, with bubble wrap, etc.), but you do not, under any circumstances, want to ship more sensitive items like laptops, which can easily stop working if they get heavily jostled.*

Stick it to 'em: There are regulations at both postal and parcel services regarding the type of tape used to seal boxes. You cannot use duct, gaffer, or masking tape. Use clear packing tape.

Weighty matters: Remember, you are going to have to lift and shift all of these items when you arrive. As all shipping costs are determined by weight, you will not save money by overloading a smaller number of bigger boxes. So break it out and ship smaller, lighter boxes. Your back (and your advance team) will thank you. You will also want to confirm weight limits with your shipper.

Lists, lists, lists: You should have a master packing list. Make sure that your advance team has a copy, as well as any breakout lists.

The once-over twice: Double-check the contents of each box against its packing list before you seal it up and send it.

Labels, not just for shipping: Do not be afraid to number or write the contents of each box on the outside. This will help your advance team know what, if anything, is missing and what to unpack first.

5 Days Before Trial Begins

Have your trial tech, graphics team, and any other support vendors arrive at the war room. The best timing is to have them arrive after you have set up the work space, but before the lawyers, client, and first set of witnesses arrive. This keeps vendors out of your way as you set up the war room, but allows them a day to set up whatever they need to start working on when the rest of the team shows up.

4 Days Before Trial Begins

The lawyers, client, early witnesses, and balance of the war room team should arrive several days prior to the first day of trial. At a minimum, they will need time to set up and get familiar with the war room. On top of that, they will need time to fine-tune and rehearse opening statements and witness testimony. In our experience, teams need at least three full working days before trial to be fully integrated and ready for opening statements.

At Least a Full Day Before They Are Scheduled to Testify

Witnesses who are not needed at the trial's start should arrive at the war room at least a day before they are scheduled to testify. This gives them time to get used to the venue and prepare for their testimony. For this to happen, however, war room staff members need to have a firm grasp of the witness list and make sure that the necessary resources (room, food, work space, etc.) have been provided for. Witnesses who plan to finalize visual presentations should plan to arrive earlier to provide adequate time for this work.

FROM "AAAAA-CHOOO" TO ANAPHYLAXIS

Allergies in the war room are no laughing matter. While pollen and animal allergies tend to be of little concern (mostly because you really do not have a lot of free time to go wandering around outside), food allergies can be very serious, especially if they result in constricted breathing or anaphylactic shock.

Fortunately, food allergies can also be managed. While making arrangements for your team, be sure to ask if anyone has any food allergies or dietary restrictions (peanuts, strawberries, etc.). If the answer is "yes," take a few steps to protect the individual as much as possible.

- *Tell the hotel, restaurant, or caterer that you have a team member with a serious food allergy or dietary restriction.*

- *Request that any foods containing allergens be removed from the hotel mini bar before your arrival.*

- *Tell anyone purchasing snacks for the team about any allergies so he can make sure that none of it enters the room inadvertently via peanut candies, wheat chips, etc.*

- *Some allergens seem to be in just about everything, so do make a special effort to provide gluten-free, nut-free, or even egg-free snacks for members of your team who react to those allergens.*

The Short-Order War Room

If you are reading this book with nine days to get ready for trial instead of 90, do not despair. We will spare you the lecture about how you need to start earlier next time; you already know that, and we fully recognize that sometimes these situations are unavoidable. Obviously, your war room will have to be scaled back (at least a bit, possibly more), and you are going to have to be realistic about what you can do prior to and during trial. Nevertheless, it is still possible to put together an effective "short-order" war room that provides essential support for the entire trial team. Here are some ways to save time.

Go big box

If your trial is not local, you need to find out-of-town support to help you set up and potentially staff the war room. If your client has local counsel, enlist their help. Also consider relying on national suppliers (e.g., equipment rental companies and hotel chains) with established reputations, rather than trying to find less expensive local ones. Sure, the boutique local hotel might be a little nicer, but at this stage of the game, you do not have time to go looking for it. Rather, choose something that is well known and well established.

WHEN YOUR HAIR IS ON FIRE

When time is short, the ultimate decision makers (usually the lead trial lawyer and/or her second chair) cannot afford to remain distant. Now is not the time to make team members guess what you want. Be involved in the process and be very explicit as to what you need.

Before you get too discouraged, it may help to know that having less time often forces people to focus on what really matters. The more you can keep this perspective and channel this focus, the better your short-order war room is likely to be.

Regularly allow yourself time to think about what makes sense. While people who are running around with their hair on fire may feel like they are being productive and contributing to the war room effort, they rarely are; in fact, they are usually making things worse. Taking a half hour twice a day to get the team together to discuss exactly what needs to be done will yield enormous dividends.

You will need to triage—that is, take some time to carefully figure out the following:

> • *Which essential tasks does the war room need to be able to do during trial and which tasks are less important? We refer to these two separate categories as "need to have" and "nice to have."*
> • *Of the essential tasks, which can realistically be accomplished, given the strict time limits, and which cannot?*
>
> *Obviously, you need to then devote resources to those tasks that are both important and doable on short notice.*

Retain your preferred consultants—STAT!

The less time you have, the more likely you are to need to outsource certain key tasks. Get on the phone with your preferred consultants and line up as many known quantities as possible. Now is not the time to experiment with new and untested people. If you do not personally know who can do the work for you, call people you trust to get suggestions. Then, when you contact those consultants, make sure they fully understand the tight time constraints under which you—and by extension they—will be operating.

Four of the most important calls should be to your preferred trial tech, trial graphics firm, strategy consultants, and jury consultant to see if they have the capacity to accommodate your case. You might get lucky!

Keep it simple

As you develop graphics or other demonstratives, realize that you may need to dial back your plans for presenting your evidence and demonstratives to the jury. With the understanding that lack of time is no excuse for subpar work, stick to the basics and keep perfectionist tendencies in check. Simple PowerPoint bullets may be less attractive (and impressive) than elaborate graphics, but your design team can create them far faster. Some other ideas:

- **Rely on your trial tech.** These days, databases can be put together relatively quickly, and a trial tech can bring up documents and highlight them for you live, on the fly, in the courtroom.

- **Cut back on video depositions** for impeachment or in lieu of live testimony. They can be expensive to produce.

- **Focus on what you need to create for your presentation.** Two hundred text slides probably will not be beneficial to your case, so take some time to really figure out what you need to convey to the jury.

- **Take it a step at a time.** You do not need to worry about your closing argument while you are putting your opening statement together.

- **Put your colleagues in charge of specific themes or witnesses.** Make sure you keep an overarching view, but trust your team to work independently.

In addition, you likely will have to cut back on the sophistication of the equipment in the war room. For example, you may not be able to set up a network of desktop computers connected to full-color printers. Again, you can find ways to work around this, such as the following:

- **Use a group of laptops.** These can be set up more or less anywhere.

- **Have plenty of flash drives** available to transfer files between computers. They are not as fast as accessing files on a network, but they work well and are much faster than copying to discs or DVDs.

- **Use a local legal copy service.** If you do not have time to have a printer delivered and installed, use a local legal copy service. Relying on the front desk or hotel business center is never wise, as the volume of printing you will need generally far exceeds their capabilities.

Time versus money

Having less time does not necessarily mean that your war room will be less expensive. In fact, short-order war rooms often cost more than those with a longer time frame. Why? If you are pressed for time, you may not be able to comparison shop for the best price for equipment or services. Additionally, just as FedEx will deliver something overnight for many times what it would cost to get it there in a week, many vendors charge rush fees for last-minute requests.

A short-order war room often calls for a larger-than-normal team. This is just simple math: If you hold the amount of work that needs to be done constant but decrease the time to do this work, you will have to increase the number of people in order to get the work completed on time. More people equals more reimbursement, a larger work space, more hotel rooms, more meals, and more transportation, all of which cost money.

Tempted to skimp? Do not do it. Err on the side of overestimating how much of a resource you need (whether it is people, work space size, hotel rooms, or food). Having too little space, too few resources, and not enough time is a horrible combination.

Finding space

If your trial is local, consider using work space at your own firm rather than at a hotel or other location. This may inconvenience others in your office, but you will spend less time setting up and you will have access to all the resources of your office without having to re-create them off-site.

Likewise, if your trial is out of town, see if you can use space at another law firm (such as local counsel). This generally means renting the space and paying for support and any administrative help you may need. You will need to work out client privacy issues with your host, but with appropriate precautions, this can work very well.

Food

If possible, line up some good catering. Military armies and legal war rooms both march on their stomachs. Soldiers usually have the advantage of being able to take some time to eat; this is not always the case for people working in war rooms. You need good food, and you need to have it available for people to eat without taking considerable time to do so. The less energy you have to spend trying to feed yourself and your team, the better—which is what makes catering so effective.

Supplies

Even short-order war rooms need office supplies. If you are hunkering down in one of your firm's conference rooms, you will have access to a steady supply of highlighters, pens, paper, staples, and binders. But if you are headed out of town, you will need all of these things. If you are lucky enough to work in a large firm with lots of resources, the easiest way to get this done is to ask someone at the firm to make you a supply care package. However, if you are bootstrapping it and need to handle this on your own, we recommend ordering online for next-day delivery to your work space, rather than trying to hunt down a local office supply store in a strange town.

Stay calm

This is perhaps the most important thing you can do, especially in a short-order war room. Panic is infectious; your staying calm will keep others calm.

Whether your trial is six months away or six days away, careful planning and strategy can make the difference between a war room—and therefore a courtroom—that is confused and inefficient and one that is orderly and effective. Every war room team has to cope with unexpected events. It is the war room team that has a coherent structure in place, as well as a sense of what has to happen, when, and why, that weathers those events successfully.

CHAPTER 6:
Where Is Your War Room?

When we ask "Where is your war room?" we are really prodding you to consider three important questions:

- Are you going to use existing office space or are you going to create an office in a location generally used for other purposes, such as a hotel conference room?
- Where is your war room in relationship to your regular office, the courtroom, your hotel, and the key resources you will need during trial?
- Is your war room located in a safe place?

As you read this Chapter, you will notice that we pose as many general questions as we suggest specific answers. We have a reason for this. Location is one of those issues that is so case-specific that it is hard to offer universally applicable general advice. Instead, the best we can do is raise a series of questions/issues to consider, offer some general guidelines, and leave you with the answers to find the best location for your war room.

Your war room can be this...   ...or this.

Are You Going to Use Existing Office Space?

The first question you need to consider is what kind of space you're going to use for your war room. The category of "existing office space" includes several options, including your own office or an office in another location. Each of these options, in turn, has advantages and disadvantages.

Using your own office space

Dorothy was right: "There's no place like home." Assuming your trial is local, staying right where you are can be enormously convenient.

Advantages of using your own office space

- **It is nearby.** You will not have to move resources and you need little, if any, setup time if you are using a conference room at your firm, because it probably already has a whiteboard, a projector and screen, and an Internet connection.

- **It is inexpensive.** But do not fool yourself—as we discuss below, using your home office still carries costs, particularly to any office mates not involved in your trial.

- **It is familiar.** Many of your team members will know how to get there, know where to get coffee, understand the office security procedures, and know where the best burrito joint is. Does this matter? You bet it does. A familiar routine is invaluable for someone working under great pressure for long hours on an important project.

- **It is comfortable.** Clients and witnesses are more comfortable working in the familiar environment of your offices during trial. They know where your coffee room is and who is in charge of getting photocopying done.

They also know some of your staff. Again, this can be really valuable during times of duress.

- **It has everything you need.** Or *almost* everything you need. Looking for a yellow highlighter? Go to the supply room or pull one out of your desk. Need a copy machine? It is not easy to get one delivered and installed at a hotel room converted to a war room. But it is gloriously easy to walk down the hall and make copies on the machine you use every day at your office.

- **It has ways of getting things done.** As we will see in Chapters 7 and 8, and some of the most important things you need to operate a successful war room are clear and effective protocols for handling everything from routine matters, like getting copies made late at night, to unexpected events, such as emergency travel arrangements. Most existing offices already have such procedures, as well as the necessary resources and people to implement them.

- **It has people.** If an emergency comes up in your war room—and inevitably it will—you will have the people you need, right there at your office. Even better: these are people you know and trust, which will make dealing with your crisis easier. Need to apply another paralegal to a witness's testimony? It is much easier to go down the hall than have to fly someone across the country at a moment's notice.

- **It is secure.** Presumably, the office security you have developed to protect your client's confidentiality (and the integrity of your work product) during normal operations will be in force during the trial. In other words, you will not have to reinvent or re-implement these protections during trial, when this type of security is particularly at risk in the hustle and bustle of the war room.

Disadvantages of using your own office space

We are not sure if familiarity breeds contempt, but we do know that if your war room is in your home office, familiarity can breed distractions. For instance:

- **There is no escape for you.** All of the other things going on in your professional life will be able to find you, distract you, and use up your time when you should be thinking about nothing but the trial. Focusing on a trial is often easier when you are working someplace other than your home office.

- **There is no escape for others.** Trials have a way of affecting everyone near the trial team, including those folks not directly working on your case. In fact, trials tend to suck all of the oxygen out of a room. Those working on the trial understand and expect this. Those not on your team may have a harder time tolerating this kind of disruption; after all, their regular work continues even when you are in trial. In other words, having the war room at your office may make life considerably more complicated for your colleagues, because you will be monopolizing administrative services, supplies, and equipment, as well as square footage.

Tips on creating a war room in your own office

When we point out these advantages and disadvantages, some clients think that we do not approve of creating a war room in their regular office. This is not the case. If circumstances permit—for example, it is a local trial and you have the in-house facilities to manage the stress and additional work—this type of war room can be incredibly effective. That being said, we do have a few suggestions to make things easier, particularly for others in your office.

- **Do not set up the war room at your normal office if it leaves your firm short of space or disrupts regular operations.** This is particularly the case if your war room will interfere with your colleagues' ability to host and service other clients. The short-term advantages particular to the war room team do not outweigh the long-term disadvantages to the firm as a whole.

- **Do the best you can to isolate the war room from other ongoing activities.** This will insulate you from non-trial-related distractions and protect others from the craziness of your war room. If your firm has several floors of offices, see if you can get space in a more isolated area or in conference rooms away from the regular action.

- **Reserve space generously.** Make the start date of your reservation several weeks before your trial is scheduled to begin so you can start storing material there. Extend the reservation for several weeks after you think the trial will end, too. That way, you can avoid either having to move out in the middle of trial or disappointing a colleague who thought he could use the space on a certain day.

- **Keep the area clean.** Without concerted effort, war rooms get pretty messy pretty quickly, even with a janitorial staff onsite. Piles of papers, empty soda cans, leftover food, and other unsightly litter do accumulate. You want to avoid or at least minimize this in any war room. But you really want to avoid this when the war room is part of the space you share with others in your office or in a location that may be visible to clients.

- **Stay within your allocated space.** War rooms tend to expand to fill all available space, including space that others may need for other legitimate purposes. Your office mates who are not on the war room team will tolerate some of this, but bear in mind that making their regular work life (which does not stop during your trial) more difficult by encroaching on their work space is not fair.

- **Share your resources.** Your first priority as a member of the war room team is to make sure that your client gets everything he or she needs. At the same time, when you have excess resources (even if you have them only temporarily), be willing to share them with others. We have one client who has learned that ordering a little extra food for dinner goes a long way when shared with others who are not on the war room team but are also working late at the office. These niceties make it more likely that future war rooms will be welcomed rather than dreaded by others in the office.

• **Keep a clear line of communication open with others at the office.** If your war room creates a problem, be sure your office mates know whom to talk to on the war room team to get the problem resolved before it escalates into an unmanageable or unpleasant situation.

Using other existing office space

If you cannot or choose not to set up the war room in your office, consider using existing office space at another location, such as the following:

• Your client's offices
• Local counsel's office
• A third party's building close to the courtroom
• A rented office facility where you have your own private offices but share a receptionist, common rooms, and some common equipment with others who are also renting space there

Advantages of using other existing office space

These options have many of the same advantages as setting up your war room at your office, but have some additional positive qualities:

• **Using your client's offices saves them money.** It is also a convenient place to base client witnesses and store documents.

- **Using local counsel's office gives you immediate access to people who know the local rules, local judges, and local services.** This can be an enormous advantage, especially when you are in an unfamiliar locale or far away from your usual trusted vendors.

Disadvantages of using other existing office space

- **You have guest status.** Setting up space in someone else's office (particularly in space usually occupied by your client or local counsel) makes you an interloper. And, as Benjamin Franklin noted, "Guests, like fish, begin to smell after three days." Do not overstay your welcome or abuse the hospitality that is being extended. (And know that the hospitality is sometimes involuntary, particularly on the part of the administrative staff, which will now be supporting not only their team but also a demanding team that is in trial.)

- **You will always need to be on your best behavior.** Even more than in your own office, keep your area clean, your stuff within the space allotted to you, and your lines of communication clear.

CONFIDENTIALITY IN THE WAR ROOM

Keeping mum about your case is one of the hardest things to do when you go onsite. People are everywhere, and so are their laptops, documents, notes, phones, and any number of other ways for information about your case to leak out. And, while you may not be handling state secrets, it is no less important to keep yourself to yourself while onsite. You never know who might be listening!

To keep you and your team on the QT, be sure to:

- *Line up a shredding service and designate just one place (usually a locked rolling bin) to put papers for shredding*

- *Remind your team that cell phone conversations in public could be overheard by opposing counsel, a reporter, or a juror*

- *Remind your team that it is not appropriate (in fact, it could ruin your case, not to mention your reputation) to mention what they are working on via any social network*

- *Keep the war room clean by holding all team members accountable for clearing up their workstation at the end of each night, including papers shredded, binders back on shelves, etc.*

- *Communicate with each team member regarding procedures for accessing the war room, so that each person knows how to make sure the room is secure at all times*

- **You will need to educate yourself and your team on how to get things done.** Just as it is always easier to cook in your own kitchen than in someone else's, it is easier to operate a war room in your own office than in an unfamiliar one. As long as you are in someone else's space, you are going to have limited say in how things are arranged, where things are stored, and what procedures are implemented. This will not bother some people; it will drive others (particularly those in long trials) completely nuts. You cannot avoid this, but by finding one person in the office whom you can contact any time with direct questions, you can avoid some frustration.

- **Security may be a greater concern.** You may not be able to leave your things out as you would in your own space. You also may not be able to talk as freely with other members of the team in areas that you are sharing with your hosts. This may be less of a concern at local counsel's office, but, as you have probably guessed by now, security is crucial wherever you set up your war room.

Potential problems presented by short-term office space at an executive office facility

- **You may have restricted hours of access.** Most of these spaces are intended to operate as work space during regular business hours—not at all hours of the night and on the weekend.

- **You will need to provide most or all of the equipment.** Most offices spaces do not have the kind of workhorse machines required by a war room. So, for example, the printer at the facility may be perfect for the typical businessperson who needs six copies of a document, but wholly inadequate for someone who needs six copies of a thousand documents.

- **Office rentals are expensive, particularly for short or abbreviated events.** Many of these places offer services, supplies, and other resources as part of an *a la carte* menu selection. While this means you will not have to pay for services or supplies you do not need, when you do use something, you may pay a lot, and you may be out of luck if you have not reserved it ahead of time.

Tips on using other existing office space

- **Establish a main contact** at the office for pre-arrival arrangements and initial setup assistance

- **Familiarize yourself with the team** and the layout of the office

- **Seek to understand** how things get done in the new environment

- **Make sure your team understands that you are guests** and should behave as such

ABSENCE MAKES THE HEART . . . LONELY

A war room is a place to focus and work, and it might seem that having family and friends visit you there is counterproductive to that. Though we value hard work and focus, our hearts are not made of stone; we won't say you must ban visitors while you are on the road.

There's a pragmatic side to our thinking on this issue. On long trials, it's not always practical for you to leave the war room for a weekend, so if family members can come to you, it can relieve the some of the stress (and guilty conscience) of being away from home and family. In the long run, this can make it easier to focus on the work at hand. One caveat: Guests need to know what to expect—your availability will be severely curtailed, and you may be called away at any moment—so that they can plan to entertain themselves.

Creating your own office space

Building your own war room usually involves converting space that is typically used for another purpose into an office. Most often this is done using a hotel conference room or suite of rooms.

Advantages of creating your own office space

- **Location, location, location.** Existing office space will be in a location that is or is not ideal for your trial. It may be close to the courthouse or it may be miles away. It may be in a safe neighborhood or it may be next to skid row. Making the decision to convert an alternative space (hotel conference room, hotel suites, etc.) into temporary office space gives you increased flexibility on the location of your war room.

- **Your team can stay in the same building in which they are working.** You can (and most often will) locate the war room in the same hotel where your team is staying during the trial, thereby making it convenient to everyone involved. This is particularly helpful during the long nights and early mornings that are the norm once trial is in full swing.

- **Your team will have access to more services.** Creating a war room at a hotel also gives you access to other resources typically associated with such locations—e.g., restaurants, workout rooms, laundry, etc. Some hotels may provide you with transportation assistance to court or to the airport. We have even seen war room teams temporarily convert a conference room into a mock courtroom, where people can practice opening statements and witness testimony. This level of service can be incredibly helpful (albeit costly).

- **Your team will have flexibility.** With certain restrictions (e.g., you cannot knock down walls), you can more or less design your war room to suit your needs. For instance, you can select the number of rooms, the size of the work space, the kind of chairs, and exactly how many shelves you want to have. Based on what stage of trial you are in, you can also grow or shrink your war room by increasing or decreasing the number of rooms you are using.

- **It is your space!** You are not sharing it with others. If your team needs to work until 3 A.M., no one else will be adversely affected and no one will complain. If you need to talk about the case, you will not have to look over your shoulder to see if you have privacy. We cannot overstate how important this is.

It's Not Easy Being Green . . .

Let us face it: the days of being able to simply chuck all your trash into one can and forget about it are over. Different firms and municipalities have different policies on waste disposal. Regardless of local practices, you can incorporate green practices into your war room several ways:

- *Find out what disposal programs are available at your war room location and ask specifically for recycling guidelines*
- *Ask your shredding company if it recycles*
- *Ship your empty toner cartridges back to the manufacturer (or your home office) for responsible disposal*
- *Ask the hotel if you can participate in a "Second Harvest" program by donating any leftover food to a homeless shelter or food bank*
- *Dispose of batteries responsibly, either through the hotel or by shipping them home for disposal*
- *Purchase locally whenever possible*
- *Participate in hotel linen programs, or request that your sheets and towels not be changed every day*
- *Work digitally as much as possible, and do not print a document unless necessary*

Disadvantages of creating your own office space

- **It is not going to be cheap.** While you may be able to work out a deal, hotels often assume you are a captive audience and charge you accordingly.

- **It is not going to be easy.** Creating an office from scratch takes time and careful forethought. Someone on your team will have to figure out what is needed and make every effort to get it there on time. And once it is there, you have to set it up, make sure all your equipment works, and keep it all functioning throughout trial.

- **It may get complex.** By that we mean that some hotels may need structural updating to accommodate your needs. For example, you may need to get an electrician to install appropriate voltage for a large photocopying machine. The Internet connection may be insufficient. You may need more phone lines. This requires a fair amount of coordination, both with the hotel and with the contractors who do this work.

- **Hotel staff are trained for hospitality, not project management.** Hotel staff may not fully appreciate what needs to be done, how fast it needs to be done, or even how to do it. The engineering staff at a hotel may be more familiar dealing with wireless access issues on a guest-by-guest basis, not high-speed connection issues for an entire work group.

Tips for creating office space

Again, this is not to say a war room in a hotel will not work. We have seen a large number of highly successful war rooms set up in hotels or other areas not usually used for office purposes. But if you go this route:

- **Try to find a place that has done this before.** Hotels (particularly those relatively close to a major courthouse) are hosting more and more war rooms. As a result, many have developed considerable expertise in assisting these clients. Ask attorneys in your office, as well as local counsel, for recommendations.

- **Take a tour (or three).** If it is feasible, go see the facilities early and make sure that a hotel will work for your team. For extra insight, take people who understand

your team, equipment, and IT needs to confirm that the
facility is appropriate or can be reconfigured to offer
what you need.

- **Get references and check them.** Hopefully yours will
  not be the first war room at this location. Check with
  others who preceded you.

- **Plan way ahead.** As we note in Chapters 5 and 8,
  securing work space takes a lot of planning. Do not
  start this the week before your trial starts; someone on
  your team needs to be thinking about this at least three
  months ahead.

- **Keep records.** Without question, your arrangements
  with the facility you are using will be complicated.
  Maintain careful notes and keep copies of all contracts
  and agreements in the Golden Binder, just in case
  confusion arises later.

FREE TIME? WHAT'S THAT?

*We've only had it happen a couple of times, but it's
always been a pleasant surprise: getting a free couple of
hours while onsite. If you are so lucky, we recommend that
you take advantage of this free time to step away from the
case to sightsee a bit. A couple of years ago while in trial
in Dallas, a free afternoon allowed Amie and the team she
was with to visit the John F. Kennedy Memorial and the
Book Depository Museum, which made for an unexpectedly
moving afternoon in the midst of a very contentious case.
On the other hand, nothing beats a shower and a nap when
you've had your shoulder to the wheel for days on end.*

Where Is Your War Room in Relationship To Other Key Resources?

Specifically, assess where your war room is in relationship to your regular office (if you are working locally), the hotel (if you are working in a venue far from home), and the courtroom. To the extent possible, you want to find a place for the war room that is relatively close to both your office or hotel and the courtroom. The less time you spend commuting to the war room from these locations, the better.

Additionally, it is helpful to put the war room close to the key resources that your team will need. Those resources might include the following:

- Adequate transportation, whether that be public (subways, buses) or private (taxis, car services)
- Supermarkets and other stores to get food and supplies
- A photocopying center—hopefully one open 24/7
- An office supply store
- Fitness facilities
- Restaurants (and bars) where people can do everything from getting a quick bite to blowing off a bit of steam
- Movie theaters, museums, and other places to which team members can escape, if they have a few hours free
- The airport or train station where out-of-town members will be arriving or departing

Is the Location Safe?

We were once involved in a war room where two different team members, who left the war room at two different times late at night, were each robbed in separate incidents by the same mugger. (Honest!) Fortunately, neither was hurt and the items stolen were insignificant, but our point should be obvious. The safety of your team is paramount!

Obviously, bad things can happen in even the best locations, but more bad things are likely to happen in the worst locations. Factor this in as you decide where to put your war room.

Unfortunately, many courtrooms sit in not-so-great neighborhoods. That means war rooms located near these courtrooms also will be in not-so-great neighborhoods. To make matters worse, many war room team members will be arriving or leaving the war room late at night or very early in the morning, as that is the typical schedule for trial work.

Staying Safe on the Road

Late nights and unfamiliar locations can lead people to forget that travelers are particularly vulnerable to crime. While we do not like to dwell on it, it is important to remember that some basic steps can go a long way toward keeping you and your team safe while on the road.

When in doubt, get out. *The best way to avoid being the victim of a crime is to listen to your instincts. If your gut is telling you that a particular location or person is potentially dangerous, remove yourself as quickly as you can. Nobody ever won a medal for bravery for hanging out in a dark parking garage.*

Lock it up. *This not only goes for your war room, but also for your hotel room. When you are in your room, make sure you use the additional locks provided beyond the standard keycard entry system.*

Safe keeping. *Many hotels offer safes in the room for your valuables, so use them for your passport, jewelry, or other items. If the room doesn't offer a safe, ask the front desk if the hotel has a safe for guest use, and store your items there so that they are secure.*

The buddy system. *There is safety in numbers, so when you are leaving the war room late at night, be sure to*

> *travel in pairs to your car. If no team member is available, ask building or hotel security to walk you out. Many places are happy to offer this service; use it. In fact, this should be a factor in choosing a location for the war room.*
>
> ***Out of sight, out of mind.*** *Never store your purse, wallet, laptop, or other valuable items in plain sight in your car or hotel room. Keeping these items in a closet, drawer, or trunk while not in use keeps them out of the line of sight (and therefore less tempting) to potential thieves.*

When choosing a work space, candidly ask yourself "How safe is this location?" If the answer is "Not very," try to make appropriate adjustments to protect your team members. For example:

- Move the war room to a different location
- Locate the war room in a hotel where team members can prepare for trial, eat meals, and sleep at night without having to leave the building at odd hours
- Arrange safe transportation for people leaving or arriving at night
- Find a location that provides extra security at night and, ideally, will escort people to their cars or taxis late at night

Accomodations Near Your War Room

Making hotel reservations

You have several options for doing this, but often the best one is to work directly with the hotel's sales department (or manager) to reserve a block of rooms. This allows you to reserve a large number of rooms at a negotiated (usually lower) rate. You also can work with the hotel staff to ensure that they can meet special needs, including a more flexible cancellation policy.

A few tips:

- **Put one person in charge of establishing and maintaining the relationship with the hotel sales department.** Sales staff will work harder for, and be more accountable to, someone they know as opposed to a faceless name. As a general rule, your designated hotel contact should be your Sergeant Major.

- **Make your Sergeant Major the go-to hotel person for your staff.** He or she should maintain the master list of hotel room reservations and manage all requests for rooms and for cancellations.

- **Do not be afraid to ask for advice from the sales department.** Chances are you will not be the first large working group at the hotel. Ask about what worked or did not work for teams that preceded you.

- **Request a corporate rate for your rooms.** This is usually lower than standard room rates and is given to groups reserving a large number of rooms.

- **Document all of your agreements with the hotel.** Do not hesitate to send an email to confirm what has been agreed to. Save your confirmations in the Golden Binder.

- **Make sure you fully understand the terms and conditions associated with booking a block of rooms at the corporate rate.** If you have questions, ask! Many Sergeant Majors cut right to the point by presenting a potential situation and asking exactly what the hotel does in such an instance. For example: "Trials can settle at any time. Let us assume a settlement takes place a couple of days before or after our arrival. Will we be able to cancel the remainder of our reservation without penalty?" Make sure that the client and the lead attorney approve resolutions to these and similar questions.

- **Insist that your rooms be safe and secure.** Consider clustering your teams in nearby rooms. This makes it easier for everyone to watch out for one another (and for people who do not belong there). Yes, your team members will lose a small amount of privacy. But we think that occasionally seeing your colleagues in workout clothes or in a pre-coffee state is a small price to pay for convenience and security.

- **Do not automatically pay for the rooms in advance.** See how long the hotel will hold them for you without payment (generally until the afternoon before the check-in date). This will make it easier to cancel the reservation if your case settles or moves, since you will not be facing lost-room fees for prepaid rooms.

- **Set up a master account so that all charges are linked to one card/cardholder.** Make sure that this is communicated to your war room team. Consider asking your client to be the master account holder.

- **Specify what charges the master account will cover.** And then follow up to ensure your team understands what charges they will be responsible for (usually phone calls, gym passes, mini bar, etc.). They will have to present a credit card upon check-in for billing extra services.

- **Do not be afraid to "wheel and deal."** Hotels would rather fill their rooms than have them sit empty. Many have an unofficial list of things they can be flexible on in order to get the rooms filled. You can, and should, ask for additional accommodations, such as:
  - Free parking
  - Free services or reduced costs at the business center
  - Room upgrades as they become available for experts and others staying at the hotel for short periods of time
  - Upgrades for a limited number of rooms for the duration of your stay (presumably these are rooms that would be used by the client or by the most senior people on the trial team)

- o   Complimentary breakfasts
- o   Liberal use of the hotel's van or town car for transporting people to and from the hotel
- o   Free Internet access for the duration of the stay and
- o   Access for everyone to the "elite" floor or other loyalty-program facilities such as the clubroom

- **Make sure that the hotel staff understands any special needs.** For example, if you are going to need 24-hour-a-day access to the business center or airport shuttle, let them know. Get them to agree while you are still negotiating, which is when you have the most bargaining power.

- **Alert the catering staff of any dietary restrictions among your team members.** The hotel may charge more for this, so get this worked out early on. If possible, get the name of someone in catering that you can call with last-minute adjustments or needs.

Without question, deciding where to set up your war room is a crucial decision, and it can be a little tricky. But by carefully considering the options discussed above—including the relative advantages of your own office versus someone else's; an existing office versus a hotel conference room; and the safest locations available—we are confident that you can come up with a solution that fits your particular trial and your trial team.

CHAPTER 7:
How to Manage Your War Room

Managing a war room is really simple. Here is the secret: All you have to do is (1) line up experienced and skilled leadership, (2) develop well-established and practiced protocols, and (3) maintain clear and open lines of communication with every member of your team. Sounds easy, right? A veritable stroll in the park!

While our insistence on what it takes to successfully manage your team's logistics is sincere, we are being facetious when we suggest that developing, assembling, and maintaining these factors is simple. The good news is that each time you manage a war room it gets a little bit easier. It is never going to be entirely easy; after all, it is impossible to foresee and plan for every possible contingency. But cultivating leadership, establishing protocols, and fostering open communications will go a long way toward keeping everything running as smoothly as possible.

The Sergeant Major

Every coordinated effort needs a leader, and a war room is no exception. You need someone with solid credentials and experience in charge of, and ultimately responsible for, all of the logistics. We refer to this person as the Sergeant Major.

As we noted in Chapter 4, in the military, the Sergeant Major is the most senior enlisted person and is responsible for the welfare of the other enlisted personnel. In this capacity, she often has a direct line of communication (and a well-established relationship) with the most-senior officers. In the context of a war room, the Sergeant Major is usually is a senior litigation paralegal, but she can also be a legal secretary or associate.

The quick answer to the question "What is the Sergeant Major in charge of?" is relatively simple: "Virtually everything in the war room."

Lest we cause undue concern among prospective Sergeant Majors, we should point out that we are not saying they actually have to do *everything*. In fact, one of the most important skills a Sergeant Major should have is the ability to delegate effectively, while at the same time keeping track of what is going on, what needs to be done, who is doing it, and when it will be completed.

While it is impossible to list everything that falls into these categories, some areas definitely require the Sergeant Major's special attention.

Scheduling and coordination

Careful attention to scheduling and timing is essential for any war room. As such, it needs to be part of the Sergeant Major's primary focus. This means making sure not only that things happen, but that they happen on time and in the right order. This daunting task includes ensuring the following:

- Witnesses are available, present, and ready to take the witness stand
- Dress rehearsals and prep sessions take place and are done in a properly equipped and staffed location
- Lawyers and in-court personnel always leave the war room early enough to get to court on time
- All necessary transportation is lined up and waiting for the team (not vice versa)
- All necessary equipment is where it needs to be at the right time

- Projects are triaged so that at any given time the most important tasks are being done first

- Projects are staged to eliminate undue congestion and confusion, as well as to maximize the utility of limited resources

- The team is aware of and meeting all of the deadlines set by the court or agreed to by the parties

- Each person knows his or her job and gets it done on time and correctly

Care and feeding of the troops

We cannot say enough about how important it is to take care of your team. Ensuring that they have healthy eating options, enough sleep, good Internet connections, a safe place to work, a strong cell signal, and a million other details, all start with your Sergeant Major. So, too, does making sure they have access to a fitness facility. Whether or not they use it is up to them—you can lead a lawyer to a treadmill but you cannot make him run. But having it there for those who need to work out in order to feel good (and work well) is crucial. While the attorneys are putting their legal strategy in place, the Sergeant Major should be working with hotels, vendors, and caterers to ensure that the team's physical, mental, emotional, and technical needs will be met in the war room. Do not underestimate how important this is or how much time these tasks will take!

MUSIC TO WHOSE EARS?

Music is a powerful tool. It can be energizing to the point where you cannot help but shake your booty in your office chair or it can be soothing enough for even the most savage trial beast. And one of the great things about modern technology is that almost any song in any genre is available to us at the touch of a button through our laptops, phones, tablets, or MP3 players. But what gets you grooving may be the worst possible choice for your coworkers. Also, you may not need the same sort of stimulation others in the room might need. While you are trying to wind down from a hard day in the courtroom with a little Brahms, your team may need a little Lady Gaga to get them through the evening hours. For the greater peace, try instituting an "ear buds only" policy in the war room (outside of the daily meeting, of course, when nobody should be distracted). That way, those who need a little MC Yogi to get into a focused mental space can do so without disturbing—or being disturbed by—their Hank Williams-loving neighbor.

Calling and scheduling daily team meetings

Your entire team needs to meet once per day. Smaller groups can and should meet more frequently, but getting your **full** team in one place for at least a 15-minute debrief right after court every day is crucial. Your Sergeant Major should ensure that all team members attend (or have a very good reason not to) and that an agenda is set and followed, thereby allowing people to get in, get out, and get on with what needs to be done afterwards. Often this requires that the Sergeant Major be a forceful moderator, cutting off discussions and moving people forward as necessary so that the meetings are succinct and productive.

Identifying and contacting vendors

It would be great if every firm had every single item needed for a war room, but that would be an expensive proposition for an event that happens only once or twice a year for even the most active trial attorneys. Therefore, your Sergeant Major needs to be able to identify and cultivate the outside vendors you might need, including (but definitely not limited to) large-format printers for boards, IT specialists, copy centers, and conference room services.

The Ideal Sergeant Major

Because she is going to be responsible for managing a lot of simultaneously moving parts, the ideal Sergeant Major is blessed with certain characteristics.

Experience and trustworthiness

Few things beat experience. Ideally, your Sergeant Major will have at least a couple of war rooms under her belt, so that she knows what to expect both generally and from the specific people on the strategic and logistic teams. Even if this is your firm's first trial and no one has this specific level of experience, find someone with considerable office experience that will directly translate into the war room. In the best situations, this experience has fostered multiple levels of mutual trust. This is important, because people on the strategic team (particularly the lead lawyers, the client, and the experts) need to feel they can rely on the Sergeant Major, that when she:

- Says something will be done, it will be, and it will be on time
- Has to make a snap decision, it will be consistent with the best interest of the client, the team, and the overall trial strategy
- Offers a suggestion or opinion, it is constructive and credible

The logistics team members also have to trust the Sergeant Major in all of the ways listed above. But, in addition, they need to believe that the Sergeant Major:

- Is watching out for their best interests
- Knows what is going on or can quickly find out what is going on both with the strategic team and with others in the war room

- Triages projects so that deadlines are reasonable and emergencies are real, not something blown out of proportion by the Sergeant Major's poor planning
- Knows what the strategic team wants so that projects need only be done once
- Knows how to work smart, not just hard
- Has backbone to spare

A "can-do" attitude

We all know them: the people whose first response to anything is "no," and whose second is "and here's why not." But in a war room you need people—especially a Sergeant Major—whose first response is either "yes," or "let me try to figure out how to do that." In other words, you need someone who instinctively starts with the presumption that with hard work, thought, and creativity, things can and will get done.

Conversely, there will be times when your Sergeant Major will **not** be able to create a miracle at the last second. Planes only fly so fast, after all, and even FedEx has a drop-off deadline. In those cases, your Sergeant Major needs to be able to "speak truth to power." This can be tough, especially if she knows that doing so might make someone very angry. Nevertheless, if the team has a strong culture, honest communication should be the least of its worries. By stating the case and the facts, your Sergeant Major will ensure that the strategists in the group know the real score and can adjust their plans accordingly.

This brings us back to the importance of making sure your Sergeant Major has a can-do attitude. It is often easier to accept that a project really is impossible when the person delivering that message is someone who does not just instinctively say "no," but instead is a person who has a history of trying to make the impossible possible.

Legal savvy

Your Sergeant Major does not need to be a lawyer, but she should know more than your average citizen about courts, legal procedures, and court personnel.

Knowledge of what the case is about

In addition to general legal knowledge, your Sergeant Major needs to have a clear understanding of the current case and its players. This knowledge will inform many of the decisions that she makes, such as what materials and equipment need to be present in the courtroom for particular expert witnesses, managing court orders and changes to the trial schedule, understanding which attorney is handling direct or cross-examination of specific fact witnesses, and a million other day-to-day decisions that have real and tangible logistical consequences.

An ability to delegate tasks comfortably

The Sergeant Major is going to have to manage an ever-changing calendar of travel and lodging arrangements for other team members. She also will be responsible for gathering documents, creating print sets, pulling together exhibits, filling out subpoena forms, finding files, ordering materials and supplies, and ensuring delivery of all equipment, as well as myriad other in-the-moment tasks.

Whoever assumes this crucial role must understand that she cannot do it all by herself; delegating these tasks is absolutely necessary if it is all going to get done. In other words, while having a Sergeant Major who is detail-oriented and a good manager is crucial, over-the-top control freaks need not apply.

The person you put in charge of your war room logistics needs to be able to recognize when she needs help (so as to provide the best service to you and the client). She should be able to ask for that help, while also remaining cognizant of the fact that sometimes she alone is the best person for a particular task and that she will sometimes just have to buckle down and take care of business.

Furthermore, the Sergeant Major will have to be able to do all this while creating and sustaining a strong teamwork ethos in the war room. Think more majordomo, less masochist.

Strong organizational skills

This really should be a given. With the variety and speed of events in a war room, you cannot have anyone running your team who is not the most organized person you have ever met. It is no good to have someone in charge who cannot find the pens, let alone make sure that your trial exhibits have all been submitted to the court—while also changing hotel reservations, arranging for a car service for your expert witness, and getting a court order so that you can bring your own equipment to the courtroom, *all at the same time.* As you can see, organization in a war room leader is an absolute must.

An ability to focus

With 25 highly pressing matters going on in your war room at once, there will be times when focused concentration is key. As such, you will need a leader who understands the power of such concentration and models it for others. For instance, at The Focal Point, we refer to Chris as the "Buddha of Chaos." With an active and energetic family and a busy professional schedule, we are pretty sure he has more patience and calm than any one human should have.[8] But Chris is also able to get an astonishing amount done in a day. By role-modeling a thoughtful, considered exterior, he is able to show the rest of the team that it is okay to be focused and to take the time to prioritize in the face of an onslaught. (In fact, it is **critical** to slow down and focus in that situation!)

An ability to multitask

Conversely, there will be times in your war room when your Sergeant Major will have to change gears and perform many different tasks at once. The key here is that your war room leader needs to be able to multitask with grace rather than getting so stressed that she loses focus, lets balls drop, or snaps at vendors or other members of the team.

---

8.   Chris's response: "That is very kind of my co-authors to write this, but the truth is I am a fan of Mose Allison, who taught me, as his song lyrics go, 'I don't worry about a thing, 'cause I know, nothin's gonna go alright.'"

Excellent communication skills

The Sergeant Major needs to be able to cultivate a really strong sense of teamwork. Long hours and stressful days call for someone who can create a feeling of "we're all in this together," but who can still get things done. This can mean "asking" rather than "ordering"; knowing how to deliver criticism (quietly and in private) and praise (loudly and in public); and understanding the fine line between strong communication and overcommunication. It has to do with being emotionally intelligent—i.e., understanding one's own emotions, the emotions of others, and how to manage both skillfully. It also has to do with the basic laws of effective communication: using "I" statements, being precise in your communications, treating others with respect, actively listening (including repeating back what you think someone is saying), avoiding interrupting and jumping to conclusions, being open to differing opinions and having the ability to affirm them, and having some control over body language. For example, it is no use saying "thanks for that suggestion" if your palms are up and you are rolling your eyes in the universal "what next?" expression.

Strong relationships with third-party vendors

Your war room will run far more effectively and efficiently if your Sergeant Major has prior experience working with your third-party vendors. Cultivating these relationships is a lot like cultivating relationships with clients: they take time and attention. If your Sergeant Major is someone who only calls vendors when she needs something for an emergency or on an expedited basis, those vendors may not be as responsive as they could be. Moreover, depending on how respectful your Sergeant Major's communications have been in the past, the vendors may or may not feel a desire to go out of their way for your team. Remember, everyone has a minimum job description, but not everyone has to stick to it. The extra mile is exactly that: extra. A respectful Sergeant Major is often able to get vendors to not only go the extra mile but to *want* to do so for your team.

Technical savvy

We all know that the first rule of repairing anything is to check to see if it is plugged in, but your Sergeant Major should have a higher-than-average degree of technical knowledge. This person needs to know the difference between Excel, PowerPoint, Acrobat, and Word, plus have a working knowledge of them. If you think that "the Cloud" is only a nice fluffy thing in the sky or that you find a "drop box" at the receptionist's desk, then you should (1) look for someone who knows more than you do to be the Sergeant Major, and (2) make sure that person is near you at all times.

We are not suggesting that your Sergeant Major needs to be a full-fledged IT specialist; but she does need to be able to troubleshoot, and she does need to know who to call to get problems resolved.

An ability to see the trees *and* the forest

It is easy, in the context of a war room, or even during the life of your case, to get lost in the details and minutiae. Your Sergeant Major needs to understand those details and, at the same time, be able to pull back and offer you and your team some perspective. Without an ability to see both the trees *and* the forest, you run the risk of having a leader who is unable to guide others on the team to what really counts.

A thick skin

This is one of the most important factors to consider when choosing your Sergeant Major. The war room is a tough environment, with tight deadlines, strong personalities, cramped quarters, and all the stressors associated with working on matters that can decide the future of individuals (such as fines, imprisonment, or disgorgement) and companies (including invalidation of patents, protection of trade secrets and trademarks, and the accompanying financial impacts). Understandably, this stress sometimes manifests in harsh comments and criticism, which is often directed (rightly or wrongly) at the Sergeant Major. To survive, your Sergeant Major needs to be willing to ignore the venom in such comments, not take them personally, and move on.

But when we say "thick-skinned" we do not mean that you should be looking for someone who is okay with inappropriate humor or off-color remarks. We are big fans of being able to let off steam in a war room; we just never forget that it is also a work environment. We bring this up so that you understand that emotionally fragile people do not fare well in a war room. If possible, allow people to *choose* to be in a war room, rather than forcing the participation of those who may not be best suited to the work.

An understanding of the principles of self-care

You might be thinking that your Sergeant Major should be someone who is (1) going to work all day and night with never a thought for himself, (2) willing to run himself into the ground for sake of "the Case," and (3) willing to make everyone else on the team do the same thing. The opposite is true. Your Sergeant Major should know when to rest, when to eat, and when to get exercise—as well as when to burn the midnight oil—in order to model that ability to pace oneself for the rest of the team.

STAY UP LATE OR GET UP EARLY?

Before Michael's daughter was born, he got little helpful advice on what to expect, but one suggestion did prove extremely useful: get your sleep whenever you can, because you do not know when the next chance will come. The same holds true for trial. In our experience, one situation where this maxim has proven especially true in the war room, is when it's late at night, and we cannot do any work until an attorney gets us the content we need—the final outline for a witness cross-examination or the page-line designations for a video deposition clip, for instance. Rather than stay up waiting for the information to come to us, we ask the attorney when the material we need might be ready. And if it is going to be more than a couple hours (because she's got three other things to do before she gets to it, as is often the case), we set an alarm and hit the sack. As long as there is no other work to be done, it's better to get some sleep and be refreshed for court the next day than to stay awake at night waiting to be productive.

Processes and Protocols

In addition to choosing the right people to lead your team, it is important to have standard ways of doing things. You need this to maintain both order and sanity. One of the most important protocols is the daily meeting.

Daily meetings

At the daily meeting, your Sergeant Major needs to establish basic ground rules, including that communication is respectful and diplomatic, so that it fosters *more* talking among breakout teams rather than shutting down lines of communication.

We are firm believers in holding a teamwide meeting once a day, at an established time, preferably about an hour after court is done (we understand this may not always be possible). We suggest factoring a brief delay between court ending and the meeting to give people some time to make phone calls, grab showers, stock up on caffeine for the evening, and anything else they may feel the need to accomplish. We suggest this for various reasons:

- Emotionally, people need time to shift from the courtroom to the war room.
- We want everyone's full attention during this meeting. We do not want them to be checking emails or returning phone calls. Those tasks should be completed before or after the meeting, not during it.
- People will be ready to jump right into work once the meeting is over.

- The delay gives the lead attorney some time to talk to the Sergeant Major about what happened that day in court and what needs to be ready for the next day.

On weekends or other days when court is not in session, these meetings should take place in the morning, also at a set time, after everyone has had time to get up, get dressed, and get caffeinated (i.e., 9 or 10 A.M.).

Daily meetings run best when there is an established agenda. That agenda should cover the same topics every time:

- What happened **today** in court?
- What is scheduled to happen **tomorrow** in court?
- What is on the to-do list for **tonight** to prepare for tomorrow?
- What is on tap for the **day after tomorrow**?
- What is on the to-do list for **tonight** to prepare for the day after tomorrow?
- Who is going to do what on the to-do list?
- What problems, if any, do people see?
- Who is going to address those problems?

The daily meeting is not a good time to eat dinner, by the way, as it is not a social event. However, once the meeting is over and everyone is clear on their marching orders, people can eat while working in their breakout groups, whether it is preparing responses to motions, rehearsing witnesses, or working on demonstratives.

The daily meeting is also not the best place to have detailed discussions about narrow problems that do not involve the entire trial team. Those discussions should take place in smaller groups with the people who will be working on those particular issues. If discussions start going in that direction, the Sergeant Major should suggest that these detailed issues can be handled "offline."

The daily meeting also is not a place for small talk. Yes, we believe there is a role for small talk among teammates, whether it is asking about the kids or comparing notes on local restaurants. Those kinds of communications promote bonding and communication. But the daily meeting is not the place for that. The daily meeting needs to be focused, productive, and serious.

One way to keep everyone focused on what needs to be done is to put up a whiteboard in the location that you conduct your daily meeting. We call this the "Sacred Whiteboard." Much like the triage board in an emergency room, the war room whiteboard is a place to keep track of what needs to be done, when it needs to be done, and by whom it will be done. This will allow everyone on your team to see at a glance what's happening and when it is due.

The Sergeant Major—or her assistant, if she is not present—should be the only person who can update the information on this board. Often the best time to do so is during the daily meeting as she reports on progress and lists remaining to-do's.

Reinforce familiar protocols and procedures

Trial is not the time to experiment with new protocols and procedures. Fortunately, most firms have a pretty well-established set of how-to's, so the Sergeant Major's real job here is to remind everyone what those are and insist that everyone stick to them. For example, if timesheets are due the next day by 9 A.M. in the home office, then they are due the same time in the war room. If the accounting department at your office requires receipts for everything over a certain dollar level, then the same requirement applies in the war room.

Does this really need to be done? Yes, because the pressures of trial sometimes cause a collective form of amnesia, which means that the protocols and procedures that everyone follows at the office get ignored.

> # WAIT—I WASN'T DONE WITH THAT YET . . .
>
> *When things get hectic, as they often do in a war room, throwing away papers or deleting emails and other old work product can seem like a good way to maintain order. But we've seen too many instances where important information gets tossed: the email sent a couple days ago turns out to be important for reasons no one could anticipate, or the earlier version of a graphic turned out to be better than the latest revision. Instead of tossing things, create filing systems for previous versions of things. It can be a folder called "Previous" or a subfolder called "Old." Whatever you call it, when you are done with something, put it in there rather than throwing it out.*

Communicating in the War Room

The Focal Point's philosophy about communication is "yes." That is, yes, communication is important and, yes, it has to happen. But in order for it to be effective, it actually has to be planned.

How will the team communicate?

With so many communication modes available now, messages can get fragmented. Are you IMing one person, emailing another, and texting still a third? The plethora of communication tools at our fingertips these days is a boon in some ways, but risky in others. Some guidelines are:

- **Instant Messaging (IM)** is good for "need a latte?" but not so great for telling someone how to load video into a trial database. In other words, it is best for questions that need an immediate response from someone you know is online.

- **Texting** is good for short-burst messages when you are away from your computer, such as "Team meeting in

15 minutes: Constellation Room," but not so good for giving directions on how a graphic needs to be changed. Remember, too, that while you may have a smartphone with unlimited text length, everyone else may not, and the recipient may have to sort through fragmented text messages before making a cogent reply.

- **Email** has become the communication method of choice, but it has its downsides. Remember these key etiquette points to help manage your inbox volume:

  o *Stop the "reply all" madness.* If the message truly applies to the whole group, go for it, but if the point you have is for one person only, start a new email chain in direct communication with that person.

  o *Do not send huge attachments to large groups of people.* If you have a central network, store the file there, and direct people to it. If you must send a large attachment, make sure you target the people who actually need it.

  o *Your subject line is just that: a line.* Do not try to communicate an email's worth of information in that limited space.

  o *Use subject lines to identify your email.* Subject lines can be useful in quickly tracking down important emails, so make sure to include specific, relevant information in them when possible. Also, remember to update subject lines if you add new information to an old email string. Or, better yet, start a new email thread if the information is not directly related.

  o *Remember: It is very easy to misread the tone of an email.* Be sure you review what you have written before hitting "send."

  o *"Send" means send.* It is always good to remind yourself and your team that once that email is sent, it is out of your hands. Double-check recipients, language, and subject matter before you hit the button; you will save yourself a ton of potential embarrassment.

○ *Go live.* If your message is longer than a paragraph, seriously consider a face-to-face discussion.

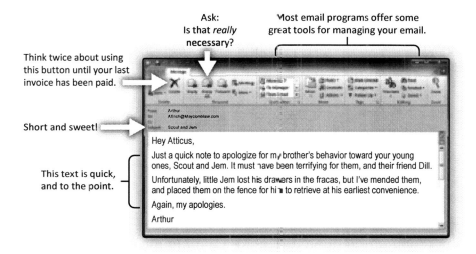

Ask: Is that *really* necessary?

Most email programs offer some great tools for managing your email.

Think twice about using this button until your last invoice has been paid.

Short and sweet!

This text is quick, and to the point.

Arthur
Afinch@Maycomblaw.com

Scout and Jem

Hey Atticus,

Just a quick note to apologize for my brother's behavior toward your young ones, Scout and Jem. It must have been terrifying for them, and their friend Dill.

Unfortunately, little Jem lost his drawers in the fracas, but I've mended them, and placed them on the fence for him to retrieve at his earliest convenience.

Again, my apologies.

Arthur

- **Cell phones** are not going to be available to you in the courtroom, so keeping phone calls to a minimum is important during court hours. All bets are **not** off once court is no longer in session, though. Remember that cell phone conversations are fairly public. Make sure the subject matter is suitable for all ears, even opposing counsel's, as you never know when a member of the opposing legal team is near you.

- **Social media:** We do not recommend using any social media tools during trial. We especially warn against posting anything related to the case on any of your personal pages, no matter how locked down you think your privacy settings are. It is inappropriate; it is not ever truly private; and it could upend not only your case but your reputation.

- **Real live talking:** Call us old-fashioned, but we still believe that the best way to talk with anyone is face-to-face. In the age of social media, smartphones, and videoconferencing, we may have forgotten how pleasurable (yes, pleasurable) a personal conversation can be. Our strongest recommendation is to take the time to walk to the other side of the room or across the hall and have a personal conversation with whom you need to speak. Keep the other methods of communication in their place.

In the Weeds . . . or Over the Cliff?

Having trained and worked as a pastry chef, Amie has spent more than her fair share of time working in a hot, testosterone-driven, high-pressure environment. When it all works though, even an overly macho restaurant kitchen takes on a practically Zen-like vibe.

There are also nights that everything goes wrong. You cannot keep up, you are overwhelmed, and, as they say in the kitchen, you are "in the weeds, man."

We have seen this happen in war rooms too. Sometimes, someone becomes overloaded and doesn't know where to start or where it will all end. He lashes out at co-workers, asks the same question over and over, and cannot figure out what to prioritize. It's important to remember that, even though you have hand-picked your team, no one is immune to this, and it's up to you to recognize and deal with it should it happen in your war room. So what do you do?

- *Offer to help*
- *Prioritize and assess progress on each to-do*
- *Delegate work where possible to less-stressed war room team members*

- *Check back in after an hour or two*
- *Check in again the next day to make sure he is back in the game*

Sometimes you may need to take more drastic action. When a cook cannot pull it together, the chef is sometimes forced to remove him from the kitchen; likewise, you may need to make a call about getting someone out of the war room for the evening. If you need to do this, do it privately, with discretion, and take extra care to follow up with the person the next day. If the situation continues, replace him on the team as soon as possible. After all, war rooms, like professional kitchens, aren't for everyone.

Making a conscious plan for how the team will communicate various needs and topics can bring order and consistency to the war room. We also recommend printing wallet cards with everyone's cell number and email address. That way people can easily get in touch with one another, even if they are away from the war room.

We know that contemplating your first (or even your fiftieth!) war room can be an intimidating prospect. But with the right people, the right principles, and the right attitude, you can approach it with energy rather than foreboding, and you will leave it with an even stronger team than ever (and, we hope, a win!).

CHAPTER 8:
How to Set Up
Your War Room

So far, we have talked a lot about planning your war room. We have discussed who should be there. We have listed what they need to bring. We have described the person who should be in charge. Now it is time to get to work.

In this Chapter we will examine how to get everyone and everything onsite, and, more importantly, what to do once you have done so. Of course, you can set up a war room in many different ways. But time and experience have taught us that there are *better* ways and, well, *less better* ways to get your war room—and by extension your team—up and running.

Two Teams Are Better Than One

In general, and especially for larger matters, we recommend that you send people to set up your war room before everyone else arrives. As we mentioned in Chapter 5, we call this group the "advance team." Your "general team" (which will include the strategic folks and the rest of your logistics support) will follow the advance team by a few days and should arrive to a functioning war room.

The advance team consists of people who will be setting up your war room from scratch, including working with the hotel staff, receiving boxes of equipment and supplies, putting together and arranging furniture, making supply runs, and setting up workstations and networks. We recommend that the advance team arrive at least three days early, but if your war room is going to be large, giving them even more time is wise.

You should have a modified advance team even if your war room is in your own office. Give the in-office advance team a couple of days to do nothing except concentrate on getting your war room set up. That way, the general team is not delayed when it starts its final push toward trial, whether that push takes place in your existing office or 2,500 miles away.

Who should be on this team? Indispensable members include the Sergeant Major, an IT person, and a couple of law firm employees who can serve as helpers. These people should be IKEA-loving folks who can quickly set up furniture, deftly wheel hand-trucks full of boxes, skillfully navigate relationships with your vendors, and gracefully articulate a wide variety of four-letter words when the going gets rough. In other words, you do not want mild-mannered people doing this advance work; you want people who can get results and are willing to work very hard for this short and intense period.

Advance team Arrive 3–7 days before trial	**Early arrivals** Arrive 2–5 days before trial	**Full team** Arrive 2–4 days before trial	**Late arrivals** Arrive throughout trial
Sergeant Major	Graphics team	Lead attorney	Expert witnesses
IT person	Trial tech(s)	Partners & associates	Specialized attorneys
1 paralegal		Paralegals	Auxiliary support staff
1 administrative person		Administrative staff	
		Client representatives	

Every trial is different, and will have different staffing needs. These are our recommended minimums.

What to Do Before You Go

Long before even your advance team gets to the war room, however, you need to handle a number of logistics. These include the following:

Making reservations for work space at a hotel

If you are planning to reserve a conference room in a hotel or office building, you will want to work with the sales staff to get a suitably sized work space that includes the following features:

- Conference tables or rectangular banquet tables for workstations (big round tables may work for meals or meetings, but they are less useful as workstations)

- Smaller break-out rooms, such as hotel guest rooms (beds removed) or small conference rooms, for focused work like witness preparation or opening run-throughs

- A clear cell phone signal

- Additional land-line phones, as well as a conference call speaker

- Straightforward delivery and pickup instructions and access for your vendors (shipping, freight, secure shredding services, etc.)

- Real office chairs rather than banquet chairs, which become uncomfortable quickly

- A location other than in the basement or other lower floor, not because you need a great view (although of course you deserve one), but because:

  o Cell phone coverage is often restricted (or non-existent) on these lower floors; and

  o Rooms on higher floors often provide greater security

- A location that will not disturb other guests if war room activities go long into the night

- A room with windows so that you remember that there is an outside world
- A high-speed Internet connection, supplied either by the hotel or an outside vendor (beware hotel wireless systems: they can be intermittent and are vulnerable to security breaches)
- A way to lock the room so that your files are secure (make sure that you also have 24/7 access during your stay, however)
- Prearranged catering, if possible, which will allow your team to eat well and save time
- A liberal cancellation policy, so that you do not have to pay for any unused time or can at least pay a reduced rate

Integrating your team into space at another existing office

If you plan to use a satellite office of your firm or have arranged to work out of local counsel's office, all of the concerns listed above are relevant. But you will also have other considerations. Specifically, take the time to do the following:

- **Establish a main contact at the office for pre-arrival arrangements and initial setup assistance.** This can be the head paralegal or other administrative staff. Remember, though, that this person has other duties to attend to and, unless otherwise stated, is not a permanent part of your team. Do not abuse this relationship.
- **Familiarize yourself with the staff and the layout of the office.**
- **Understand how "things are done."** Never assume that just because you do things one way, everyone else does them that way, too. This applies to everything from kitchen duty to copies to conference room reservations. Our experience is that in this one particular situation, it is better to ask permission than beg forgiveness.

- Be gracious guests. Make sure that everyone on your team understands the etiquette and behaves accordingly.

How long should you reserve the space?

You can never be sure of the exact length of a trial, of course. But with the help of your lead attorney, you can make a good estimate. Then add a few days to a week for wiggle room, depending on your venue (we have found that state courts are more likely to go over schedule than federal ones) and the size of your trial. Bottom line? It is always better to pay for a couple of extra days than to lose productivity by having to move people to another war room right before closing argument.

What to Send to Your War Room

No matter where you set up your war room, you are going to need *things*—office supplies, furniture, and all sorts of equipment—in order to function. But deciding what to bring, how much to bring, how to pack it efficiently, and when you should just say "it would be easier to rent onsite" can be confusing. No doubt your own team will come up with its own way of stocking a war room, but in the meantime, here are some general guidelines.

Office Supplies

Determining what you need

It is safe to say that you are going to need the same office supplies in the war room that you use in your home office—and likely a few extras. If your war room is going to be in a law firm (either your own or someone else's), office supplies are not going to be a big issue, since you will probably find an already assembled supply available. Just be sure that everyone has what they need (or want). For example, some people prefer #2 pencils to retractable ones, or some insist on fine felt-tip pens as opposed to roller-ball pens.

We like to create standard supply lists that we pull out every time we pack up for a war room, although we also keep in mind those individual preferences. A list for a moderate-sized war room looks something like this:

Supplies and Office Products

Item

Staplers
In/out trays
Staple removers
Pen cups
Scissors
Rulers
Color copier paper
Blue pens
Black pens
Red pens
Black Sharpies
Red Sharpies
Mechanical pencils
Yellow highlighters
Small Post-It notes
Regular Post-It notes
Large Post-It notes
Notepads
Large paperclips
Medium binder clips
Large binder clips
Correction tape
Binders
File folders
Scotch tape
AA batteries
Stopwatch
Staples
Flash drives
Powerstrips
Extension cords
Mousepads
Laser pointers

In addition, we suggest that you bring:

- A tool kit (with a hammer, pliers, several screwdrivers, wire cutters, and both duct and gaffer's tape)
- An emergency kit (including a list of emergency contact numbers for all your staff, plus a first-aid kit)
- Hard copies of local maps and/or driving directions to key services (hospital, airport, hotel, office supply shops, grocery stores, drug stores, copy centers, etc.)
- An eyeglass repair kit and/or an extra pair of glasses
- Mints and gum—never underestimate the power of fresh breath
- A small sewing kit for quick repairs before heading to court (we once saw opposing counsel give an entire closing argument with a paperclip holding his shirt closed, and we are pretty sure the jury noticed, too)

Keeping track of it all

You want your team to use the supplies; that is why you provide them. But the more people use the supplies, the faster they run out. Make sure that someone on your team is charged with checking the supplies **daily** and either replenishing them directly or alerting the Sergeant Major that specific items are running low and need to be supplemented.

GO FOR THE BEST YOU CAN AFFORD

Ordering a roomful of supplies can be expensive, and we know it can be tempting to try to cut costs by buying cheaper products. But we highly recommend investing in good-quality office supplies. They work better, last longer, and keep your team members happier. For instance, given a choice between cheap ballpoint pens and nice ones, go for the highest quality you can afford. The aggravation saved in stains and unintentionally blue fingers is well worth the slightly higher price.

Supply Storage

Once you get to your war room, do not make your team members dig through cardboard boxes for their supplies. Your advance team will set up your systems and your storage plan for the duration. We recommend that you reserve or buy a set of shelves specifically for supplies so that your entire team knows where to go for more pens, highlighters, toner, paper, etc. The key is that it be simple, visible, and accessible.

Determining how much storage you will need

If you have a large and complex matter requiring an equally large and complex team, consider devoting a breakout room for your supply storage needs. Conversely, if you have a short (but brutal) war room planned, you may only need a shelf or two.

In addition, we suggest that you bring these items:

- Plastic storage bins in which to unpack boxes of pens, pencils, binder clips, correction tape, etc.
- Extra bankers boxes for the work product that will be produced during the trial
- Extra shipping supplies

Keeping track of it all

Develop a system for keeping track of all of your supplies and inventory as it arrives and, equally important, as it departs. Nothing is more irritating (to you/the hotel/conference space/local counsel) than having to chase down things that have been left behind. Make sure you check everything into and out of your war room against a master spreadsheet or packing list.

Small war room – an example layout

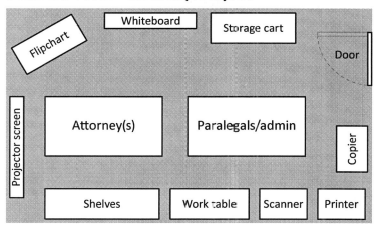

Medium war room – an example layout

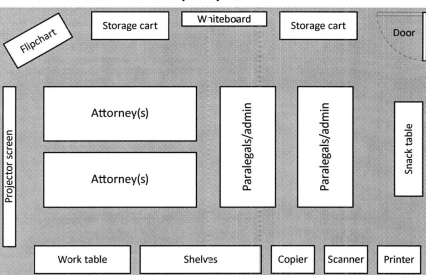

Large war room – an example layout

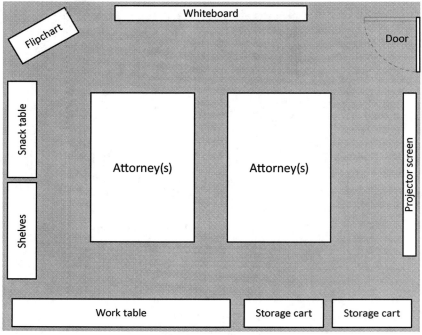

Main war room

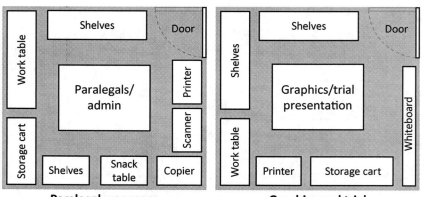

Paralegal war room

Graphics and trial presentation war room

Equipment

Given how much of your communication and work product will be digital, you want to be certain that you are bringing all the electronic equipment you need. At a bare minimum, we recommend:

- A laptop or other computer for each team member's exclusive use

- A printer connected to every team member via a local network, or at least able to accept a connection via USB cable (a color printer is nice, but often not necessary)

- A portable copier/scanner or a rented high-speed copier

- High-capacity external hard drives for hosting files on a local network (if you do not have access to files on your home server) and for backing up files

- Flash drives, both for transferring files between personnel and for bringing files to court (consider getting both regular and encrypted flash drives for confidential material)

- Extra cables (network and USB), power cords, surge protectors, mice, keyboards, and mouse pads

- An LCD projector, desktop speakers, and a projection screen for rehearsals

You Can Get a Virus in a Flash (Drive)

Flash drives (or thumb drives) are a convenient way to transfer files from one computer to another. However, due to the popularity of these small backup devices, many hackers design computer viruses that are transferred through them. If your computers have anti-virus software (and they should), use it to scan your flash drives frequently. And when inserting someone else's flash drive into your computer, hold down the left "Shift" key for a minute; this disables the computer's auto-run function, which very often will keep viruses on the flash drive from launching.

In addition, we suggest bringing a list of your vendors and their support numbers. That way, when the printer starts choking at 11 P.M., you will not be scrambling to find the right number to call, in addition to keeping the attorneys calm.

Equipment needed to produce display materials for court

The hardware that you need for working on display materials in the war room is fairly straightforward. First, you need a powerful PC with ample hard drive space, preferably but not necessarily a laptop, that is at or near the top of the line. Second, you need a duplicate (or comparable) PC, in case something goes wrong with the first one.

Why PC? It is not because they are better than Apple computers; each of us owns multiple Apple products for personal use. It is simply because almost everyone in the legal industry uses them, and you want to be as compatible with your clients, co-counsel, and courts as you possibly can.[9] As we have said dozens of times by now, the war room is a stressful, fast-paced, deadline-driven environment where the most important resource is time. You do not want to spend that valuable time hassling with a computer that cannot easily share files with other computers.

In terms of software you have many options. Some common types of software used during trial are listed in Chapter 10. This is not to say that these are the only types of software that will work, but they are the types of software we see most often and what we use ourselves. Some of that software is very powerful and specialized; it is not necessary for you to have skills in all of the programs. We recommend leaving the specialized software to the specialists, and bringing the standard software you use every day at the office with you to the war room.

---

9.   Having said this, we will note that as of the writing of this book, PC laptops are the current industry standard for the legal field and in courtrooms, but other types of technology are becoming increasingly common. It is definitely worth your time to investigate alternative technologies, such as tablet computers and smartphones, to round out your trial preparation toolbox. Many tablets offer robust apps for the legal industry using a variety of operating systems. Just make sure that whatever you decide to use in your trial prep and presentation, be it PC or iPad, is compatible with the rest of your team's equipment or your files may not be readable by anyone else, and you may not be able to display them in court.

What you need to practice for court

We have said this before, but it bears repeating: Everything done in the war room is done in the service of one goal—prevailing in court. This takes more than just preparation; it also takes practice.

Sometimes it isn't pretty...

You should do a full dress-rehearsal of your opening statement at least once before giving it to the jury, with graphics and any other materials you plan to use. If your experts are going to show graphics or charts, you will want to run through those with them in the war room. And witnesses, especially those who have never testified before, will benefit greatly from a dry run that approximates the same conditions they will experience in the courtroom.

Keeping track of it all

It is possible, and even probable, that when you get the war room up and running, you will discover that you do not have something you need. It could be something as small as a stapler or as big as a scanner. Whatever it is, take the steps to get what you need as soon as you realize you do not have it. The problem will only get bigger if you procrastinate.

Telecommunications Equipment

Everything happens over phone lines these days, from a simple call to large data transfers. In order to accomplish all that you will need to do in a war room, you are going to need these items:

- **A smartphone for every team member.** This allows
  everyone to not only call or text but also send and
  receive what may be critical emails or documents at a
  moment's notice. A basic cell phone is no longer enough
  when you are working in a war room.

- **A hard-wired, high-speed Internet connection.** This
  means that there is an actual cable that comes into the
  room to connect your computers to the Internet. This
  is faster and more secure than any wireless connection
  you could establish. The high-speed connection will
  allow your team to access the Internet and transfer large
  documents quickly. You also will need an Internet hub
  (also called a switch).

- **A wireless network as a backup.** One big advantage
  of a wireless network over a hardwire connection is
  that it can be easier to set up, with just a few pieces of
  equipment and no need to install wiring in places that
  may not have the capability. But a reminder: They are
  not as secure as hard-wired connections, so be very
  thoughtful when making your decision.

- **A strong cell phone signal is a must for every war
  room.** Being stuck in a basement or in a room with little
  or no signal will stop you in your tracks faster than an
  adverse ruling in court.

*i*CONNECT

*An Internet hub or switch is a device that splits one
Internet signal and distributes it to multiple computers. It
is the same principle as using a power strip in a room with
only one wall socket; it expands the number of people who
can plug in their devices.*

In addition, we suggest the following:

- If you can afford it, have the hotel put a dedicated Internet line into your war room that is separate from the hotel's line for guests. This will ensure fast, reliable, and secure service.

- If your room does not have a wired Internet port and you cannot afford to have one installed, bring extra-long Internet cables and a couple of Ethernet hubs so you can split the signal from another room.

- It is always a good idea to bring extra analog phones for larger war rooms in the event of dead batteries or lost chargers.

- We also recommend that you pack an extra cell phone charger in your bag. Someone always forgets theirs, and in small towns they may not be very easy to find. Know, too, that you can buy chargers that fit multiple types of phones at major drugstores and office-supply stores.

Furniture

As a very basic guide, you will need tables, chairs, and shelves, as listed below, but you should not be shy about asking the hotel to provide more or fewer as you need them. Do you have team members leaving midway through the trial? If they are gone for a week or more, dismantle their workstations to provide more room for remaining staff. Using a hotel room as a breakout space? Have the hotel remove the bed and add an extra desk or a table.

When planning your furniture needs, make sure you have the following:

- **Workstation space of at least 36" for each team member.** We list this in inches rather than seats, as you will want to make sure that people have a little space to spread out. Ensuring a set amount of space per table also means you will not crowd people.

- **Comfortable chairs.** We cannot stress this enough. Standard banquet chairs will not keep people feeling good throughout the trial. Look for solid office chairs and offer to rent or even buy them if your facility does not have them.

In addition, we suggest bringing:

- **Extra tables** for clear work space (if you have room)
- **Halogen lamps** for each worktable to reduce eyestrain and ease long working hours under harsh overhead lights
- **Large dry-erase boards** for brainstorming

PERSONAL SPACE—IT MATTERS

Edward T. Hall created the concept of proxemics in his book The Hidden Dimension. *In it, he describes the varying unseen dimensions that surround individuals in relationship to others, depending on the nature of that relationship.*

In a war room, it's important to foster close working relationships, but "close" shouldn't apply to physical distance—you do not want people to feel like they are in a submarine. Provide enough personal space at workstations and dining tables for each member of the team to feel comfortable; that's generally at least 2 to 4 linear feet of space between individuals. This is what's known as "personal distance," which is what people from Western societies generally expect with acquaintances and casual friends. So only put two people at a typical 8-foot conference table, even though, technically, three would fit.

This is not just touchy-feely stuff; findings by Hall have shown that when people are forced to be too close to others with whom they are not intimate, they get uncomfortable, distracted, and do not focus as well. While people from different cultures have different requirements, Americans, interestingly, need more personal space than any other culture. Taking the time to plan for the personal space needs of your team will go a long way toward ensuring a more relaxed working environment and thus a better-functioning team.

Keeping track of what you have

Be sure to confirm that you got what you asked for and that you fill in the gaps. For example, if you discover that the furniture-rental company provided you with five, not six, conference tables, call and ask for another to be delivered. And if you then discover that you really need seven, call again.

Case Boxes and Files

Determining what you need

The legal strategy team generally calculates the exact number of case boxes and files, as well as when they will be delivered. You also should order more of the supplies needed for case boxes and files, including correctly sized binders, file folders, and boxes for shipping.

You will need to arrange an infrastructure and location for the materials. You might consider putting all the supporting materials in one room (or one part of a room), for instance, and all reference materials in another room.

In addition, we suggest bringing:

- A heavy-duty, three-hole punch so that you can make binders quickly and easily
- A label maker so that you can identify and store case files with ease (and not have to decipher someone's handwriting)

Keeping track of it all

You will need to create a checkout system to help keep track of who is using materials. This goes for the smallest war rooms as well as the largest. Nothing is more frustrating than looking for a file, only to discover it three hours later on a colleague's desk. Your checkout system does not have to be complicated; a slip of paper will suffice, as long as it includes the material's identifying name or number, a date, a time, and the name of the person using it.

GET MOVIN'!

Think about how you will move your stuff (including boxes, equipment, and furniture) around the war room. Hotels or maintenance departments can provide hand trucks and carts for that; you just need to order them ahead of time.

Personal Items

Determining what you need

In these times of extra baggage fees and limited airline services, almost everyone tries to fly without checking bags. If you know you will not need them before you arrive onsite, we recommend sending the following items ahead.

- **Suits or other dress clothes.** These tend to take up the most space in your luggage.
- **Books or other free-time supplies.** You may want to have something to read or play in the hotel room to help you wind down before knocking out.
- **Extra shoes.** Wear your most comfortable pair on the plane and send the dress shoes you will use in court.

- **Toiletries.** If your trial is exceptionally long, leave them at home and purchase what you need when you arrive.

- **Extra glasses.** These can be hard to come by on short notice, and are a critical piece of equipment.

It is a travel truism that you always come home with more than you left with. Pack a smaller, empty bag inside of your suitcase to accommodate items that accumulate with time on the road.

Keeping track of it all

Your personal items really should not migrate from your hotel room to the war room, but we all know how it goes. Make sure that team members returning home early do a sweep of not just their work space but the entire war room to locate any stray MP3 players, chargers, batteries, cables, notebooks, etc., before they depart for home. The last thing you want to deal with when you are packing up the war room is matching up staffers with random bits and pieces of personal stuff.

Food and Sustenance

War room still life

Determining what you need

We cannot emphasize enough how important it is to keep your troops well fed in the war room. This entails not only scheduling catering for breakfast, lunch, and dinner, but also having a constant supply of snacks and beverages on hand. If you are in a hotel, in your firm's offices, or at local counsel's, these things may already be taken care of. But be sure to call ahead to confirm the number of people you are expecting. At minimum, you will want to ensure that your team has:

- Bottled water
- Energy and/or protein bars
- Fresh fruit
- Coffee and tea, along with cream and sugar
- And, of course, candy

LOCAL FLAVOR

If you are relying exclusively on hotel catering for your meals, you may want to consider bringing in food from a local restaurant at least a couple of times per week. This will help break up the monotony of hotel catering (which is generally a pretty limited menu), as well as give your team a taste of some local specialties. After all, you wouldn't want to miss barbecue in Kansas City, jambalaya in New Orleans, or lobster rolls in Maine.

If you are managing the supply of snacks and beverages on your own, a quick trip to the grocery store by you or your advance team should do the trick.

Remember, you can always go back and get more, but making sure you have a fair supply on hand at the start will help you understand how much you will need later.

In addition, we suggest that you bring:

- **A limited number of soda options.** You do not need to meet everyone's needs. Honestly, unless the person who wants vanilla diet-cherry sparkling water can commit to drinking a case, plain water will do the trick. We cover our beverage bases by providing still water, bubbly water, iced tea, a cola, a diet cola, a clear soda, and a diet clear soda, as well as hot coffee and tea.

- **A wide range of healthy snacks, such as roasted nuts, trail mix, beef jerky, fruit leather, etc.** Keeping these on hand provides a satisfying snack and helps your team keep the candy consumption down.

Storage issues

As you might imagine, storage of food is a big issue in a war room, both because you want to keep it fresh and because you want to discourage vermin from taking up residence. We have found that keeping food items in a plastic storage bin with a lid, rather than in open boxes or on shelves, is the best option.

Keeping track of it all

As with office supplies, snacks need to be monitored and replenished on a regular basis. (If you run out of dried fruit and nuts, your team will survive, but if you run out of coffee or peanut M&M's? Heads will roll.)

WHAT ITEM IS MOST OFTEN FORGOTTEN?

Amie: If I had a dime for every emergency call for a projector, I'd be a (moderately) rich woman. Remember, you'll need to do run-throughs of your various presentations, as will your expert witnesses, supporting attorneys, etc. Make sure you have at least a rudimentary projector in the room for just such practice sessions (you can always use the wall for a screen).

Chris: I have a far less technological take on what people forget to bring. I cannot count the times I, or another member of the team, have walked out from a windowless war room, only to find that it is pouring outside and there is not an umbrella to be had. How disappointing to arrive in court with a killer argument and a fantastic visual presentation, only to be undermined by a damp suit and dripping hair. Do yourself a favor: get your hands on several good travel umbrellas, and have them readily available for the war room.

Michael: People always forget what it's like to sit in the gallery of a courtroom day after day. One thing they can do to make this easier is to bring a cushion to absorb some of that impact. Got a favorite sports team? Get a stadium cushion to park under yourself. Your posterior (not to mention your back) will thank you (probably even before the lunch break on day one).

Transportation

You will not always need rental cars—but you will pretty often.

Determining what you need

Just how many (if any) cars you need depends on a number of factors, including:

- Where you are going
- How far from the courtroom you will be
- How big your team is
- Whether you are in a "taxi town"

For example, if you are going to be in New York City, getting a rental car is basically a death wish. Only New Yorkers can drive there and survive, and most choose not to. Subway, taxi, and messenger services will more than suffice. But if you are going to be in Denver, where you will find little public transport and few cabs, having a rental car to get from the airport to the war room, from the war room out to restaurants, and from the war room to the courtroom would indeed be helpful.

Still not sure if you need a rental car? Go ahead and reserve one anyway. You are generally under no obligation to pick it up if, once you arrive, you find that a taxi makes more sense.

Keeping track of it all

It is possible that once you are in your war room, you will discover that you need another rental car or driver. Just remember: if you add a driver to an existing account, you need to take that person to the rental car office and sign him or her up. As far as we know, no rental car company will let you sign someone up over the phone or by email.

GET UP, STAND UP

We do not claim to be experts, but we do know that good ergonomics is one of the most overlooked areas in any war room. Long hours in a hotel-issued folding chair hunched over a laptop is a surefire method for inducing back and neck pain, eyestrain, headaches, and sore muscles everywhere.

We have a few tips, but we also recommend talking with your firm's HR professionals for more guidance and resources.

Before the war room:

- *Make good ergonomics part of your planning right from the start by packing your supply and equipment boxes reasonably so that anyone can move them if needed, not just the strongest person in the room.*

- *Post instructions on exercising at your desk or stretching recommendations for those who will be burning the midnight oil.*

- *Get good chairs. Really, we cannot stress this enough. If the facility you are working in cannot provide them, rent them. The payoff of a good chair will be immediately evident.*

During trial:

- *Take frequent, short walking breaks, even if it is just down the hallway and back. Use this time to stretch, get the blood flowing, grab a glass of water, and give your eyes a much-needed rest.*

- *Encourage people to use the exercise facilities. Keeping up normal fitness routines is one of the best ways to fight the "war room 10," while also helping to keep your team on an even physical (and mental) keel.*

- *Use a checkpoint-friendly rollerbag for your laptop and files that you need to transport to and from the courthouse.*

- *Do not ignore team members who complain about physical strain. Rather, work with them to implement the right solution so that they can continue to be productive and effective throughout the trial.*

How to Get Your Stuff to the War Room

We have told you *what* to pack. But how you get your materials *to* the war room is equally important.

Let's face it, short of having your luggage go missing, having your stuff arrive in pieces is the most dispiriting thing on any trip (business or otherwise). And even though you have your advance team on the ground several days ahead of your arrival, hunting down or replacing missing or broken items is the last thing you or your team members need to be doing as you prepare for opening statements.

Packing

We have lots of tips for you on packing, but the most important thing is to ensure that your team has enough time to do it properly and thoughtfully. By following our tips below (or even just a few of them), you will be well on your way to making sure that your items arrive safely and in good condition, and that you'll be even better prepared for packing up and going home once trial is over.

Make sure you have enough of the appropriate shipping supplies on hand before you get going. We recommend these materials:

- **Cardboard boxes in a variety of sizes.** Do not fall into the trap of getting only big boxes, thinking they are easier to organize or cheaper to ship. Shipping is priced by weight. The bigger the boxes, the more you can put in them, and consequently, the more they will cost to get from Point A to Point B. By using a variety of sizes, you can ensure that items can be appropriately cushioned, and that boxes will not be too heavy for your team to move around.

- **Bubble wrap.** It will protect your items from damage. It's also great fun once you have unpacked.

- **Packing tape.** Have two or three tape guns on hand during the packing process (one always gets misplaced—or packed!).

- **Marking pens.** To write box numbers or contents on your packed boxes.

- **Box cutter.** To customize box sizes and re-open prematurely closed boxes.

Next, we suggest that you make several lists:

- **Master packing list.** This will help you understand just how much you need to ship, as well as allow you to make packing lists for each box (which will be key, as you will see in just a bit). This also will be your master inventory as you unpack and, ultimately, repack for the journey home.

- **Smaller packing lists.** The second list is actually several lists. Take your master inventory and break it out into sensible groups (office supplies, case files, equipment, etc.). Print each of these groups as individual packing lists and use them as your guide as you start packing. As your advance team unpacks, they will be able to see what should be in the box, and can identify and replace any missing or broken items.

Once your advance team is onsite, they should be instructed to not throw any shipping materials out. Rather, the boxes should be stored (either assembled or broken down) with the individual packing list attached to each box. Your team will know exactly what to look for to pack up when returning.

One sanity-saver: Make one box your "First to Unpack" box. This box should be clearly marked and include these key items that your advance team will need:

- Basic office supplies (a few pens, scissors, pads of paper, etc.)
- A basic tool kit, with at least a screwdriver, hammer, wrench, and box cutter
- Basic first aid items
- A hard copy of the contact list for all members of the team, including vendors
- A few snacks (protein bars, mints, gum)
- A packing-tape gun
- An extra extension cord or power strip
- Wet wipes to clean surfaces

- Zip ties
- Gaffer's tape (for taping cords down on carpet)
- A hard copy of your master inventory list

One final tip on packing: Do you use equipment that comes in heavy-duty shipping containers (e.g., printers and projectors)? If so, make sure you inspect the exterior for any holes, cracks, or other imperfections that might cause damage to your equipment before you ship it out.

Insurance

Some people are dedicated to the idea of insurance when shipping. But since insurance will not help you locate lost items (it only pays for replacements), we believe you get the most value from your insurance by covering only expensive technology or equipment. Things that are easy to replace, such as office supplies, do not warrant the additional cost of insurance, whereas expensive equipment, such as printers and monitors, should be covered for at least the replacement value.

DOUBLE-DUTY

Remember earlier when we mentioned heavy-duty shipping boxes for equipment? Well, rather than roll them away into a storage space while you occupy your war room, think about using them as extra furniture. Many are just the right height for extra seating, work space, or even rolling tables.

Labeling

One of the biggest favors you can do yourself while packing is to write a list of the contents on the outside of every box. That way, as boxes are delivered, you can immediately take them to the room or area where they belong—whether it is the case materials area, the snack area, or the hang-out room.

Choosing a delivery method

So your office is in Boston and your trial is in Chicago. Which delivery method should you use? It depends on a number of factors:

- When does it need to be there?
- How much lead time do you have?
- How much do you need to send?
- What is your budget?

If you want to be extra careful, you can hire a truck and a driver to personally deliver everything you need to your war room. We know of one firm that does that no matter where their case is (even if it is cross-country) and they have yet to lose a thing.

THE SHIPPING NEWS

One thing is for sure, when you are arranging for shipping, you could easily be overwhelmed by the number of options you have at your disposal. It's important to consider several factors before you make a decision as to how to get your supplies and equipment from Point A to Peoria.

Cost: If you have a cost-conscious client, you are going to want to spend more time than money on this process and send your equipment early, either through ground shipping with a parcel service or through the USPS. The potential downside to this is that the earlier you send something, the greater the chances the matter will settle in the interim, and the cost of shipping proves unnecessary.

Timing: Are you short on time? Then, by following the maxim of "fast, cheap, or easy . . . pick two," you will wind up spending a bit more to get your stuff where it needs to be via an overnight (or close to overnight) shipping service, but it will be fast and easy—two commodities worth the extra money to compensate you for the lack of time.

Delivery: Will the location to which you are shipping have space to store your items? Call ahead to find out, and if so, we recommend that you ship your equipment to arrive two to three days before you, so you can correct for any missed deliveries or damaged goods. If no storage is available, pick a shipper that can offer you a delivery window that works for your recipient. This is far more efficient than having the items sent to a third location (e.g., local counsel's office) and then having to figure out how to transport them to your war room.

Mix and match: If you have items ready and there is space for storage, consider shipping some items ahead on the slow boat (ground or standard shipping). Save overnight delivery for more time-sensitive items.

Do not bother: When she used to come out from the Midwest to California to visit, Chris's mother stuffed her suitcase with all kinds of items she was afraid she might not find in San Francisco—things like her favorite nationally distributed instant coffee or cinnamon-flavored Pop-Tarts. Eventually, after repeated assurances by Chris that such items were easily purchasable at hundreds of locations in the Bay Area, she stopped shipping all of this stuff and bought it once she arrived. If she did not use it all before she went back home, she left it and Chris's kids would get a windfall (particularly with respect to the Pop-Tarts). Our point is one we mentioned earlier and bears repeating: Consider buying whatever supplies you need locally to further save on shipping costs.

Return shipping: Once the verdict is in and you are packing up to head home, do not waste funds shipping items back to your office overnight. Unless they are critical, ship all items back via ground or standard shipping. You will

> *save your clients hundreds of dollars, and in all honesty, you will not be in a rush to get back to the office to file everything away anyway.*
>
> *Lastly, whatever method you choose, make sure that all outbound and inbound shipping information, tracking numbers, delivery specifics, and other key information is in your Golden Binder so that you have it available for reference should an issue arise.*

What to Do Once You Are at the War Room

If you are reading this because it is your job to set up the war room, you will be part of the advance team. In an ideal world, you will arrive several days early so that you can set up furniture, receive shipments, and get materials organized. Even if that cannot happen, you (and your team) definitely need to arrive one day early to get the room(s) set up so staff can hit the ground running when they arrive.

Here is what you will need to do:

Unpack boxes

Check each box against each individual packing list and against your master inventory sheet so that you are sure you have gotten everything you sent. Mark any items that are missing so that the Sergeant Major can make sure gaps get filled before the team arrives.

DAMAGED GOODS

The first thing to do when you discover that equipment is not working is to check and make sure it is plugged in. If it is still not functioning properly, or has been damaged in shipping, immediately order a replacement. Only when that replacement is on its way can you go about (a) figuring out what happened, (b) figuring out if it was insured, and (c) reporting it. Remember to take photos so you can show the shipper/vendor/insurance company what happened.

The war room in action and under deadline

Configure the war room

It takes a little experience to figure out what goes where in a war room, but even just a little forethought will get you a working layout. We suggest the following:

- **Identify all attendees and designate their work spaces.** Paralegals, associates, consultants, and witnesses will all need working space in addition to the attorneys. By grouping like teammates together, you will ensure a stronger work flow and be able to lay out your resources and technology to greater effect. For instance, we like to put ourselves (that is, graphics consultants and trial tech) in one area; expert witnesses in another; paralegals in still another; and lawyers in their own rooms.

- **Create breakout spaces.** Once you have your workstations laid out, designate another room, or a portion of a larger work space, as extra work spaces.

These areas should be free of storage, printers, food, and other distractions.

- **Designate storage space.** You will need to store, but not regularly access, shipping materials, redundant equipment, backup supplies, and other materials. Ideally this is in another room, but if you need to use space in the main work area, we suggest that you break down what you can and use a discrete corner of the space.

- **Designate supply space.** Binders, books, snacks, and other backup items should be in an area that is easy for the team to access.

Establish the network

We would love to give you specific instructions on how to set up your computer network once you get onsite. But as each war room is going to have different requirements, not to mention different types of equipment, it is not possible for us to create a step-by-step manual. However, we can make some strong recommendations for setting up a secure network for your team.

- If you are working at a satellite office of your firm, have your Sergeant Major begin discussions regarding equipment and networks early in the process. This will help your team determine what can be provided by the firm, what needs to be handled by each individual, and what you will need to rent.

- If you are working at local counsel's office, you will want to have the same discussion with their IT team, but include the following additional questions:
  - Will you be able to access your firm's servers for file sharing? If not, do they have recommendations on how best to do that, using what they have available?
  - Will you be able to print in color or just black and white? If so, how will that work, in a step-by-step fashion?

- o Will bringing in extra equipment (computers, laptops, printers, etc.) overload their network in any way?
- As we have mentioned before, if you are working in a hotel, you will need to bring all of your equipment with you. In this scenario, we strongly recommend having an experienced IT person from your firm, or from an outside vendor, work with the hotel prior to your arrival. We also recommend having that IT person arrive with your advance team to create a secure, stable network for you and the team.

Test your equipment

Make sure that laptops power on, that they can communicate with the printer, that they can talk to each other (if networked) or to the servers at the home office, and that that the fax machine, printer, and copier work properly.

Stock the refrigerator

With any luck, you are somewhere with in-house catering that can meet your team's food and drink needs at any time of day. That said, it is still much easier for everyone if they can just walk over to the fridge and grab a Diet Coke or mineral water. Buying a dorm fridge, or having the hotel put one into your work space, will be a big plus for your team and will allow you to stock not only the energy drinks your team asks for, but also some healthier choices like juice or bottled water.

Make side trips

Once you have unpacked everything, you will know what other supplies you need. Now is the time to make side trips to local grocery or office supply stores for things like wet wipes, water, pens, extra paper, and so on.

Establish relationships with hotel staff

You have dealt with them by phone and email; now it is time to meet them face-to-face. Despite what you may think, the front desk is not your best contact at the hotel. You want the sales representative who sold you your block of rooms or conference room. Then you need to know who the go-to person is for after-hours help. Do not wait until a problem occurs to have this first meeting; introduce yourself right away. Talk about what your team will be doing in the war room. Let your contact know of your expectations and confirm any prior arrangements, such as 24/7 catering, etc.

LINENS AND THINGS

One thing we strongly recommend is removing all linens from tables immediately upon arrival. You do not want cloths on the tables, particularly when you will be setting up equipment that will prevent changing them in the coming days. Removing them prevents future spills, dinners, and broken pens from becoming more of a nuisance than necessary. It also prevents people from getting tangled in the tablecloths and sending expensive equipment crashing onto the floor.

Confirm war room access

Be very sure that everyone who needs to get into the war room can do so at any time. That generally means making sure you have a sufficient number of keys or magnetic cards for getting into conference and hotel rooms (if you are staying at a hotel) or building security cards (if you are working out of a law office). You do not want anyone stranded outside the war room at 2 A.M. in the rain, frantically trying to get the alarm code, as once happened to Amie.

When the Troops Arrive

Early arrivals

You will want a couple of folks to arrive after your advance team but before the full war room team: namely, your trial techs and trial graphics consultants. All of these people will need time on the ground to set up their own networks and workstations and receive any materials they may have shipped. By giving them this extra bit of time, you can be assured that they will be ready to go the instant the strategy team arrives. As an added bonus, if things are a little crazy, you have a knowledgeable and experienced group of people to lend a hand.

The strategic team

If all has gone as planned, by the time your strategic team arrives, the war room will be set up and ready to go. Your first step will be to schedule your first team meeting, during which you will:

- Introduce the team
- Show people where things are located
- Introduce the Golden Binder and Sacred Whiteboard
- Issue ground rules on ordering from room service and other billing issues
- Provide directions on getting from the war room to the courtroom
- Tell everyone what time to meet before court
- Plan for who will be in court daily (versus occasionally)
- Establish the regular time for the daily meeting and reinforce the mandatory nature of the gathering
- Do another systems check to make sure everyone can turn on their laptops, print something, log on to the home office server, and access the Internet

HANDLING LATE ARRIVALS AND EARLY CHECKOUTS

Late arrivals and early departures are a regular part of war rooms, as case needs and courtroom events dictate. Early departures are easy; just make sure that they have checked out of their room and have everything packed up from their workstation so that the next person can take a seat and get down to business. Late arrivals need a little extra attention. At minimum, make sure that you provide them with:

- o *A clean workstation*
- o *A quick orientation to the work space*
- o *An overview of who is in attendance and what they are working on*
- o *A quick systems check*
- o *A review of security systems*

Once you have your people, equipment, and supplies in place, what do you do? Go get a scotch and a good dinner, because you know what is about to hit the fan.

What Goes Up . . .
Packing Up Your War Room

By the time closing arguments have been finished, we can guarantee that you will be dying to get out of the war room and go home. But, just as everything that goes up must come down, everything that gets set up in a war room needs to be taken apart. And that means your war room—and your job—are not finished until the very last package is delivered to the home office and the very last team member is on her way home.

In general, your wrap-up team is going to be the same as your advance team. The wrap-up team will need to complete the following tasks:

- Rebuilding (if necessary) and repacking boxes
- Checking that all items on each packing list and the master inventory are returned to the home office
- Shutting down the network and connections
- Making sure that all rented equipment and furniture is returned to vendors in good condition
- Checking that all personal items have been removed from the war room
- Closing out billing with the hotel
- If you are at another firm's (or your own firm's) offices, thanking the staff and giving a gracious farewell, so that you will be welcomed back next time

This is not a two-hour job, by the way. It is generally an all-day job, and you do not want to rush it, because you might end up compromising the security of your documents, equipment, and other sensitive items in the desire to get home (which can be overwhelming at this point, trust us!).

HOMEWARD BOUND

It may not be worth sending some things back. If you have a few extra boxes of pens, one three-hole punch, and several reams of paper, for instance, you might be better off donating those to a local school than paying for shipping. If you have purchased furniture or other more durable goods you do not want to ship home, a local shelter or other charitable group may be more than happy to put it to good use.

CHAPTER 9:
How to Set Up (and Survive) in the Courtroom

Technology plays an increasingly important role in both the courtroom and the war room. It is not unusual to see computers and monitors in the courtroom, along with everything from blown-up, highlighted deposition testimony to 3D animations. But using technology in the courtroom takes considerable preparation and practice.

This Chapter focuses on how members of the logistics team should:

- Choose, set up, and use the right equipment in the courtroom to display evidence and related demonstratives to the judge/jury/arbitrators

- Choose, set up, and use the right equipment in the war room so the courtroom presentation goes off without a hitch

The order of these topics (i.e., examining courtroom needs before outlining how the war room can support those needs) demonstrates two key points of this book. First, you do what you do in the war room so your client will prevail in the courtroom. Second, what happens in the courtroom only works if it is first perfected in the war room. In other words, make sure that the courtroom and the war room complement each other.

Assessing Courtroom Equipment Needs

Your presentation equipment needs will vary depending on the venue, the audience, and the nature of your event. In every case, the person on the war room team responsible for assembling, running, and maintaining this equipment must consider a series of key questions.

Do I Need to Bring My Own?

Even if your venue provides presentation equipment, you might need to bring your own as well, for a few reasons.

First, the court's equipment may not be very good. It may be out of date or worn out, or maybe it was never that good in the first place. It's worth having someone knowledgeable test it, if possible, or at least get the model numbers and research them online to make sure they are adequate.

Second, the court may not provide everything you need for your presentation. For instance, the federal courthouse in San Francisco has courtrooms with monitors in the jury box, but they do not provide a projector and large screen. Some courts provide a projector and screen, but neither a document camera (Elmo) nor monitors at the witness stand and counsel tables. An experienced trial tech can help you determine what your setup needs are and whether your venue meets those needs.

Third, it is easier to use equipment with which you are familiar. It also is easier to troubleshoot it should something malfunction or need repair.

Where is the event taking place?

While every location is unique, you generally can make a couple of assumptions:

Federal courtrooms

Federal courtrooms tend to be large and well funded. As a result:

- These facilities often have their own basic built-in presentation equipment, which the court generally expects all parties to use.

- Most federal judges and court staff are already familiar and comfortable with electronic presentation equipment and, since they understand the benefits of such technology, are not leery of letting counsel use it.

- To the extent that you have to provide your own equipment (either because the courtroom has none or you need to supplement what is already there), the size of the courtroom often means you need larger and more equipment. This usually makes the presentations more complicated and expensive.

- The size of the courtrooms often means more work and storage space for the person running your presentation. This is a real advantage once you are in trial.

State Courtrooms

State courtrooms vary widely, but they are often small and old. As a result:

- Many state courtrooms have no electronic presentation equipment. This means you may very well have to provide everything yourself

- Many state courtrooms do not have the infrastructure to easily support extensive additional electronic equipment. Bring lots of extension cables and power strips, and talk to the facilities manager to make sure their circuits can handle the extra power load.

- State court personnel often have less experience with such equipment and sometimes are reluctant (or refuse) to let you use it. This does not mean you should not try to get the equipment into the courtroom. It just means you may have to do some polite persuading before you are allowed to do so.

- Courtroom space is often so limited that even when you can use your own equipment, you may be limited to what is absolutely essential. Sometimes this is less than ideal.

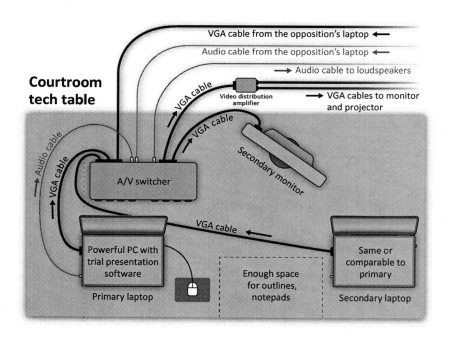

This tech table has the mark of an experienced trial tech.

Arbitrations

Arbitrations usually take place in confined spaces (hotel conference rooms or offices) that were not originally designed for adversarial proceedings. As a result:

- Be prepared for anything (think L-shaped rooms, double-wide trailers, hotel ballrooms, pillars in the wrong places, too few electrical outlets, etc.).

- Most of these locations have virtually no built-in equipment, so you will have to bring whatever you need.

- The administrators in charge of the arbitration generally do not care what equipment you want to use, so often you can be relatively creative in how you display your material.

EXCHANGES

Many courts require that the parties exchange their demonstratives prior to trial or at a predetermined interval during trial (e.g., 48 hours prior to putting on the witness who will rely on the material). This is one of those important local rules that we urged you to uncover and commit to memory.

Whatever your venue requires is likely to put a strain on the war room team. Because the demonstrative exchange can be a delicate dance, you and opposing counsel should have worked out the details long in advance of trial. Whether your exchange deadline for trial is three days or three hours before court, it is critical that you meet that deadline.

This requires a little planning on your part to ensure that your demonstratives are developed, produced, and checked for accuracy before you hand them over to the other side. So consider the following when a new idea for a demonstrative strikes:

Plan for reasonable production time. *While computers and other technological advances mean that we can produce more, and faster than ever before, it will still take some time to conceive of and create graphics, charts, boards, and graphs.*

If you want to create a new demonstrative on the fly, make sure the raw data is available. *It can take a lot of time to, hunt down documents or plow through pages of deposition testimony to find that key quote or number. If you are unsure whether you will ultimately need this material, err on the side of caution and assemble it anyway.*

Determine if you really need to create a demonstrative to exchange with the other side. *You could retain some flexibility by having your trial tech bring up and highlight the already-submitted document using TrialDirector live in court rather than tip your hand by exchanging a pre-treated text pull graphic.*

Do you need to provide print sets? *If so, this is just another reason to have a networked printer available in the war room (make sure it is a color printer if you have to provide full-color prints). If you do not have a printer, give yourself (or someone on your team) extra time to run to the local copy shop to have them printed.*

Double check your work. *Nothing is worse than having your demonstrative hit the big screen in court and seeing a misspelling or data error. We catch errors before we exchange with the other side by providing enough time to do a thorough check of our work. Bear in mind, an error in your demonstrative could also raise an objection from the other side—just another reason to make time for this critical task.*

What kind of event is it?

The nature of the event also can influence your choice of trial presentation equipment. Factors to consider include (1) the audience (e.g., one judge versus a judge and 12 jurors) and (2) the degree of formality associated with the proceeding (e.g., a formal federal jury trial versus a less formal pre-trial motion or contractually mandated arbitration).

Jury trials

As a rule, jury trials require more equipment and are more complicated than bench trials for the simple reason that you are showing your material to more people. In addition, it is crucial that all of the jurors see everything you want them to see. A judge can review certain materials in her chambers after court, but you only get one shot at showing your most compelling evidence to the jury—and that is during trial. (The jury sometimes can review a limited amount of material during deliberations, but that is at the discretion of the judge and is severely limited. So you need to make sure the display during trial really counts.)

Making things visible for all 12 jurors can be more complicated than you might think. For instance, space restrictions in some courtrooms often require you to set up a single screen and projector far from the jury box. This may not allow the jury to see documents that have very small fonts, even if your trial technician zooms in on it. As we discuss below in greater detail, this may mean that you will want to set up supplemental monitors next to, or even inside of, the jury box.

Bench trials

Unfortunately, while many people routinely fret about what equipment to use for a jury, they routinely ignore what equipment the judge may want and need in a bench trial.

We once spoke with a judge concerning what he thought lawyers could do to improve their presentations in bench trials and major pre-trial hearings. He smiled and said, "I hate that juries get all the fun stuff." He went on to explain that while attorneys will give a jury the full audiovisual treatment (especially at opening and closing), they sometimes assume that such techniques would be out of place in a bench trial or hearing, thereby forcing judges to rely solely on verbal arguments. He admitted that he was puzzled by this and could not understand why lawyers were reluctant to use the same technology in bench trials.

The judge did point out that lawyers should alter the content of visual presentations for the bench (probably fewer visual analogies and icons, for instance), but he politely reminded us, "Judges—and this is something that some attorneys unfortunately forget—are people, too." That is, they want to find the fastest way to get a full understanding of the issues (factual and legal) that have been brought to them for resolution. Judges, like everyone else in the courtroom, also want evidence to be displayed in an efficient, focused, interesting, and professional manner.

Many judges, like many jurors, are visual learners who do not entirely "get it" until they can *see* what you are talking about. And like many jurors, most judges like the live action of video deposition and the dynamism of simple, buildable graphics as opposed to the monotony of an imageless presentation.

We have **never** seen a judge who does not pay attention when a salient exhibit or deposition designation is shown on the screen in her courtroom. Putting an exhibit on the screen for the judge and blowing up the relevant section will get her attention, just as it would any juror's. Displaying the exact deposition testimony you are quoting on the judge's monitor, rather than pausing to find the printed version or having the judge thumb through it, will be appreciated as an efficient use of the court's time. Most likely, it will also be far more memorable for her.

Key Pre-trial Hearings

Pre-trial hearings play an increasingly important role in complex litigation. For example, in patent disputes, the Markman or claims construction hearing (which often is held months before the jury trial to determine the meaning of key terms in a patent) can be as important as the subsequent trial. Similarly, preliminary injunction hearings, at which the court views evidence concerning the appropriateness of enjoining commercial activity, often prove dispositive. Given the importance and potential complexity of these hearings, more and more attorneys are creating war rooms to support these efforts.

In terms of equipment, you should treat these key pre-trial hearings as bench trials, with one major logistical complication. Unlike bench trials that generally last for days, pre-trial hearings, though highly critical to a case, are relatively short—often only a few hours. And the court sometimes wedges them between other unrelated events (e.g., on an afternoon when another trial is dark or as part of a series of hearings on motions for several different cases). This means you may have limited time to set up your equipment. And when your hearing is done, you may have virtually no time to get everything out of the courtroom before the next event gets under way.

The net result is that (1) your options may be severely limited, and (2) even when you have options, the implementation may be challenging. The safest bet is to use technology to enhance your argument, but keep the technology as simple as possible.

Arbitrations

The major consideration with arbitrations is the size of the room in which you will be presenting your case. Arbitration facilities vary widely. They can be held in cavernous hotel conference rooms or offices so small you can barely turn around. If you are going to be in the Grand Ballroom, make sure that your screen is big enough—at least 8 feet, and bigger if possible. If you are in the equivalent of a broom closet, make sure that your screen (and all other equipment) is compact enough to fit. And if you are thinking of using boards, do not assume they will be workable at any venue. We have been in arbitrations where the boards that the attorneys were planning to use literally would not fit in the room once all the equipment was set up and all of the parties were in their seats. In the Grand Ballroom, your boards may be so far away from the audience that they are unreadable.

Which brings us to the best aspect of arbitrations: you can get away with presenting things a little differently than you can at a more formal trial. In other words, get creative and let the less-formal structure work in your favor.

What are you going to be doing during the event?

This is a relatively straightforward question to ask yourself and your team, repeatedly, right up to the time you start trial. Are you using video depositions? Are you playing animations? Do you have to show a lot of documents to the jury? If so, how are the key documents going to be displayed? The answer to each of these and related questions will determine what equipment you need for the courtroom.

Equipping the Courtroom

What equipment and infrastructure already exist at your venue?

As indicated above, some locations have built-in equipment; others do not. Some courtrooms have infrastructure that can handle the strain of adding significant audiovisual equipment; others cannot. With this in mind, you need to determine the lay of the land at your venue.

Sizing up the venue

Check with the person in charge of your location. Ask about both the equipment and technical limitations in the room.

- **If you are setting up in a courtroom,** start with the clerk. He can get you in touch with the designated technology staff person if the court has one.

- **If you are setting up for an arbitration,** the sponsoring organization (for example, the American Arbitration Association) usually appoints an administrator or similar person to take care of logistics for the arbitration panel. Start with this person.

Do not take everything you are told at face value. With all due respect to the venue administrator, you really will not know what you are dealing with until a tech-savvy member of the war room team actually checks it out. This is because administrators do not always fully understand what they have. Or if they do know what they have, they may not realize that their equipment may not be in the best shape.

Because that is a possibility, ask the clerk if a member of your team—preferably the person running the presentation—can test court-provided equipment before your presentation. Set up this appointment well in advance.

Once again, manners matter. As we stress often in this book, etiquette is a key consideration when you are dealing with court personnel. So, if you do ask to test the equipment, you should:

- **Be flexible** – Usually the clerk is doing you a favor by letting you in the courtroom at an odd hour to do this testing;

- **Be prepared** – The objective is to get the information as quickly as possible and get out of there with minimum disruption to the clerk or court; and

- **Be polite** – We hope this goes without saying. Remember: this is the clerk who will be supervising your trial and, as we discussed before, this is not a good person to upset.

Testing equimpent

If your venue provides equipment, make an independent assessment as to whether the existing equipment serves your specific needs. Let us look at a couple of common examples. Assume that you have key documents that you need the jurors to carefully read and review. Alternatively, you may be relying on hours of taped deposition transcripts from witnesses that are unavailable at trial. In both instances you may need monitors installed in, or near, the jury box. The courtroom may provide a monitor, but if it is only a single, unmovable, small monitor halfway across the well, half (or more) of your jurors will not be able to see it clearly enough to thoughtfully review your materials.

To accurately make this determination, you may need to bring specific examples of your key exhibits/demonstratives with you (e.g., deposition clips or key documents that you need the judge/jury to be able to read) and test them on the court's equipment.

If the results are less than satisfactory, consider finding a diplomatic way of sharing this information with the venue administrator. When you do, make sure you have a reasonable alternative plan to discuss as well. The worst thing you can do is to complain and then leave it up to the courtroom deputy to figure out what to do. In such an instance, we can virtually guarantee that you will do nothing but alienate the wrong person.

Will you be allowed to supplement the existing equipment?

Let's assume that you decide you need to supplement the court's existing equipment. Do you immediately start assembling a long list of what you will be bringing to court? Well, yes and no.

Yes, you should put together a list of what you feel is needed. But before you go out and rent or buy this equipment, make sure that the court will let you use it. Here we remind you of the observation from one of our greatest modern philosophers, Mick Jagger: "You can't always get what you want . . . but if you try sometimes, you just might find, you get what you need."

Why would the court refuse to let you bring in lot of equipment to the courtroom? The court generally has three reasons:

- **The location is too small for the equipment you want to use.** For instance, you cannot automatically assume that an 8-foot-wide screen will fit. And if it is a question of whether the screen goes or the jury box goes . . . well, you get the point.

- **The court simply will not let you bring equipment into the courtroom.** This may not seem like a rational decision, but if that is what they say, try to see it their way. You are asking them to alter their environment for your needs; they may think that you are going to disrupt their process, too. They may not know a lot about technology or they may have had a bad experience with it in the past. They may envision you bringing a projector the size of a Volkswagen and strewing cords all over the place. It may be possible to dissuade them of these mistaken notions, but it takes time and a diplomatic effort.

- **Even when the equipment is there, you might not get to use it your way.** Judges often have strong opinions on what should be shown during presentations, and those opinions do not just concern admissibility. Sometimes judges just do not like what you want to do. Here is actual trial testimony from a case we worked on that demonstrates this tendency.

  ATTORNEY: Your Honor, I would like to show an excerpt of the video deposition. . . .

  THE COURT: Why don't you just read it? Is it something that is going to be [so] shocking that we have to see? It is just an answer. Just read the question and answer.

The attorney, of course, read the deposition excerpt, rather than playing the video clip we had prepared. It is one of the basic rules of trials: The judge always gets what the judge wants. Do not get too attached to what you want to display or how you want to display it. But do not give up either; if you have a good reason to show the clip, ask to show it. Most judges are willing to let you use the equipment if it is there. We just want you to know that this is not always the case.

> ## Judge's "Golden Rule":
> **Do unto judges as they would want you to do unto them.**

Arbitrations

When it comes to equipment in arbitrations, the administrator generally will allow the parties to do whatever they want (within reason). So the real question is whether the room in which the arbitration will take place can accommodate your technological needs. If it cannot, many arbitrators are willing to change locations; after all, the parties are usually paying for the arbitrators' time and renting (either directly or indirectly) the location. If the parties are willing to pay for a larger room and moving will not cause undue prejudice, many arbitrators will accommodate you. That being said, there is no guarantee, so check before you go out and procure expensive technology.

Courtrooms

Things are often less certain when it comes to courtrooms. Most courts do not care if you bring in additional equipment (within reason, and bear in mind that the judge will have the final say). Other courts are very reluctant to let you do so—often with good reason. The courtroom may not have the necessary infrastructure (electrical plugs and power) to tolerate much additional equipment, for instance. Or an extremely heavy docket will not allow sufficient time to set up and remove additional equipment. Other times, the court just does not want the perceived hassle.

Whatever the reason, be ready to deal with this reluctance. To increase the chances of getting what you need in the courtroom:

- **Be politely diplomatic.** We are repeatedly shocked at stories of trial techs belittling the existing courtroom equipment, flashing their admittedly superior knowledge, and demanding that they be able to completely redo the courtroom just for their trial. This kind of crass behavior is embarrassing on many levels.

- **Be politely persistent.** Try to educate the clerk as to how the technology will work and look, as well as why it is important. For instance, if you are asking to put monitors in the jury box, explain that you need this so the jurors can see the fine print in the contracts that are at issue. And always tell them that you will tape down all your cables with gaffer's tape to make sure no one will trip over them; this is often a big fear for court staff.

- **When possible, get both parties to make a single request.** The fact that two adverse parties agree on what is needed and that there is a single request and not a series of them is always appreciated by the person who has to make the decision whether to admit more equipment into the courtroom. At minimum, work to ensure that you do not have to double up on equipment such as projectors, screens, etc.

- **Show the court the advantages of adopting your suggestion.** A court that is used to using an Elmo may not appreciate the benefit of an integrated database system that projects the key material onto a screen or monitor. Be clear about the advantages, including the fact that such systems benefit the jurors by making their job easier and also help the court by moving testimony along more quickly and with fewer interruptions.

- **Bend over backwards to accommodate the court.** Additional equipment often requires time to install. Be willing to work with the court on its own schedule. When you go to install the equipment, be prepared—do it on a single trip; do not forget something and then have to come back a second time. Remember, your credibility is on the line.

- **Ask if your equipment should be taken down at night.** Some clerks will ask you to do this if the courtroom will be used for other matters during the course of your trial. Often, if you respectfully point out that you are placing your equipment and taping down all the cables to avoid inconveniencing people, you can get permission to leave it up overnight. You can also point out that you are not afraid that the equipment will be damaged or stolen— another typical concern—as you have always left the equipment set up in other courtrooms.

THE MAGIC OF GAFFER'S TAPE

Because a war room and a courtroom are a bustling places, taping down the myriad cables that will be criss-crossing the floor is crucial if you want to prevent tripping (and the awful possibility of having someone file a lawsuit as a result of working on your lawsuit). Not all tapes are created equal, gaffer's tape is the best. It tears easily, it adheres well to carpet, and it doesn't leave residue behind when you pull it off, unlike duct tape.

What equipment should you bring?

Let us assume that (a) you need equipment and (b) the court is willing to accommodate your bringing in such equipment. Now the obvious question is, what equipment do you need?

- **Big projection screen.** One of the most common mistakes that people make is getting a display screen that is way too small. If you have the budget and the space, get a big screen, at least 6½ feet wide. A screen of up to 10 feet wide may be necessary to effectively display materials to the jury if it is more than 25 feet away. At the same time, keep room constraints in mind to avoid overcrowding.

- **Projector.** This should be powerful enough to display an image clearly in full lighting conditions, since many judges will *not* dim the lights for such presentations.
  - Choose an LCD projector over a DLP. Many DLP projectors display graphics poorly. Your demonstratives will be crisper and your highlights clearer if you use an LCD model.

DO NOT SKIMP ON COURTROOM PRESENTATION EQUIPMENT!

Get the best. Or, at the very least, do not simply choose by cost or convenience. When you rent equipment from vendors, make sure they know what they are doing—if you can, find one who specializes in litigation—and ask them for recommendations if you aren't sure what you need.

While it's important to make sure you have high-quality equipment, prioritize your equipment budget by eliminating what you do not need. Loudspeakers and microphones may not be necessary in a small courtroom. If your display materials have been digitized, do you really need an Elmo? Does every table in the courtroom need a monitor if the main presentation screen is clearly visible? Focus on what really matters to keep your costs in check. Also, do not let the media drive the message. If a blackboard and chalk will get your idea across better than using 3D animation, we say use the blackboard. But if you are relying on digital graphics, prioritize your projector and an adequately-sized screen above all to ensure a clean, crisp, visual presentation for your jury.

Make sure that whatever equipment you decide to use is up to the task. Consider the general size and power of the larger pieces of equipment.

LESS IS MORE

*You do not want screens tipping over or projectors getting knocked off tables, and you do **not** want your judge getting cranky because you have crammed so much stuff into her courtroom that it has become a distraction. When you are thinking about how to present your materials and how much equipment you can cram into that courtroom, remember the wisdom of Coco Chanel, who advised women to always remove one accessory before leaving the house to ensure that they didn't overdo it. In other words, more is not always better; sometimes more is just more.*

DO LUMENS REALLY MATTER?

Yes! Most consumer-level projectors range from 1,500 to 10,000 lumens. And, while lumens are not the only thing to consider when choosing a projector—the difference between a 3,000-lumen and a 4,000-lumen projector can be slight, and the 3,000-lumen one might actually produce a better-looking image—it is an important specification.

We recommend not going lower than 3,000 lumens, because you would have to dim the lights to see the image clearly on any projector with a lower rating. For most normal lighting situations, you do not need to go above 7,000 lumens, so shoot for something in the 4,000- to 6,000-lumen range.

In addition to the equipment described above, you may need a variety of other equipment, such as:

- **A backup projector and/or a spare bulb.** Ideally you will have both, but at a minimum have a spare bulb.

Why? Because a burned-out bulb is one of the most common reasons for projector failure. And we are here to attest that it is not so easy to find an extra projector bulb on short notice. Unlike a regular household lightbulb, projector bulbs are not standardized and often need to be special-ordered. So unless your trial is in a major metropolitan area, just assume that it will take at least a couple of days to get a replacement—unless you bring one with you. If you are using the court's projector, make sure you get the specifications so that you can secure a spare bulb, should the court not have one on hand.

- **Portable projector stand.** Surprisingly, many venues do not provide this. The alternative is to try to find an existing table to put your projector on, but even if you can move the table (which sometimes is not permitted), it takes time and is awkward. It also limits where you put the projector and screen. A portable stand with a small footprint allows the most placement options.

  o Do not use a chair as a substitute for a stand. It is almost impossible to get projectors level on chairs; they are not designed for such an expensive piece of equipment. Plus, it looks terrible and should be embarrassing.

  o Be sure your projector stand is steady, and consider strapping your projector to it. We once saw an attorney accidently nudge an unsecured projector on a small stand, sending it crashing to the floor and rendering it inoperable.

  o If you want to get fancy, get a skirt to go around the table. This will conceal wires and look more professional.

- **LCD monitors for key people in the courtroom.** To the extent that you need to augment the large projection screen for key courtroom personnel, we suggest that you consider adding LCD monitors for:

- ■ Counsel tables in federal court (2)
- ■ Podium (1)
- ■ Witness (1)
- ■ Clerk (1)
- ■ Courtroom deputy (1)
- ■ Judge (1)

- **LCD monitors for the jury.** To the extent that you need to augment the large projection screen for the jurors, consider placing LCD monitors in the jury box. These can be arranged so that each juror has access to his own screen (in which case you will need up to twelve) or every two jurors can share a monitor (in which case you will need six). Be sure to account for alternate jurors.

  o Monitors can be placed in the jury box on stands

  o Some courts, especially district courts, have these built in, so be sure to check with the clerk

  o Note: if you are going to get resistance from court personnel not accustomed to electronic equipment, these monitors are likely to trigger it

- **Two powerful laptops**—one primary, one backup

  o These should be fairly new, near or at the top of the line, and thoroughly tested (do not purchase a laptop from a store on the way to trial!).

  o They should have a video port—preferably VGA— that can output to a projector or monitor.

  o Each laptop should be equipped with the following software:

    ■ Windows XP or later (we have nothing against Apple, but as of the date of this book, PCs are ubiquitous in the legal field[10])

    ■ Microsoft Office

---

10. If you do have an Apple laptop, know that in some courthouses you cannot plug it into the court's video presentation system without an adapter (which you have to bring yourself).

- ■ Adobe Acrobat Pro
- ■ Basic video and graphic editing software
- ■ TrialDirector, Sanction, or other trial presentation database (for more on trial presentation technology, see Chapter 10)

- **Speakers.** Desktop speakers will not suffice; use a loudspeaker. But for goodness sake, do not do what we saw one vendor do in court—use an electric guitar amplifier instead of a real speaker. The only thing tackier than using a guitar amp as a loudspeaker is using a chair as a projector stand.

  - o Bench trials may not require speakers because many judges prefer to have impeachment deposition testimony read into the record rather than watching video of it.

  - o Make sure your speakers are loud enough for your venue.

  - o A separate volume control nearby is helpful for quick adjustments—often needed when playing video depositions, where the volumes fluctuate.

- **Video kill switch.** Some judges require this simple on/off video switch so they can immediately remove an image that has been erroneously put up on the jurors' screens, or to stop the action when there is an objection. Even if the judge does not take personal control of the kill switch, the person presenting in a jury trial may. This is not an expensive piece of equipment; we guarantee it will cost less than a new trial if the court declares a mistrial for improper and prolonged display of inadmissible material.

- **Video switcher.** This piece of equipment allows multiple parties to share the same base display equipment. Specifically, it allows each party to have its own computer but use the same projector, screen, and monitors. This saves considerable time, because neither party has to stop, unplug its computer, then wait for the other party to plug in its computer and get set up.

- o Generally speaking, unpowered switchers are simple to use but can be slow (i.e., there is a lag when switching to different computer inputs)

- o Powered switchers are more complicated but switch faster

- **Video distribution amplifier (DA).** This sends the video signal from a laptop to multiple sources (i.e., projector *and* monitors). It helps prevent video quality loss by amplifying signal strength.

- **PowerPoint slide advance remote control.** This gives the lawyer (or anyone working on behalf of the lawyer) the option of advancing the graphics on his own when using PowerPoint rather than relying on a trial technician to do so.

- **Laser pointer.** In fact, we recommend that you bring several, as this is an item that tends to disappear.

- **Stopwatch or other easy to read timer.** Judges often limit the amount of time lawyers have to present, and this simple item helps you keep track of it.

- **Tech table.**

  - o We recommend letting the trial technician sit separately from counsel. The tech needs room, and many lawyers find it very distracting to have someone working at the same table where they are trying to talk to clients, get ready for cross, and manage all of the intense activities that take place at counsel table during trial.

  - o This table should be big enough for one trial tech and two laptops, but small enough to have many placement options (4 feet by 2 feet is ideal).

- **Power strips and extension cords.** Many courtrooms have limited power outlet access. Do not scrimp on these. Use premium-gauge cables and power-surge protectors to protect your equipment.

- **A document camera.** This is often referred to by the brand name Elmo. Use this to display physical evidence or paper documents through the projection system. Think of it as the old-fashioned overhead projector—on steroids.

- **Annotation screen.** Allows the presenter to make virtual markups on the presentation screen. Alternatively, you can give it to the witness.
  - o This equipment often allows you to save marked-up images for later use.
  - o Practice with this before trial to make sure you really want it. We have seen many trial teams enthusiastically rent one, no doubt with John Madden fantasies in their heads, only to find them harder to use than anticipated.

- **VGA cables.** These are cables that send video signal from computers to monitors and projectors.
  - o Use high-quality cables.
  - o Make sure to have an assortment of lengths, including very short and very long (3 feet to 50 feet).

- **Gaffer's tape.** Use it to secure cables in the war room and courtroom.

- **Two easels.** Remember, you will not be displaying everything electronically. Most courts do have easels, but they tend to be flimsy. We prefer metal over wooden easels and those that have fixed legs rather than telescoping legs.

THE WORLD'S BEST EASEL

In this age of lumens, gigabytes, and 3D animations, do not overlook the importance of a good easel, for both displaying boards and holding up blank flip charts for writing on in front of the jury.

Unfortunately, most courtrooms either do not provide easels or the ones they provide are so flimsy as to be useless. For this reason we routinely bring our own easels or make them available to our clients. We recommend spending a little more on this piece of equipment, and going with a metal easel with fixed legs and a bar on top for flip charts.

Here's why:

- *They are sturdy, so they will not collapse on you. You can beat them up pretty badly (not that we encourage this) and still use them for many more trials and hearings.*

- *They allow you to display material in portrait and landscape format.*

- *The legs are fixed, not telescoping. While this makes them a bit more difficult to transport, they have three advantages over "portable" easels: they are quicker to set up, they are always level, and there is no danger of a leg collapsing in the middle of your presentation.*

Whatever model you ultimately choose, make sure you put your firm's name on it, since they tend to disappear after the hearing. That may be the best endorsement yet of how superior these types of easels are.

- **A flip chart with a pad of butcher block paper, plus permanent color markers**
  - o Material on this board can be saved, marked, and introduced into evidence.
  - o Get a model that is big enough for the jury to see, but small enough to move around the courtroom as needed.
- **A dry-erase whiteboard, plus dry-erase markers**
  - o Often the court will have such a board. Unfortunately, it is often permanently fixed on a single wall of the courtroom and is not very convenient to use.
  - o We create portable versions of these by taking a foam-core board that is usually used for trial exhibits and treating it with an erasable laminate. You can put this on an easel and move it around as needed.
  - o Anything you write on this will not be permanent, so if you need a record, a flip chart is a better choice.
  - o Do not use permanent marker on this board. (The permanent markers are just for the butcher-block flip chart.)
- **A digital camera.** Use this to take pictures of anything that is drawn and needs to be admitted in evidence. Note that you cannot take a photo, even for legitimate reasons like this, without getting court approval.
- **A signed judicial order.** Not technically a piece of equipment, but very likely to be required to get your equipment into the courtroom.

"Oh No, Wrong Marker!"

It's bound to happen at some point. In the heat of the moment, you pick up a permanent marker and start writing on your dry-erase board, then realize you're not using a dry-erase marker. Here's a tip from The Focal Point: If you liberally go over the permanent mark with a dry-erase marker several times, you can wipe off both layers of ink, thus saving your whiteboard (and you will look like a genius).

Where can you obtain the equipment?

You can rent almost all of the equipment listed above from companies that deal in A/V equipment; some even specialize in litigation. Just make sure they are experienced, reliable, and able to provide quality equipment. How do you know? See if the company provides references or a list of events for which they have provided equipment.

If your trial is going to last more than a couple of weeks, it may be more cost-effective to purchase equipment rather than renting it. Owning it allows you to use it at future trials or sell it at the conclusion of this trial, further reducing your expense to use it (though increasing your time dealing with it).

Setting Up Your Equipment the Right Way, Step by Step

Once you have figured out what equipment the court has and what equipment you should bring, you will need to make plans for setting it up. This takes some time; you cannot just show up at the courthouse 30 minutes before your trial starts and assume you can set up your projector and screen. Once you have called or met with the clerk to find out what you are allowed to bring, you need to do the following:

Call opposing counsel

Presentation equipment (other than the laptop on which each side's data is stored) is almost always shared by both sides at hearings and at trial. Even the biggest federal courtrooms are too small to accommodate two projectors, two screens, and two monitors for every table. And most judges would not allow each side to bring in its own equipment anyway. Equipment sharing is one area on which judges insist the two sides come to agreement.

With the right equipment, this is easy to achieve. Each side can plug into a video switcher that is attached to all the monitors and the projector, and, with the push of a button, either side can present from their own computer. This does require some coordination with the other side, of course. We recommend that you make the first move by starting this process. Arrange for it with the court and secure the equipment with a vendor as soon as possible. Then reach out to the other side, tell them that you have everything in place, and offer to share. Chances are you will have beat them to it, which may force them to cede the setup to you, which means you get the kind of equipment *you* want for your presentation.

What if you get the call from opposing counsel first? You can still exert control over the situation. Ask them to send you a list of exactly what they are providing, compare it to the list you have developed using the information on the preceeding pages, and make sure that what you need is on it. If you have to request supplemental equipment, ask them in an email so you have a record of the request. Also, ask who is providing the equipment. If you are not familiar with the vendor, or if the law firm is providing it themselves, ask for more information about the equipment, like the make and model of the projector and the size of the screen, so you can determine its suitability. If it is not up to your standards—say they want to bring a DLP projector, and after reading this book you know that LCD is the way to go—ask them to bring something different. If they do not agree, you can bring your own piece of replacement equipment to the court. If you explain that you have concerns about the quality of a specific part of the other side's setup, the judge likely will allow you to substitute yours.

Finally, remember that sharing equipment means sharing costs. If your side provides the equipment and the other side uses it, even for a small part of the trial, they can be on the hook for half the rental costs. To help keep them honest, you can always mention to the judge on the record that you have agreed to share equipment and costs with the other side. Likewise, it is really tacky to use someone else's equipment and then not offer to foot part of the bill.

Call the court clerk

Ideally, this is not your first call to the clerk; in your first call you introduced yourself and found out what equipment was available. This subsequent call is to get permission to set up your equipment and to find out when you can get into the courtroom to do so.

If the clerk suggests the morning of the event, politely explain that might not leave enough time (unless of course your setup is extremely simple) and that you would not want to run the risk of delaying the scheduled court proceedings. Try to get a couple of hours the day before. Remember, you need to do more than set up the equipment; you need to test it to make sure it works and troubleshoot any possible problems. Be sure to allow plenty of time for parking and getting through security (which probably will entail standing in line and dealing with lots of scrutiny of the equipment). Since most trials start on a Monday, we suggest asking if you can get into court on the Friday afternoon prior (which is often, but not always, a slow time for the court) to set the equipment up. That way it will be ready to go first thing the next week.

ARE YOUR DEMONSTRATIVES COVERED BY THAT ORDER?

Increasingly courts (particularly United States District Courts) are requiring that the parties exchange "potential exhibits" earlier and earlier—often 30 or more days before trial. We think this is a good idea. But we want to offer a clarification that is overlooked in the war room and, as a

> *result, causes unnecessary concern. Too often we see less-experienced counsel and war rooms panic because they think that this order includes such items as material for the opening statement or (heaven forbid) the closing argument, both of which may be months away. This is usually not the case. Most courts, when they refer to potential "exhibits," are not referring to demonstratives or material that is being offered for illustrative purposes. Instead, the court is looking for the **exhibits**, the items that may reasonably be formally marked and admitted into evidence as part of the official record. Most demonstratives do not rise to this level.*
>
> *We are not saying that such material is never covered by such a pre-trial disclosure order. We are just suggesting that they are generally not covered, and that this failure to clarify can cause unnecessary work and panic. Before you do panic, check with the court! Make sure you fully understand what needs to be produced months in advance and what is not covered by the order and can be exchanged (often as a matter of courtesy) just before it is used in court.*

Get a judicial order allowing you to bring equipment into the court

Security is obviously a great concern for all courts. All federal courts that we know of require a written order from the judge to bring equipment into the courthouse. Some state courts do as well, or they require some form of judicial approval. To get this, you need to list exactly what you intend to use, type that list up in the form of an order, and get the judge to approve it. This takes time; you cannot do it at the last minute. Check ahead of time on exactly what you need to accomplish this task.

Also, do not forget to find out if laptops need to be listed in the order. Most jurisdictions do not require them to be, but some do—and that is a piece of equipment you do *not* want to be without.

This is often a *pro forma* procedure where you simply list everything you propose to bring on pleading paper, submit it to the court as you would any other proposed order, and then get the signed copy back from the judge. It usually can be done the week before the setup. Finally, *make sure to bring the signed order with you to the courthouse to show security.* If you forget, try to contact the courtroom deputy and have him talk to security, but do not count on this. In fact, try to avoid it. Remember, your professionalism and credibility are on the line.

While the lists of equipment and issues to be considered can seem daunting, we can guarantee that not planning for what you need and what might happen (with opposing counsel, with your judge, and with court personnel) will create situations that are even more daunting. As with all aspects of the war room, an ounce of prevention is worth a pound of cure—and will give you 10 pounds of peace of mind.

CHAPTER 10:
How to Organize Your
Material for Trial

In the old days you could watch a strange ritual just before each trial started. A parade of lawyers, paralegals, and other members of the war room would form just outside the courthouse and proceed in solemn fashion into one of the courtrooms. Participants would march more or less in single file, carrying various objects or pushing carts stacked high with boxes of documents. The volume of this material was often tremendous. Boxes would fill all available space in the well and occasionally much of the spectator gallery. Chris even remembers a particularly kind court clerk providing 20 or so filing cabinets, each about 5 feet tall and almost 3 feet deep, for the parties to temporarily store the documentary material they needed for trial. This ritual of bringing forth all the physical material needed to try the case was seen as a sure sign that settlement was impossible and the parties really had to try their dispute.

Fortunately, the importance of this parade has diminished over the years—or at least the number of people needed to participate in it has gone down substantially. Without question, the trend in litigation is toward creating more and more digital databases of this material. In fact, over the last 20 years the practice of digitizing material—from contracts to surveillance video, from photos to depositions—and putting it in databases has become the norm for most medium to large cases. These days, a trial presentation technician from the war room walks into the courtroom simply carrying a laptop—but one with the equivalent of hundreds of bankers boxes of material loaded onto it.

We see three obvious reasons for this trend. First, material in these databases is easier to organize, access, and display in the courtroom. Second, the cost of doing so has decreased dramatically. Third, as anyone who routinely uses email or other aspects of the Internet can attest, more and more key material exists only digitally.

Granted, some material cannot be digitized. Certain physical evidence, such as the tire that exploded and allegedly caused the accident, still needs to be brought into court. The law does sometimes require that the parties produce at trial the actual physical contract with original signatures. And for tactical reasons, some material *should not* be digitized. For example, certain illustrative material, such as an overall time line laying out what happened in chronological order, is better displayed blown up on a board. This allows the trial team to leave the information up on an easel more or less throughout the trial, so that jurors can look at it whenever they choose.

This Chapter examines how the logistics team can go about assembling all of the material that the strategic team needs to display at trial.[11] The early part of this Chapter deals with the digital databases that attorneys can use first as part of trial preparation and then eventually in the trial itself. Assembling these databases can be very complex and so is probably best done by someone on your team who already has extensive experience, even if this person is an outside vendor. Providing you with everything you need to understand this topic is beyond the scope of this book; nevertheless, we hope that after reading this Chapter you will have

---

11. Let us pause for a minute to examine our deliberate use of the word "material." Some people refer to anything that is brought into the courtroom as "evidence." This is both technically wrong and potentially confusing, particularly for the judge. "Evidence" is a term of art; it is the material that the judge formally admits into the official record after she determines that it meets often very strict rules as to authentication, fairness, relevance, etc. Whatever is used in opening statement or closing argument is not evidence. Graphics used to illustrate an argument or clarify witness testimony are generally not evidence. The blown-up version of a key document with sections highlighted and parts annotated is not evidence. Yet all of this "stuff" is important to those in the war room. For convenience's sake, we refer to all of this as "material." When we use the word "evidence," we do so in its technical sense and as a subset of the "material" commonly used by the parties at trial.

a better basic understanding of how these database systems work and how to prepare to use them.

The latter portions of this Chapter deal with other materials that your team may use during trial, e.g., physical evidence and boards. We make various practical suggestions for making sure that this material is available when it is needed.

TRIAL PRESENTATION FILE FORMATS

Digital trial materials literally come in dozens of different file formats. Some work better than others in trial presentations. Here's a list to help you pick the best file types for use with the top two trial presentation databases.

Trial material	File Format / Quality / Software
Documents	PDF Adobe Reader for opening files Adobe Acrobat for creating files 300 dpi
Graphics and photos	Maximum-quality JPEG Microsoft Paint Adobe Photoshop At least 150 dpi for graphics At least 300 dpi for photos
Deposition video	MPEG-1 Microsoft Windows Media Player Resolution: 352 x 240
Synchronized transcript	CMS (TrialDirector) MDB (Sanction) PTF & VID (LiveNote)

Non-deposition video	*WMV, MPEG-1, AVI are best* *Microsoft Windows Media Player for playback* *Microsoft Movie Maker or Adobe Premier for* * editing* *Original resolution*
Animation	*Interactive: SWF (Adobe Flash Player)* *Non-interactive: WMV, MPEG-1, AVI are best* * (see above for software)*

Litigation Databases

Unless your case is very small or you are using only physical objects for your trial, chances are you will use some form of digital database to store, organize, retrieve, display, and enhance at least some of your presentation material.

Litigation databases fall into two categories: pre-trial and trial presentation databases.

The pre-trial database

If we could look deep inside the memory of a computer, we imagine the pre-trial database would look something like the warehouse scene at the end of the movie *Raiders of the Lost Ark*, only (hopefully) much better organized. The pre-trial database is the larger of the two databases. It is the repository for virtually everything that you gather in discovery that is related to your case, including, among other things, documents, deposition transcripts, videotaped deposition testimony, and expert reports. This is the database you will rely on most heavily as you collect and analyze material in discovery. The most commonly used of these databases are Summation, Concordance, and Relativity, which primarily allow you to store, organize, and retrieve this information.

It is sometimes helpful to think of the pre-trial database as the universe of everything gathered that might be of any use—not just for the trial, but for the overall case. It is the digital equivalent of a holding pen. But, we need to emphasize, this is a very well-organized holding pen, one that contains everything that has been assembled related to the case, whether that material is legally relevant or not, legally admissible as evidence or not, even ultimately useful or not.

Anyone familiar with the modern discovery process will know that the vast majority of the material in the pre-trial database will never see the light of day in the courtroom, even if the case goes to trial. Mountains of documents are produced during discovery; only a small percentage of them ultimately prove useful in trial. Similarly, hundreds of depositions can be taken (by video or not), and then summarized, digitized, and otherwise organized. But in the end only a handful will prove useful in the courtroom as actual trial testimony or for impeachment.

The pre-trial database has three primary functions: storage, organization, and retrieval. That is, you store material on the system as it becomes available; as you store it, you organize it in a logical way. This organization then allows you to retrieve this raw data whenever you need it.

While the pre-trial database plays an essential role in your overall case and you will likely have it with you in the war room, it should not be what you take with you into the courtroom. If you do find yourself taking it into the courtroom and relying on it as your main source of trial material, you probably did not have enough time to fully prepare for trial and reduce the case down to what really matters. Also, since its primary use is for organizing material, it has only rudimentary tools for presenting that material. Having said that, we do not want to create the impression that the pre-trial database is unimportant. How you set up and maintain this database will substantially impact how effective you can be in both the war room and the courtroom.

The trial presentation database

The second type of database is the trial presentation database. It contains the crucial subset of material (culled from the pre-trial database) that you will take with you into the courtroom to use as you present your case to the judge/jury. Like the pre-trial database, the trial presentation database may include all forms of material, such as digital versions of original documents, deposition transcripts, deposition videos, demonstratives, and photographs—any digital material that might be shown in court.

How to Get Your Trial Tech to Do Anything (in Court)

You know your documents forward and backward and have probably memorized the dates and titles of key documents and graphics. But your tech most likely hasn't, which is why it's crucial to use agreed-upon names to call up your material in court. Use exhibit numbers and file page numbers when calling up documents; make sure your graphics have a unique number on them; and refer to them by that number ("Can you please show exhibit 144, page 15?"). And when calling up deposition testimony, use the deponent's name, depo date, and page/line range. Not only will this result in a faster, more accurate display at court, it will create a much better record for the jury to refer to when deliberating.

Like the pre-trial database, everything in the trial presentation database must be well organized so that it can be located and displayed at a moment's notice. In fact, it could be argued that trial presentation databases need to be even better organized than the pre-trial databases. Why? If you cannot find material in the pre-trial databases in your office during discovery prep, you just keep looking, and probably no one will know about the delay. If you cannot find something in the trial presentation database in court, everyone in the courtroom knows you could not find it, and they all (judge, jurors, witnesses, and lawyers) are inconvenienced by the delay.

Two things to keep in mind about the trial presentation database:

- **It is a subset of the pre-trial database.** Remember, the pre-trial database is the universe of *everything* collected in the life of the case. During trial preparation you will go through this universe and pick the material that you will actually need for trial. The result of this effort, not surprisingly, is the trial presentation database.

- **Still, it likely will include more than you will use at trial.** People who teach trial practice classes talk about how the trial team needs to find the "handful of documents that really matter." Since most cases come down to a handful of really important documents, your trial team needs to eliminate most of the junk that gets collected during discovery and focus your trial presentation on what really matters. That being said, your trial presentation database contains a fair amount more than that handful of documents. The trick is finding ways to substantially reduce the overwhelming amount of material in your pre-trial database, but still create a trial presentation database that includes all that you might need to actually present.

To make your documents useful in trial, a trial presentation database performs five functions: storing, organizing, retrieving, displaying, and enhancing the material. It is these last two functions that make this database, and the system that runs it, so crucial in the courtroom. Specifically, the presentation components of this database allow you to display this material to the jury electronically on a screen or monitor and then enhance what is being shown by highlighting, annotating, and zooming in on key portions of evidence, or otherwise emphasizing what really matters to your case. These enhancements can be done in advance or on the fly while the lawyer is talking or a witness is testifying. Needless to say, these are incredibly powerful advocacy tools.

Trial Presentation Glossary

In the war room and at trial, things run more smoothly if the attorneys and their support staff speak the same language. To that end, here is a list of common trial presentation terms.

Exhibit: Anything obtained in discovery that is on the trial exhibit list and has the potential to be admitted into evidence, especially documents.

Graphic: A demonstrative aid created to persuade and/or instruct the judge or jury. A graphic is distinct from an exhibit in that it is not obtained in discovery, but created afterwards, and is rarely admitted into evidence.

Board: A graphic or demonstrative that has been printed on a large, flat foam-core surface for display on an easel.

Slide: An individual unit of a presentation. Note: A graphic may be put on a slide, but the two words are not interchangeable; if you ask to see a slide, it will be assumed that you are talking about something displayed electronically.

PowerPoint: The software commonly used to create and/or display a presentation. PowerPoint is far less versatile than TrialDirector or Sanction in some ways: slide order is generally predeterminded and there are no options to zoom in or highlight on the fly.

TrialDirector/ Sanction:	*The two most common commercial trial presentation databases. These store and present digital materials to be shown at trial and allow the user to zoom in on documents and highlight them. This differentiates them from PowerPoint, which is used only for presentation of slides, not storage of digital trial evidence.*
Synchronized video:	*A video deposition that has been matched—or synced—with its corresponding transcript so it is searchable by word or page/line. Video depositions that will be played at trial should always be synced and for optimal use should be presented with TrialDirector, Sanction, or other trial presentation software.*

Assembling Your Databases

The war room team can put almost any digital material it wants into one or both of these databases. As with all trial-related tasks, the process of assembling this material is considerably easier if you plan ahead.

Documents

After discovery, even in our electronic age, you are going to end up with a lot of paper documents. In order to get your documents into a database, you have to scan them. In mid-sized to large firms, that scanning task often happens in-house. If your law firm does not have such resources, you will need an outside vendor. Look for a scanning vendor that specializes in litigation, or at least has experience with it.

Even an experienced litigation scanning company (or the scanning expert in your office) may not ask you all the right questions about how you want your documents scanned and what you want the resulting files to be. You are going to have to tell them what you want. Consider the following questions:

What constitutes a document?

Where most documents start and end is pretty obvious, but for some documents it is not clear, or you may want to handle them differently than a scanning vendor might assume. For instance, if an email has two attachments, should that be scanned as one document or split up into three documents?

There is no right answer; do it the way that makes the most sense to you. The point is that you want to make the decision, not have the scanning vendor make it for you. Additionally, once you decide how to handle the situation, be consistent!

What exactly should be scanned?

This also may seem obvious, but it often requires clarification. If you give a box of documents separated by file folders or slip sheets to a scanning vendor and say "scan this," they will likely scan the folders or slip sheets and make them part of the resulting document files. The problem with this is that anything you scan other than the document will affect the page numbering of the file you get back from the scanner—the slip sheet becomes page 1, and the document's true first page becomes page 2. This can cause confusion down the road at trial. If an attorney asks to show page 20 of exhibit 55 to the jury, the trial tech will have to account for the extra page, which can be hard to do under pressure.

A good rule of thumb is to avoid scanning anything that did not come to you through discovery or that was added by your office or another service. And if you are not sure of something, such as Proof of Service papers that some jurisdictions add to the front of a document, consider having them moved to the back. That way they will still be in the scanned file but will not affect the page number of the true document. In other words, the page with number 1 will be the first page of the document. Again, once you make this decision (whatever the outcome), do not change your mind mid-way through trial preparation. Apply your specification consistently.

How should the files be named?

A file name is crucial—it is how you locate documents in any system of organization, whether an exhibit index, file cabinet, or database. That is why most documents in litigation are marked with document control numbers (i.e., Bates numbers) and, later, exhibit numbers (but those are a long way off at trial, not when you are scanning documents during discovery). While you may assume the scanner will name your files by Bates number, if you do not specify that, the vendor may give you files named with a generic number, which *will not* help you find them in a database.

Into what file format should they be scanned?

PDF is becoming the new standard because it works across the widest variety of software and computers. TIF, once the standard format for litigation, also still works well. But if you have documents that are a mix of color and black and white, making the files PDF is your best option.

The main point with all of these decisions is that you need to plan ahead, make the decisions, and be consistent with them. If you have documents coming in different batches throughout discovery, have each set of documents scanned in and divided up the same way you did your first set.

Video depositions

Video used in the courtroom can be divided into two categories: Video depositions and non-deposition materials (such as surveillance video, CCTV footage, news clips, etc.). The vast majority of video shown during any trial is likely to be video depositions.

The most important thing to know about video depositions is that they can be synchronized to their corresponding transcripts. This process matches the video to the transcript and allows you to search for words within the video as if it were a text document. This search functionality, in turn, allows you to make video clips quickly, because you can immediately find any word in the video simply by clicking on the transcript. Video clips can be used for impeaching live witnesses or can be played in lieu of live testimony if a witness is either a party witness or outside the subpoena range and cannot be compelled to testify at trial.

Syncing deposition videos also allows you to make last-minute changes to your clips very easily, so you can alter them—in court, if necessary—to respond to objections or last-minute rulings by the judge. And we all know that these last-minute changes are the rule, not the exception, in litigation. Un-synced videos can be used to create clips, but it takes much more time than synced video, and last-minute changes are difficult and time-consuming. Creating a clip on the fly in court is essentially impossible with un-synced video, and that is a major disadvantage. So sync those videos!

Because of this, we believe as a general principle that if it is worth having a deposition videotaped, it is worth having it synced. Sometimes legal teams try to save money by not syncing their videos (it does cost extra), with the idea that the trial will not happen or is a long way off. But videotaping depositions and not syncing them is like buying a flashlight for storm season but skipping the batteries because you do not think a storm will hit your house. If a storm *does* hit, you not only did not save money on the batteries, you lost the money you spent on the flashlight, because it does not work. More important, you had a lot tougher time getting through the storm.

Some legal teams wait to see if the trial goes away before they have their videos synced. This is fine up to a point. Just do not wait too long, because the syncing process can take time, and some vendors will charge a rush fee if you need quick turnaround.

Options for syncing video

- **Hire a videographer.** Video syncing has gone from a highly specialized service to something that most litigation videographers now offer. But beware: many videographers are fairly new to this technology, so their work may not be of the same quality as that of someone who has more experience syncing. If you do hire a videographer to sync video, make sure the transcript and the video match up properly and that the sync transcript has the same page numbers as the official court transcript.

- **Hire a sync specialist.** Some vendors do syncing as their primary service or as part of a wider array of trial support services. If you have a large litigation with deponents all over the country, or even all over the world, it will be inefficient to use a different company for each deposition. Instead, try to find an experienced nationwide company. They are more likely to have a standardized process for syncing video (and for videotaping as well), including quality control. That means you will get consistent quality, no matter where the deposition was taken.

- **Do it yourself.** You can purchase software that will allow you to sync the videos yourself. Such software costs between $400 and $1,000, depending on which product you get, and can pay for itself over time. But only do this if someone on your team has the time to learn how to do it properly, including how to test the sync files, or if you have someone who has experience with this form of trial technology.

What you need to sync video

If your video files did not come to you synced after the deposition, you can still have them synced later, as long as you have the video file and the transcript file. Different video file formats can be synced, but MPEG-1 is the best, because it works with the most types of software. The type of transcript that you need is the court reporter's official ASCII text file. Word documents, TIFs, PDFs, or condensed transcripts (such as Min-U-Scripts) cannot be used.

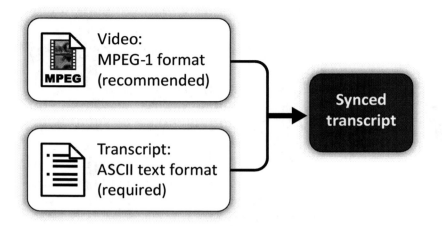

What you will need to sync video depos

Types of sync files

It is best to request a variety of sync files from your vendor, because they are not standardized. That means you will need one type for your pre-trial database and a different type for your trial presentation database. So, while you may only need a LiveNote sync file or a Summation sync file for your pre-trial database, if your case does go to trial, you will need sync files that are compatible with your trial presentation database. Most vendors will not charge extra for giving you multiple file types, so just get everything synced in more than one format. However, if, for whatever reason, you wind up with only one type of sync file, your vendor can convert it to whatever type you need for trial. Again, get it done well ahead of time. This is not something that you want to deal with a week before trial starts, especially if you have a lot of deponents.

If you ask for these different types and your syncing vendor does not seem to know what they are or says, "Oh, no, you only need one," that is a good indication that your vendor is not experienced at syncing and you need to find someone else. Fast.

If you do not have the budget or expertise for the software listed above, some companies will provide you with synced depositions packaged with self-contained video-editing software.

Other types of material

You may need myriad types of other materials for trial, including graphics, photographs, wiretaps, audio, and non-deposition video. These materials can cause a lot of problems during presentation at trial, because they come in multiple formats and are not as standardized as documents and video depositions. Here are some tips for dealing with them and choosing the best formats to use for trial.

Graphics

If you are dealing with a graphics vendor, ask her to provide you with a JPEG. Other file types will work, but JPEGs are the industry standard. They also work with a wide variety of operating systems and software.

A few other tips:

- **Size:** Ask that your graphics be at least 150 dpi (dots per inch, a measure of the quality of graphics). This size offers good enough quality to project on a screen for jurors. But it also keeps the file size small so it can be emailed easily and downloaded quickly. If the graphics are information-rich—like a time line, for instance—and might need to be blown up for the jury to see, then 300 dpi is recommended. If you are not sure, go with 300 dpi; you will rarely need to go higher than that.

- **Scans:** Avoid scanned printouts of graphics whenever possible. If you have a PowerPoint, you will get much higher quality with the original digital file than a printout.

- **Color:** Finally (and we know this is getting technical), make sure the graphics are saved as what is known as RGB, *not* CMYK. We will not bore you with the distinction except to say that RGB is the standard for digital graphics. CMYK is the color setting for print graphics; files saved in this format may not display correctly in trial presentation software. Your graphics vendor *should* know this, but it never hurts to specify. Plus it will make you look smart!

Photos

Like graphics, the best file format for photos is JPEG. Though other formats will work, the JPEG format was created specifically for digital photos (it is an acronym for Joint Photographic Experts Group). Try to get photos at the highest possible quality, as it can be really useful to zoom in on them in court, and if you have a low-resolution photo, any zoomed image will be pixelated and grainy. Whenever possible, use the original digital file, not a scan of a printed picture. If you do have to scan a picture, make sure it is scanned at 300 dpi, at minimum, and go higher—up to 600 dpi—if there is fine detail that will need to be shown. Just note that higher dots-per-inch results in larger files, so transferring and opening them may be a challenge for older, less powerful computers.

Animation

Moving images are becoming increasingly common in our culture, so common that people now regularly watch videos on their smartphones. They also are becoming increasingly common in litigation as the technology to create them becomes better, faster, and cheaper to use. At The Focal Point, we create a lot of animations in Flash, which allows the animation to be interactive rather than linear. So instead of having one defined start and stop point, Flash allows the user to decide which portions of the animation to play, and when. Think of animations on car websites that allow the viewer to use a mouse to rotate the car to look at it from different angles, as well as focus in on different features. This is done with Flash, and the interactivity is a boon when you want to be able to respond to changing events in the courtroom.

But guess what? All this functionality takes a long time to create. So if you know that you (or your attorney) are going to want Flash, you need to get that project to a vendor quickly. You also want to make sure the attorney sees the rough drafts of these animations and responds to them well ahead of trial so that the necessary revisions can be made.

Some other tips:

- **File types for Flash animation:** In a trial presentation database, the best file type is SWF. If it is going to be played outside of a database—say, by the court or co-counsel—you can request an EXE file that contains software to play the animation so that no additional programs are necessary.

- **File types for non-Flash animation:** For linear, non-interactive animations (the kind where you just press play and let it go), ask for a common file type, like Windows Movie File (WMV) or QuickTime (MOV), rather than proprietary formats, which often only play with one type of software. Even if your vendor offers use of its proprietary software for free, go with something standard that you know you will run on most computers without having to download additional software. By the way, even with these simpler animations you will need to plan a fair amount of lead time to get them created, much more than with still graphics.

- **The importance of testing:** No matter what type of animation you use or what kind of file type it is in, you truly have to test it on the computer that is going to be used to present the animation. You do not want to just grab a laptop, take it to court or a focus group, and assume it is going to work. Animations are not like Word documents or Excel spreadsheets or JPEGs; they often require specialized software or plug-ins that will not necessarily be installed on all computers.

Non-deposition audio and video

Surveillance video, wiretaps, videos of conferences, and site surveys might make up only a tiny percentage of the materials you have, but they can cause a lot of problems if you do not deal with them correctly. This is due to several reasons. First, you may need to convert these materials to a digital format. Or if they are already digitized, you might need to convert them into a more common digital format so that they will work better in a presentation database.

Second, unlike video depositions, these materials are not usually synced to any transcript, which means that they are not searchable—you have to view the entire video to find the portions you want to show. Because of this, allow ample lead time if an attorney wants to make smaller clips from these.

If any of these types of evidence have audio tracks, though, you can get them transcribed by a court reporter and then sync the resulting transcript to the media. This extra process may be worth it if many clips of this material need to be made, because you will be able to edit them quickly. But again, this needs to be done well before trial begins.

Out-of-date media formats

VHS, Beta, floppy disks, LaserDiscs, MiniDiscs, cassette tapes, and microfiche are all out-of-date media formats that almost do not exist anymore. But there are just enough of them out there that they sometimes crop up in litigation. You will need to find a vendor who can convert these to a common digital format, which is not always easy, since most vendors have moved away from these formats. You may have to ship them off to another city, which means you need to allow still more time for preparing these materials. But once they are digitized, they can be treated the same way as the non-deposition audio and video discussed above.

Websites

Because websites are such a ubiquitous part of our lives, they are showing up more and more in litigation. But how do you present them in court? You have a couple of choices here:

- **Replication:** This method, which requires no Internet connection in court entails taking a JPEG screen shot of, say, a website's home page and showing that to the jury. It demonstrates the look and content of that page but not the functionality.
- **HTML files:** You also can save different web pages as HTML files. This keeps the links between the pages

active if they are saved in the same folder. This is a good option if you do not have Internet access in the courtroom but want to show how the pages link together. This can be complex, so you have to ensure plenty of lead time. You can buy software that will do it for you, but in our experience the results are inconsistent.

- **Internet connection in the courtroom:** You can present a website via the court's Internet connection if it provides one (more and more are doing this). Or you can get a temporary, wired (*not* wireless) Internet connection installed in court by a vendor. This can be expensive, but it can be worth it if the website is a key component of the trial. Just make sure you ask the court's permission before you make arrangements to do this. It is true that courts used to frown on Internet access in the courtroom. But as the Internet becomes more common in our lives and in business, courts are much more willing to allow its use, especially if it is important to your litigation.

- **Wireless card:** Finally, if you cannot get a connection installed, and your computers are not already configured for wireless, you can obtain a card that will plug into your laptop and get Internet access through a cell phone connection. This may require a contract with your cell provider. Just make sure you test it in the courtroom prior to trial. A lot of courtrooms have poor cell phone reception, and you do not want to discover that mid-presentation.

Note: Even if you plan on using an Internet connection and you are sure the connection in the courtroom is good, have an offline version of the website available as backup, even if it does not totally mimic how the site performs online. As a cautionary example, consider an iPhone product reveal Steve Jobs once gave to Apple shareholders. He planned on running the demo live, but it did not work, so he had to ask the audience to turn off their cell phones because their signals were interfering with his wireless connection. If Steve Jobs had problems displaying something online to an audience, it is safe to say that problems can arise for anyone.

Organizing Your Trial Presentation Database

Now that we have gone over all the different types of material you could encounter, we will move on to some best practices for organizing and displaying them for trial. The suggestions below focus on organizing material in litigation databases. However, the principles also apply to creating evidence indexes in text documents or spreadsheets.

The first step before adding anything to a database is to create a plan for how to organize and label the incoming material. That plan should include these elements:

Use consistent naming conventions

Always use the same naming system for your documents (or any type of file), and use one that makes sense. For instance, if you decide to name your files by the documents' Bates numbers, make sure the number in the database exactly matches the one already on the scanned page. For material with no Bates number, assign control numbers. Just make sure they are consistent—always use the same number of characters (see below) and consider using a simple prefix that will help identify the material ("p" for photo, "v" for video, etc).

Choose a date format

Searching by date is a very efficient way to find a document in a database, as long as the date information is entered consistently. Decide whether you are going to use a six-character date (06/13/07) or an 8-character date (06/13/2007). It does not matter which you use; just be consistent so that you can search with only one date format. Always use a zero in front of the month and day, if it is a single digit, so that the number of characters stays the same (01/08/12 not 1/8/12). Inconsistent entries make searches harder, because you may have to type in multiple entries of the same date before you hit on the right combination of numbers.

Add exhibit numbers

Databases organize numbers differently than humans do. To get a database to organize numbers sequentially, like we do, each number has to have the same number of characters. This is done by adding what are called "leading zeros" to your exhibits. If you have 1,000 exhibits, for instance, you need to have four characters for every exhibit number. Exhibit 1 becomes 0001; exhibit 10 becomes 0010; exhibit 100 becomes 0100; and so on.

Proper sorting:			**Non-sequential sorting:**
Add leading	001.pdf	1.pdf	Without leading
zeros to make	002.pdf	10.pdf	zeros, this is
the file names	003.pdf	100.pdf	how a database
have the same	004.pdf	11.pdf	organizes files
number of	005.pdf	12.pdf	
characters	006.pdf	13.pdf	
	007.pdf	14.pdf	
	008.pdf	15.pdf	
	009.pdf	16.pdf	
	010.pdf	17.pdf	
	011.pdf	18.pdf	
	012.pdf	19.pdf	
	013.pdf	2.pdf	
	014.pdf	20.pdf	
	015.pdf	21.pdf	

The importance of naming files with leading zeros

If you do not know how many exhibits you will ultimately have, or if you do know but there is a chance you will add more, add an extra leading zero to be safe. For instance, if you have 950 exhibits, use four characters (e.g., 0950) just in case you wind up adding 50 more exhibits, putting your total at 1,000.

Create just one document database

In litigation that has a lot of different issues, you may be tempted to create a document database for each issue rather than one big one. But this can cause serious problems down the line if you have to combine all those databases into one trial database (and you should plan as if you will have to do this). Instead, create one document database, then mark your exhibits with issue codes. An issue code is a field in the database that you can use to organize potential evidence. This avoids having the same document in several databases, which can cause problems of duplication later on when you try merge everything into one trial database (see more on that below).

Trial Presentation Databases

As we mentioned earlier in this Chapter, your trial presentation database will contain all the documents and other digital material that you want to present at trial. You should create this database about the time you start assigning exhibit numbers to your documents—i.e., a month or two before trial starts.

The key to creating this database is to name the material in a way that allows for easy call-up at trial. Primarily, this pertains to your documents.

Naming conventions

In your pre-trial database documents are usually identified by Bates numbers, but since those numbers are often at least 10 characters long, they are difficult to key in at trial, when speed is of the essence. It is better to name your documents in your presentation database by trial exhibit number. These are shorter than Bates numbers—usually only three or four digits—so they are easy to type in and bring up on screen. And since you have to submit your trial exhibit list to the court, using exhibit numbers in your presentation database means everyone is speaking the same language. This not only allows the attorney to communicate what she wants to see on the screen, it also creates a clean record for the trial transcript.

Changing the names for your trial presentation database: When you move your documents from a pre-trial to a presentation database, you can change their names in one of two ways.

- The first is to print out just your trial exhibits, have exhibit stickers put on them (many vendors do this), scan them using the same parameters in the scanning section above, and have the resulting files named by their exhibit numbers. These files can then be loaded into a presentation database, which by default names the document by the file name.

- If you want to skip the step of printing and scanning, you can add a trial exhibit field to the documents in your pre-trial database. Then export the trial exhibits and have the software name the files by the exhibit number field. The software also can put digital exhibit stickers on the documents. However, this method requires someone knowledgeable, like a database administrator or a paralegal with a lot of experience.

Branding your exhibits

Whichever method you use, we recommend "branding" each page of your exhibits with its exhibit and page number. This creates what is essentially a simplified Bates number for trial, and, it is extremely helpful to attorneys when they want to call up a page in the middle of a document that may not have page numbers (a multipage email, for instance, or an attachment to a declaration). For instance, if exhibit 100 has 50 pages, each page would have a unique number on it: 100-01, 100-02, 100-03, and so on. If at trial the attorney wants to bring up the 25th page on the screen, she can quickly look at the brand (100-25) and ask for exhibit 100, page 25. Just make sure that the branded version of the exhibits is printed out and made available for the attorneys to use during their preparation.

SHARE AND SHARE ALIKE

*If you have an outline, make sure your tech does, too.
And to be really effective, go one step further—create your
outline with your tech in mind. That means making it a
map of what you want to display so your tech can put them
in order beforehand, or, barring that, so the tech can know
what's coming next and be ready to bring it up. Making
a good map means putting exhibit numbers with page
numbers or in bold letters where you want them to appear,
and doing the same for graphics or deposition citations.
Make sure it stands out, and be precise as to what you
want to show and when you want to show it. So, instead
of putting "March 13 email" in the margin, put "Show
Exhibit 10, page 3—March 13 email" at the exact point
in your outline where you will want it brought up on the
screen.*

Non-Digital Materials

Actual documents

Despite many digital advances, the legal field is nowhere near being
paperless. Instead, we now have a hybrid situation where paper is still
given to the court, marked into evidence as part of the official record, and
often provided when questioning the witness. But increasingly attorneys
are using digital evidence instead of (or as a supplement to) paper and
other analog material for the courtroom presentation itself. In other
words, the witness may be holding a piece of paper, but a digital version
of that document is displayed and enhanced on a screen or monitor.

This means that the logistics team will still need to assemble hard
copies of certain documents for the courtroom. Fortunately, this does
not mean that you have to have shelves of preprinted material on hand.

Instead, with sufficient planning you should be able to print hard copies the night before you need them, or even while you are in court.

Physical evidence

You may have some old-fashioned, nondigital, just plain physical evidence. Michael was in a trial once where the main piece of evidence was a 6-foot-tall, 200-pound residential heating unit. As with boards, you need to plan for how to get such materials to court ahead of time. You may need a messenger service with a big truck, for instance, and a dolly to get it to the courtroom. You also want to make sure you can get the evidence past security. That may require a court order, especially if it is any kind of weapon or something that the court thinks could be used as a weapon. If it is a small or fragile piece of physical evidence that you do not necessarily want to give to the jury, you can display it with a document camera, commonly known by the brand name Elmo. These are modern takes on overhead projectors that can display a physical object—no transparencies needed—but they do require connection to a projector or monitor.

Exhibit boards

Although most of your materials are going to be in a digital format, attorneys do still use foam-core boards with documents or demonstratives on them, because they still have a purpose. Exhibit boards work well for displaying time lines, for instance, while other evidence that supports the time line is displayed on the screen. Also, if you do not have a lot of evidence to display, or if you do not have a big technology budget, exhibit boards are relatively easy to produce and require only an easel in court.

However, just because boards are simple does not mean they are quick or easy. Again, you should not just call up your vendor and say "I'd like a board, please." Following are a few things you need to consider.

Image quality

If you are providing a graphic or image to the vendor to put on a board, use the highest quality possible. Otherwise, the image will pixelate (or show all its tiny dots) on a large board, which will not look good. If you cannot find or create a high-quality version of a file, ask the vendor to create one for you or recommend someone who can.

Size

One size does not fit all. Courtrooms are often tight, and the location in which a board can be displayed is often very specific. Try to have somebody scout the courtroom to see where the board might go (often the clerk can help determine this), and then calculate the distance from the jury box. Give that measurement to your vendor to help determine the board's final size.

Material

Boards come in several different types, including foam-core, which is the cheapest, and GatorBoard, which is more durable and better for shipping. You can also request different surfaces, such as dry-erase or magnetic.

Printing schedule

Boards take time to print, and if changes need to be made, they usually have to be reprinted. Take this into account before pulling the trigger; make sure they are final before giving the print order. Or have them printed with enough lead time to get them done again if changes need to be made. As a safety net, also ask your vendor for redaction tape that matches the background color of the board. If there is a problem (e.g., the judge upholds opposing counsel's objection to one element of your board), you can cover the offending parts with something that blends in better than masking tape or black marker.

How to display boards

Boards do not look very good if they are propped up on the floor or if the attorney has to hold them up while talking. Courtrooms sometimes provide crummy easels, if they provide them at all, so it is best to bring one yourself; just make sure it is the right size for your board, of course.

Transportation

Plan ahead for how you are going to get your boards to court. You do not want to have to somehow tuck a bunch of 6-foot boards under your arm and try to get them into a cab.

The Benefits of Preparation

Michael's mother lives in Florida, which, as everybody knows, is hurricane country. Hurricane Hugo, which struck in 1989, was one of the biggest storms to hit Florida. It did not hit his mother's area, fortunately, but it did get her thinking about the importance of being prepared.

So a few months after Hugo, she put together a hurricane survival kit. And now every year, just before hurricane season, she takes a look at the kit and stocks up on anything that has expired or been depleted: canned food, bottled water, batteries, and other emergency supplies. Then she makes sure that all those supplies are in good working order, as she does not want to end up scrambling at the last minute to find something—or discover that it does not work.

Michael's mother does all this even though her home has never been hit by a hurricane. But she knows it *could* happen, and she has friends who might not have survived past disasters if they had not been prepared. In other words, she puts money and effort in ahead of time so she will be prepared if a hurricane actually does hit.

Trials are a lot like hurricanes. You know that they happen and they also often go away (hurricanes veer off course; trials settle), but you should still prepare as if they are going to hit, because being prepared will make a huge difference. Otherwise you are going to be scrambling like crazy just at the time when you most need to be focused on other things.

If you wait until the last minute, your pre-trial preparation will likely be more expensive (vendors often charge rush fees for syncing video depositions or scanning exhibits) and actually less effective than if you took the time to get it done earlier. In fact, if you wait too long, it may not get done at all. And then you have lost the opportunity to present the most complete and organized case possible.

Having your material prepared and organized for courtroom presentation allows you to focus in trial on the things that you were specifically trained for, whether you are a paralegal or an attorney. In fact, we believe that good preparation confers on you four major advantages, not just in trial but in the run-up before trial:

- **Time:** All trials are different, but in our experience, the one thing they all have in common is a lack of time. Preparing in advance lets you do the most with the little time you have before trial when you are focused on briefs, motions, witness prep, and opening statement.

- **Speed:** A big part of preparation is being organized and knowing where everything is so you can access it quickly in court, where taking 20 seconds to find an exhibit can seem like 20 minutes with the judge and jury watching.

- **Completeness:** You will know that everything you need will be in your trial database, essentially at your fingertips.

And what all of this gives you is probably the most important benefit of all:

- **Sanity:** Because you know where all the material is, how to display it, and that it is all truly there.

CHAPTER 11:

How to Deal With Costs

In previous Chapters we talked a lot about what you should bring to your war room. By now it must seem like we pack everything (including the kitchen sink) and only work on cases that are bet-the-company, no-holds-barred, unlimited-budget extravaganzas.

While any war room is going to cost some money (even if it is just the cost of a local hotel room where you can concentrate and prepare), we are just as focused on the bottom line for our clients as you are for yours. Rest assured, we work on a wide variety of cases—from the aforementioned unlimited-budget extravaganzas to highly cost-conscious pro bono matters—and we know that a war room can be created, staffed, and adequately supplied at any spending level.

FOOLS AND THEIR MONEY ARE SOON PARTED

Unthinkingly spending money on a war room does not make it more effective. Instead, the most successful war rooms are the ones that combine a strong spending plan with tight team management. The key with war rooms (as with so much in life) is being thoughtful, knowledgeable, and accountable (or having someone who is), not just throwing money at the problem.

Different Types of Clients Mean Different Spending Plans

As more clients are focusing on the bottom line, requesting new and unusual billing packages, requesting detailed expense sheets, and dictating what types of activities can and cannot be billed, it is not surprising to hear that clients also are setting ceilings on war room budgets and wanting to be involved in the planning process. This can be great, because knowing where the boundaries are helps you to stay within them. But it also can be frustrating, as clients may not know what an Elmo is and why you might need one, or why a color printer is key when a black and white printer is so much less expensive, or why going for the cheapest vendor may prove to be an expensive disaster.

Experience has shown us that clients come in a wide variety, but war rooms basically come in three different types:

No holds barred

Admittedly, these are rare and tend to fall into the patent or corporate grudge-match types of trials. They involve huge teams (20 attorneys, multiple firms, defendants/co-defendants/cross-complainants, consultants galore, an army of paralegals, and so on) and can be overwhelming simply to hear about. Not too many attorneys come across these types of cases or war rooms, but if you do, keep these two guidelines in mind:

- **An unlimited budget does not trump forethought.** You still need to take time to think, really think, about what you need in your war room and how to deliver the best possible result for the client.

- **Bigger is not always better.** Again, the fact that you can bring the entire force of your firm to bear on a matter does not guarantee high-level thinking or strategy. So do not be afraid to bring a smaller, more effective strategy team if that is going to get you a better result in the end. After all, it worked for England against the Spanish Armada!

Medium, not mediocre

The majority of the war rooms we work in tend to fall into this category. In general, they feature a single, mid-sized team (one lead attorney, one or two additional partners, three to five associates, three legal assistants, along with a jury consultant, graphics team, and a trial tech to round it out). However, the teams that work these cases go to trial *a lot* and have developed specific skill sets to keep costs in check and war rooms functioning. What do they do differently from the big budget teams?[12]

- **They define things as "need versus want."** In other words, they know what they need to have in a war room and consider anything additional to be convenience items. For instance, they know that having a backup printer is key, whereas having a backup Elmo is overkill.

- **They define roles clearly and early.** In the best-run war rooms, everyone is crystal-clear on their responsibilities and they hold themselves accountable. Even better, when they have completed their basic responsibilities, they offer to assist others who may be falling behind.

- **They understand the "fast, cheap, or easy . . . pick two" principle.** In other words, "It can be fast and cheap, but it ain't gonna be easy. Or it can be easy and fast, but it sure ain't gonna be cheap." This means they can make intelligent decisions about where to invest their war room dollars.

- **They plan early.** They do not wait until 30 days before trial to lay the groundwork for a war room. They reserve everything that does not require a deposit or cancellation fee. They book equipment and vendors, and lock in consultants as soon as they even *think* they might be going all the way to trial.

---

12. The best big-budget teams also do these things, but for medium-sized teams they are a necessity.

- **They understand that small luxuries are necessary.**
  For example, that slightly-nicer-than-average bottle of
  wine after a long court day can be more necessary than
  you think from this distance. But they also know that
  keeping an eye on excess (and reining it in) is just as
  necessary. It never hurts to have an explicit discussion
  with your team about what is acceptable and what is not.
  For instance, at The Focal Point, we cover the costs for
  laundry, but only after a staffer is onsite for seven days.
  We also set clear guidelines on meal and entertainment
  costs and have easily understood rules about which
  personal expenses team members can bill.

- **They follow through on policies.** They hold their team
  members accountable for personal expenses and business
  related spending limits.

- **They provide catering to their team.** This can save
  a great deal on food costs (not to mention time lost in
  trying to decide where to eat and then how to get there).

CAN I EXPENSE THIS?

*All businesses have their own set of guidelines
regarding business and travel expenses, but gray areas
often arise. It is worth your time (and worth it to your
bottom line) to have a clear-cut policy and to regularly
communicate it to your team. If you do not currently have
a policy, now is a great time to develop one. Here is an
example.*

Okay to expense to the client:

- *Airfare, in coach*

- *Lodging (defer to client specifications if stated)*

- *Cab fare, rental cars, or other transportation to
  and from the war room*

- *Meals: Breakfast $20, lunch $25, dinner $75 per person per day, including tax and gratuity*
- *Parking fees*
- *Mileage on personal car*
- *Laundry services when traveling for one week or more*

What is okay to expense to the firm (but not the client):

- *Gym or fitness center fees charged by the hotel*
- *Cell phone expansion plans (international, data)*
- *In-room movies*

Not okay to expense to the firm or the client, unless you have approval:

- *Toiletries or other personal grooming items*
- *Shoeshines or tailoring services*
- *Travel expenses during time off*
- *Entertainment (sightseeing, movie tickets, etc.)*
- *Travel upgrade to Business or First Class*

Small, but mighty

Okay, so you are looking at creating a war room for a client with a very limited budget. Never fear, it is still possible to make a great war room happen. In fact, it could be argued that cases that have fewer resources really need to focus on getting a war room together, so that the team that may not have been able to buckle down on a matter has a chance to come together and truly focus on the facts and strategy of the trial.

But with limited resources, how do you make a war room happen? Start with the things that medium-sized teams do—plan early, define roles, use the "need versus want" principle, etc.—and then add:

- **Think outside the box.** Do you need a huge conference room to work or would a hotel room with all the furniture removed do the trick? It is important to not fool yourself here—if you have 12 people, a hotel room is not a viable choice—but if it will honestly work for your team, this is a great option.

- **Work digitally as much as possible.** It is faster than printing and carrying copies all over the place; you will have fewer things to ship or store; and if your computers are networked, you need to search only one place for documents or case folders.

- **Keep people on call, not necessarily onsite.** If you have limited resources, limiting staff's time on the ground and working with people remotely is a great way to keep costs in check.

- **Consider purchasing rather than renting.** Long rental periods (two weeks or more) for equipment such as projectors, printers, and monitors can be more expensive than outright purchase of those items. Be sure to confirm rates with your vendor, then do some serious comparison shopping.

- **Ask about long-term rental rates.** Often, companies that rent equipment offer a discounted long-term rate, which can save you (and, by extension, your client) hundreds of dollars.

Come Up With a Budget

When you are trying to determine costs for a war room, keep in mind that, with a few exceptions, you can only ballpark the number for your client. Court rulings may shorten or extend a war room, you may need more or fewer people onsite, and there may be only one hotel in town. All of these factors will affect your eventual bottom line.

The first step is to map out your ideal staffing, equipment, lodging, and travel plan, along with some basic cost assumptions. This requires that you know the following:

- How many people, ideally, you would have on your team and what roles they will play. Calculate an average billing rate to understand how much (in general) each person will cost the client in the end.

- What equipment you will need to accomplish what you want to do, in both the war room and in the courtroom. You should rely on your firm's IT department for this list, but a vendor or consultant also can provide you with an estimate for a variety of equipment packages.

- What other needs your team will have. Make sure your budget includes travel, lodging, freight, meals, rental cars, etc.

- Do not forget about regional variation. Things in Manhattan are bound to be two to three times more expensive than in Minneapolis.

But what if you are in the second or third category of war room and you know you cannot afford all of your ideal items? We still want you to create a list of your ideal scenario, because it will give you a clear baseline from which to start, and your decisions on any adjustments will be more informed, more conscious, and more geared toward your team's needs, rather than a stab in the dark.

Once you have added up all of these rough costs, you will have (most likely) a shockingly high number. Hey, we never said this was going to be cheap, right? Sit with that number for a few hours or days and let it sink in. If you are lucky, your ideal plan will be within your reach, in terms of your client's expectations.

However, you may be in the somewhat disappointing position of having to trim a bit (or a lot) here and there. Do not worry; you can still create a war room for you and your team. And as we said above, it may run better and more efficiently, as roles and resources will be condensed to the elemental pieces. But you will need to make some changes, so consider the following possibilities:

- **Alter the structure of your team.** Reduce the number of attorneys onsite to what is essential and have others work remotely or travel in and out of the war room as needed. This way you can concentrate on staffing your team with paralegals, who really need to be on the ground in order to be at their most effective.

- **Consolidate equipment where possible.** In other words, get one piece of equipment that can print, scan, and copy rather than three separate machines.

- **Go mid-range on the hotel.** At 3 A.M., your team is not going to care that the hotel does not have a pool, but we never recommend going low-end unless you absolutely have to.

  o Staying in a low-budget hotel creates a negative perception for your client, your team, and even the opposition. In addition, budget hotels offer no (or very few) amenities, and remember: Your team is busting their humps for you and the case. So yes, you can save by staying at All-American Suites, but not by staying at the No-Tell Motel.

- **Have one person manage all travel.** This will reduce cancellation fees, control swings on ticket prices, eradicate bad judgment calls (e.g., booking business class when the client has only agreed to pay for coach), and ensure adherence to billing contracts.

- **Use a company credit card.** Whenever possible, use a company credit card instead of a personal one, preferably one that has a points program or spending rewards to increase the value of each dollar spent.

- **Pay your invoices on time.** Late fees and interest generally are not billable to the client, so making sure invoices get paid is key to ensuring that war rooms do not become a losing proposition for your firm.

- **Do not be penny-wise and pound-foolish.** Understand the real costs of your personnel and equipment. By knowing where expenses can grow unexpectedly, you can make better decisions about staffing, strategy, and morale.

Put Your Plan Into Action

Now that you have developed your baseline and trimmed down costs if necessary, it is time to put your plan into action. The first step is bringing your Sergeant Major up-to-date on the spending plan and client expectations. As this person will be making spending decisions, you want him to be as well informed as possible. Issues you want to discuss with your Sergeant Major include:

- Does the client have a spending limit or tolerance threshold for updates? (See more below.)

- Are there companies that you should not patronize due to client contractual obligations?

- What about spending details and invoicing requirements?

- What is the plan for unexpected urgent matters? What if the team needs to fly in an expert witness? What if the war room needs extra equipment? Make sure that your Sergeant Major is clear on how to handle fiscal surprises, because they happen more often than not.

- Consider adding a 20 percent "CYA" amount to your estimate for the client, to cover—well, you know . . .

As you go along, you will want to have your Sergeant Major keep the worksheet up-to-date and provide you with regular spending briefs that will allow you to keep your client up-to-date as well. Your Sergeant Major also will want to keep a sharp eye on any major discrepancies in billing. Is someone's room service bill as high as their room cost? That is an issue the Sergeant Major will need to look into immediately.

By making sure your Sergeant Major has all this information, is receiving regular invoicing updates from all vendors, and is empowered to make choices, attorneys can focus on developing a solid case strategy. Resolving billing disputes while your war room is in progress is always easier than having to backtrack after the war room is closed.

But what if you are doing this on your own or with a very small team? Our recommendation does not change. Make one person in charge of the spending decisions (even if it is you), and you will save yourself a lot of time and effort having to track down information when you start the billing process.

Keep the Client Well Informed

Every firm has its own way of invoicing and billing clients. To further complicate the matter, clients have their own expectations as to how invoices should be developed and delivered. However, standard principles do exist, including:

- **Avoid the "But I only ordered salad!" debate when your client gets the bill.** We have all been to that dinner with a friend who wants to split the bill evenly at the end of the evening, even though she had two glasses of wine and a huge steak, while you enjoyed a lighter salad and sparkling water. It is critical that you and your client understand each other's billing practices at the outset, so make sure you clarify your practices and give your client a chance to provide input. Then document it when you are retained, by including onsite costs in any engagement or retention documents you or your firm regularly uses.

- **Keep your client informed of costs periodically.** A surprised client is (almost always) an angry client.

- **Send updates via email.** One of the best things about email is that it never goes away. (This is also one of the worst things about email, but that is a whole other book.) By updating your client electronically, you create a trail to follow should a dispute arise in the future.

These principles should serve as guidelines when you start to develop your spending plan. We recognize they are very general. What we really want you to remember is that a large and expensive war room is not going to win your case, but a thoughtfully planned and executed one certainly will help you get there. And, as with all aspects of war rooms (including staff and equipment), making conscious decisions early on is what ensures the most smooth-running, efficient operation possible.

Appendix A, CHAPTER 1:
Overview

There Are Five Types of Questions to Ask Yourself

There are four key questions you need to ask yourself when considering whether you need to establish a war room for your event. They focus on the who, when, where, why, and how of setting up and running a successful war room:

- Who should staff your war room?
- When should you start planning your war room?
- Where should you set up your war room?
- How should you configure your war room?

Appendix A, CHAPTER 2:
War Room Basics—Asking the Right Questions

A war room is a space that you set aside to prepare for a major legal event. It is typically for a trial, but can also be useful for an arbitration or a major hearing, such as:

- A Markman in a patent case

- A preliminary injunction hearing in a trade secret case

- A major significant summary judgment hearing

A war room is the place you go to concentrate and plan. A war room should be:

- Far away (psychologically, if not always physically) from the day-to-day distractions of home and office

- A place for the entire team to gather to work out key case themes, theories, and critical next steps

- An inner sanctum, where a team can craft case strategies and make major decisions both before and during the heat of trial

The "Who" Questions

Your war room is nothing without the right staff—in both the courtroom and the war room. When planning your staff, you must consider:

- What is each person likely to need in order to do his or her job, in terms of both support and supplies?
- Who is your intended audience?

The "When" Questions

- When is your trial?
- When should you set up your war room?
- When do you need to set up your equipment in the courtroom?

The "Where" Questions

- Where is the trial being held?
- Where will you set up the war room?
- Where is your staff located?

The "How" Questions

- How will you set up your war room?
- How will you run and manage your war room?
- How much is this going to cost?
- How will you make one of those databases that organizes all the materials you will want to show in the courtroom?
- How will you set up in the courtroom?

Appendix A, CHAPTER 3:
Who Is Your Audience?

Two Types of Teams to Build

- **The strategic team:** those people who focus primarily on making the record in the courtroom at trial
- **The logistics team:** those people who work behind the scenes and in the war room to make sure that the strategic team has what it needs to accomplish its goals in court

Who Is Your Audience?

Your first audience is the decision maker in the matter. This could be:

- A judge sitting as the sole "finder of fact" during a bench trial
- A judge presiding over jurors who are charged to reach a final verdict
- One or more arbitrators in a binding arbitration

Your second audience is the courtroom support personnel, including:

- The judge's courtroom deputy
- The staff attorney and the judge's law clerks
- The court reporter
- The IT/AV specialist

- The jury administrator
- The case administrator

The Courtroom Deputy

When dealing with the courtroom deputy, we recommend the following general rules:

- Be respectful
- Ask, do not tell
- Be careful
- Remember: the courtroom deputy is your conduit to the judge
- Be professional
- Avoid making special requests
- Be prepared
- Work it out
- Ask for help when you need it
- Do not be a pest
- Work together
- Designate a single point of contact on your team
- Maintain your credibility
- Ask about what to do or who to contact in an emergency
- Be cooperative

Appendix A, Chapter 4:
Who Should Be There?

Principal Characters in the Courtroom

What the logistics team does in the war room is done to support those who are in the courtroom:

- The client or client representative
- The lawyers
- The percipient witnesses
- The expert witnesses

The Needs of the Strategic Team

Ask your strategic players:

- What are they expecting by way of support?
- Whom do they see as being vital to the trial efforts?
  - Is there any specific person (by name) that they feel needs to be there?
  - Is there any type of person (by category, e.g., trial technician) that they feel should be there?
  - Is there any special project (e.g., cross-examination by video clips) that they think needs to be done for trial?
- What did they do/need in prior trials?

- What services do they typically rely on in the home office?
- What are their typical work hours?
- When will they need support?
- When they are not in trial, what resources do they routinely use to get their work done?
- Whom do they regularly rely on?

War Room Team

- **Logistics support:** This group includes what we call the "Sergeant Major," who oversees what is going in the war room, as well as the paralegals, and the administrative support.
- **Technical support:** This group includes both IT personnel and your presentation technology specialist (or "trial tech").
- **Strategic support:** These are the jury consultants and trial graphics consultants you bring in to help with strategic decisions regarding persuasion messaging and graphic presentation.
- **Remote support:** People at the home office, who marshal and focus the support located there.
- **Vendor support:** These individuals have a very specialized focus and assist at discrete moments in the case; they include messengers, process servers, and printing and copying specialists.

The "Sergeant Major"

The Sergeant Major should be at the center of all war room information. She should be the person through whom all logistics questions pass—from travel and lodging to equipment rental, from vendors to court deadlines. The Sergeant Major does not need to know the answer to every question, but she should know (or be able to find out) who does.

The ideal Sergeant Major has the following characteristics and skills:

- Experience and trustworthiness
- A "can-do" attitude
- Legal savvy
- Knowledge of what the case is about
- An ability to delegate tasks comfortably
- Strong organizational skills
- An ability to focus
- An ability to multitask
- Excellent communication skills
- Strong relationships with third-party vendors
- Technical savvy
- An ability to see the trees *and* the forest
- A thick skin
- An understanding of the principles of self-care

The Paralegals

Your ideal paralegals have:

- Experience with the case
- Experience with the key lawyers
- A good working relationship with the client
- Experience in other war rooms
- Knowledge of the fundamental issues, theory, and themes in your case
- Knowledge of key technical issues
- Patience and endurance

Administrative Support

Unfortunately, war rooms often lack adequate administrative support. To the extent possible, look for someone to fill your administrative role who:

- Has a good working relationship with the Sergeant Major
- Has as many basic skills in as many areas as possible
- Has the ability to multi-task

The IT Specialist

The IT specialist is responsible for setting up your computer, network, and Internet systems; preventing problems before they arise; and fixing these problems when they do occur. Do not assume you can just take your in-house IT person to the war room.

- The IT needs of the war room are almost always different and more complicated than those of the home office
- Your war room IT person will need sufficient people skills to work smoothly with a group of people he is unlikely to have met or worked with before
- Taking your in-house person away to trial may be great for the war room; it could spell disaster for the home office

IT staffing requirements in the war room:

- **Best staffing solution:** If your trial, your staff, and your budget are large enough, we recommend having someone who is fully capable of undertaking all of the IT tasks onsite for the entire trial.
- **Next-best staffing solution:** If it is not feasible to have an IT person at the war room for the entire trial, do your

best to have him set up the war room and then stay at least through opening statements.

- **Minimum staffing solution:** At the very least, have a knowledgeable IT person talk to someone at your venue well before you set up the war room. Make sure that you continue to have someone available by phone 24/7 to answer technical questions and fix problems.

The Trial Tech

More and more companies are providing trial tech services, but consider these questions to find the *right* trial tech:

- Has he gone to trial before?
- Has he worked on complex cases?
- Does he plan on using software specifically designed for trial presentation?
- Does he know not only how to work with the equipment, but also how the equipment itself works?
- Can he go into a courtroom and immediately figure out how to set it up in a way that makes it useful for everyone (including opposing counsel)?
- Is he familiar with your specific court and particular judge?
- Will he be fully dedicated to your case?
- Does he communicate well?
- Is he proactive?
- Does he have a broad range of technical skills?
- Is he calm under pressure?

The Jury Consultant

While the jury consultant may play a variety of roles in the life of the case (e.g., organizing mock trials or other research exercises), her primary role at trial is to provide strategic insight and jury selection support. For the most part, jury consultants work on their own. While they probably will need space at the war room and access to some of the logistics team's resources (copiers, computers, Internet service, etc.), most jury consultants need only minimal support from other members of the war room team.

Trial Graphics Consultants

It is a fact of the modern age that almost every trial relies on a visual presentation of some sort or another. If you are using graphics consultants, plan to bring them onsite with you as part of your team, rather than as an afterthought.

Remote Support

Technology increasingly makes working remotely an option for certain members of your war room team, whether your war room is a few blocks or several thousand miles from your main office. Ask yourself what role people back at the home office might play to supplement your staffing and ensure that your needs are met.

Other Vendors

In most venues, you can find excellent vendors that offer services such as:

- Deliveries
- Process serving
- Photocopying and assembling of documents
- Transportation
- Food services

You need to take four steps to find vendors:

- Determine if such services are available in the local area
- Find out who is good and who is not
- Choose one person in your war room to supervise and keep track of your vendors
- If you cannot locate a trusted vendor, add a staff person to your team to do this work

Appendix A, CHAPTER 5:
When Is Trial?

Tasks That Are Never Too Early to Start

- Notify everyone of the trial date and keep them advised of changes

- Start the "Golden Binder" (see Appendix B). This is **the** place for information related to the war room. One designated person has sole responsibility for updating the Golden Binder; all changes have to be funneled through that person. It should contain answers to basic questions for anyone who may be serving in the war room, including:

  o Contact information for all vendors

  o Contact information for all the war room team members, including emergency contact numbers

  o Flight, hotel, and rental car logistics

  o Contact information and schedules for witnesses

  o Instructions for getting an exhibit board made

  o Directions for changing toner cartridges in the printer (and what to do with the empties)

  o Hotel contact names and numbers for catering or other services

  o Relevant account numbers

  o Maps of the local area

  o A map and driving directions to the nearest hospital

- o   The customer service number for your firm's health insurance provider
- o   Location and directions to the nearest shelter in areas subject to extreme weather
- o   Map and directions to the nearest police and fire stations
- • Create, publicize, and regularly maintain a master calendar.

Things to Do as Soon as You Know Which Judge Will Preside Over Your Case

- • Know your court's rules, and make sure everyone on your war room team follows them
  - o   The four categories of court rules:
    - ▪ **Jurisdictional-level rules.** Apply to every court at a particular level of the judicial system.
    - ▪ **Venue-level rules.** Apply to a particular geographic division within a jurisdiction.
    - ▪ **Courtroom-level rules.** Judge's and courtroom deputy's preferences
    - ▪ **Common custom.** Certain ways of doing things, rarely formally adopted or even written down.
  - o   How to find out about the rules:
    - ▪ Check with the lawyers on the case
    - ▪ Check with any contacts your firm has in the trial venue
    - ▪ Contact the court clerk and ask about any courtroom-specific rules
  - o   Look for specific rules concerning:
    - ▪ Exchange dates for exhibits and other demonstratives

- Guidelines for pre-marking exhibits
- Exchange dates for deposition transcript designations
- Length of advance notice you must give before calling a witness
- Procedures for getting equipment and other material into the courtroom
- Special rules for providing for jurors
- Anything particular to the judge or courtroom
- Get background information about the courtroom, the judge, and the courtroom staff
- If possible, visit the courtroom:
  o Learn it's layout
  o What kind of display equipment is available?
  o How does the clerk handle admitting exhibits or displaying video clips?
  o Does the courtroom have sufficient room to store material and equipment?

At Least 90 Days Before Trial

- Organize your internal support team
- Coordinate with the in-court team
- Retain your external support team
- Start your list of to-do's and determine who is responsible
- Reserve hotel rooms
- Locate potential work space
- Stake a claim on extra space at your office

At Least 60 Days Before Trial

- Get a hard fix on who is going to be part of the war room
- Sign contracts for work spaces
- Assemble your preliminary list of equipment
- Start assembling your database of potential exhibits and video depositions

30 Days Before Trial

- Finalize your hotel rooms
- Finalize vendor contracts
- Order or rent your equipment
- Finalize transportation
- Visit the venue
- Lay out the anticipated schedule through the conclusion of trial

14 Days Before Trial

- Confirm your equipment and office-supply deliveries.
- Make preliminary travel arrangements
- Finalize your database of potential exhibits and video depositions
- Lay out your war room
  - Who is going to be working where
  - Tables, chairs, and other pieces of equipment

7 Days Before Trial

Send out your sergeant major and a small advance team to set up the workspace. They should:

- Confirm that the Internet and other technology are functioning smoothly
- Coordinate the deliveries of equipment and supplies
- Unpack boxes and organize their contents
- Physically set up the war room
- Problem-solve for any issues prior to the rest of the team's arrival

5 Days Before Trial

Have your trial tech, graphics team, and any other support vendors arrive at the war room.

4 Days Before Trial

The lawyers, client, early witnesses, and balance of the war room team should arrive several days prior to the first day of trial. They will need time to set up and get familiar with the war room.

At Least a Full Day Before They Are Scheduled to Testify

Witnesses who are not needed at the trial's start should arrive at the war room at least a day before they are scheduled to testify. This gives them time to get used to the venue and prepare for their testimony.

The Short-Order War Room

It is possible to put together an effective "short-order" war room that provides essential support for the entire trial team. Here are some ways to save time:

- **Go big box.** Find support to help you set up and potentially staff the war room. If your client has local counsel, enlist their help. Also consider relying on national suppliers.

- **Retain your preferred consultants—STAT!** Do not experiment with new and untested people; call people you trust to get suggestions. Then, when you contact those consultants, make sure they fully understand the tight time constraints under which you—and, by extension, they—will be operating.

- **Keep it simple.** As you develop graphics or other demonstratives, realize that you may need to dial back your plans for presenting your evidence and demonstratives to the jury.

  o Rely on your trial tech

  o Cut back on video depositions

  o Focus on what you need to create for your presentation

  o Take it a step at a time

  o Put your colleagues in charge of specific themes or witnesses

  o Simplify the equipment you take

  o Use a satellite office of your firm, or local counsel's office for work space

  o Book catering ahead

  o Have supplies sent ahead

  o Stay calm

Appendix A, CHAPTER 6:
Where Is Your War Room?

Three Important Questions

- Are you going to use existing office space, or are you going to create an office in a location generally used for other purposes, such as a hotel conference room?

- Where is your war room in relationship to your regular office, the courtroom, your hotel, and the key resources you will need during trial?

- Is your war room located in a safe place?

Using Your Own Office Space

Advantages

- It is nearby
- It is inexpensive
- It is familiar
- It is comfortable
- It has everything you need
- It has ways of getting things done
- It has people
- It is secure

Disadvantages

- There is no escape for you
- There is no escape for others

Tips

- Do not set up the war room at your normal office if it leaves your firm short of space or disrupts regular operations
- Do the best you can to isolate the war room from other ongoing activities
- Reserve space generously
- Keep the area clean
- Stay within your allocated space
- Share your resources
- Keep a clear line of communication open with others at the office

Using Other Existing Office Space

Advantages

Same advantages as using your own office, plus:

- Using your client's offices saves them money
- Using local counsel's office gives you immediate access to people who know the local rules, local judges, and local services

Disadvantages

- You have guest status
- You will always need to be on your best behavior
- You will need to educate yourself and your team on how to get things done

- Security may a greater concern
- You may have restricted hours of access
- You will need to provide most or all of the equipment

Tips

- Establish a main contact at the office for any pre-arrival arrangements and initial setup assistance
- Familiarize yourself with the team and the layout of the office
- Seek to understand how things are done in the new environment
- Make sure your team understands that you are guests and should behave as such

Creating Your Own Office Space

Advantages

- Location, location, location
- Your team can stay in the same building in which they are working, if located in a hotel
- Your team will have access to more services
- Your team will have flexibility
- It is your space!

Disadvantages

- It is not going to be cheap
- It is not going to be easy
- It may get complex
- Hotel staff are trained for hospitality, not project management

Tips

- Try to find a place that has done this before
- Take a tour
- Get references and check them
- Plan way ahead
- Keep records of your agreements

Making Hotel Reservations

A few additional tips for making hotel reservations:

- Put one person in charge of establishing and maintaining the relationship with the hotel sales department
- Make your Sergeant Major the go-to hotel person for your staff
- Do not be afraid to ask for advice from the sales department
- Request a corporate rate for your rooms
- Document all of your agreements with the hotel
- Make sure you fully understand the terms and conditions associated with booking a block of rooms at the corporate rate
- Insist that your rooms be safe and secure
- Do not automatically pay for the rooms in advance
- Set up a master account so that all charges are linked to one card/cardholder
- Specify what charges the master account will cover
- Inform your team members that they still will have to present a credit card upon check-in
- Do not be afraid to "wheel and deal"
- Make sure that the hotel understands any special needs

- Alert the catering stuff of any dietary restrictions among your team members

Where Is Your War Room in Relationship to Other Key Resources?

To the extent possible, you want to find a place for the war room that is relatively close to both your office or hotel and the courtroom. Additionally, it is helpful to put the war room close to the key resources that your team will need during trial. Those resources include:

- Adequate transportation
- Supermarkets and other stores
- A 24/7 copy center
- An office supply store
- Fitness facilities
- Restaurants
- Movie theaters, museums, and other places to which team members can escape
- The airport or train station

Is the Location Safe?

Candidly ask yourself, "How safe is this location?" If the answer is "Not very," make the appropriate adjustments to protect your team members, including:

- Move the war room to a different location
- Locate the war room in a hotel
- Arrange for safe transportation
- Find a location that provides extra security at night

Appendix A, Chapter 7:
How to Manage Your War Room

The Sergeant Major's Duties

- Scheduling and coordination
- Care and feeding of the troops
- Calling and scheduling daily team meeting
- Identifying and contacting vendors

(See Appendix A, Chapter 4, for the ideal Sergeant Major's characteristics and skills.)

Daily Meetings

Perhaps the most important protocol in a war room is holding a daily debriefing, shortly after court closes.

Agenda for the daily meetings:

- What happened today in court?
- What is scheduled to happen tomorrow in court?
- What is on the to-do list for tonight to prepare for tomorrow?
- What is on tap for the day after tomorrow?

- What is on the to-do list for tonight to prepare for the day after tomorrow?
- Who is going to do what on the to-do lists?
- What problems, if any, do people see?
- Who is going to address those problems?

Communication Guidelines for the War Room

- Instant messaging (IM) is good for questions that need an immediate response from someone you know is online
- Texting is good for short-burst messages when you are away from your computer
- Email—Remember these key etiquette points to help manage your inbox volume:
  o Stop the "reply all" madness
  o Do not send huge attachments to large groups of people
  o Your subject line is just that: a line
  o Use subject lines to identify your email
  o Remember: It is very easy to misread the tone of an email
  o "Send" means send, so be careful before you hit that button
- Cell phones are not going to be available to you in the courtroom, so keep calls to a minimum during court hours.
- Do not use any social media tools during trial
- Real live talking: We believe that whenever possible the best way to talk with anyone is face-to-face

Appendix A, CHAPTER 8:
How to Set Up Your War Room

Making Reservations for Workspace at a Hotel

Work with the hotel sales staff to get a suitably sized workspace that includes the following features:

- Conference tables or rectangular banquet tables for workstations
- Smaller break-out rooms for focused work, like witness preparation or opening run-throughs
- A clear cell phone signal
- Additional land-line phones, as well as a conference call speaker
- Straightforward delivery and pickup instructions for your vendors
- Real office chairs rather than banquet chairs
- A location other than in the basement or other lower floor
- A location that will not disturb other guests
- A room with windows
- A high-speed Internet connection
- A way to lock the room so that your files are secure
- 24/7 access during your stay

- Prearranged catering
- A liberal cancellation policy

Office Supply Checklist

In addition to basic supplies and office products, pack:

- A tool kit (with a hammer, pliers, several screwdrivers, wire cutters, and both duct and gaffer's tape)
- An emergency kit (including a list of emergency contact numbers for all your staff, plus a first-aid kit)
- Hard copies of local maps and/or driving directions to key services
- An eyeglass repair kit
- Mints and gum
- A small sewing kit
- Plastic storage bins
- Extra bankers boxes
- Extra shipping supplies
- Case boxes and files
- A heavy-duty three-hole punch
- A label maker

Equipment Checklist

- A laptop or other computer for each team member's exclusive use, plus the laptops for use in court
- A printer connected to every team member via a local network, or at least able to accept a connection via USB cable
- A portable copier/scanner or a rented high-speed copier
- High-capacity external hard drives for hosting files on a local network (if you do not have access to files on your home server) and for backing up files

- Flash drives, both for transferring files between personnel and for bringing files to court
- Extra cables (network and USB), power cords, surge protectors, mice, keyboards, and mouse pads
- An LCD projector, desktop speakers, and projection screen
- A list of vendors and their support numbers

Telecommunications Equipment Checklist

- A smartphone for every team member
- A hard-wired, high-speed Internet connection
- A wireless network, as a backup
- A strong cell phone signal
- A dedicated Internet line that is separate from the hotel's line for guests
- Extra-long Internet cables and a couple of Ethernet hubs so you can split the signal from another room
- Extra analog phones in the event of dead batteries or lost chargers
- An extra cell phone charger

Furniture Checklist

- Workstation space of at least 36 inches for each team member
- Comfortable chairs
- Extra tables
- Halogen lamps for each worktable
- Large dry-erase boards
- Shelves and rolling carts

Personal Items Checklist

Consider sending the following items ahead:

- Suits or other dress clothes
- Books or other free-time supplies
- Extra shoes
- Toiletries
- Extra glasses
- An extra empty bag for the things you accumulate while on the road

Snacks Checklist

- Bottled water
- Energy and/or protein bars
- Fresh fruit
- Coffee and tea service
- Candy (of course)
- A limited number of soda options
- A wide range of healthy snacks, such as roasted nuts, trail mix, beef jerky, fruit leather, etc.
- Storage bins specifically for food items

Packing Supplies Checklist

Make sure that you have at least the following shipping supplies available to you as you start to pack up your supplies and equipment for shipping to the war room:

- Cardboard boxes in a variety of sizes
- Bubble wrap
- Packing tape

- Marking pens
- Box cutter
- Packing lists

One sanity-saver: Make one box your "First to Unpack" box. This box should be clearly marked and include these key items that your advance team will need:

- Basic office supplies
- A basic tool kit, with at least a screwdriver, hammer, wrench, and box cutter
- Basic first-aid items
- A hard copy of the contact list for all members of the team, including vendors
- A few snacks (protein bars, mints, gum)
- A packing tape gun
- An extra extension cord or power strip
- Wet wipes to clean surfaces
- Zip ties
- Gaffer's tape (for taping cords down on carpet)
- A hard copy of your master inventory list

What to Do Once You Are at the War Room

- Unpack boxes
- Configure the war room
  - o Identify all attendees and designate their work spaces
  - o Create breakout spaces
  - o Designate storage space
  - o Designate supply space
- Establish the network

- o   If you are working at a satellite office of your firm, have your Sergeant Major begin discussions regarding equipment and networks early in the process
- o   If you are working at local counsel, you will want to have the same discussion with their IT team, but include the following questions:
    - ■   Will you be able to access your firm's servers for file sharing? If not, do they have recommendations on how best to do that, using what they have available?
    - ■   Will you be able to print in color or just black and white? If so, how will that work, in a step-by-step fashion?
    - ■   Will bringing in extra equipment (computers, laptops, printers, etc.) overload their network in any way?
- o   If you are working in a hotel, we reccomend having an experienced IT person arrive with the advance team to create the network
- •   Test your equipment
- •   Stock the refrigerator
- •   Make side trips
- •   Establish relationships with hotel staff
- •   Confirm war room access

When the Troops Arrive

Early arrivals: Trial techs and graphics consultants should arrive in between your advance team and the full war room team, to set up their own networks and workstations and receive any materials they may have shipped. When the remainder of your team arrives set up your first team meeting:

- Introduce the team
- Show people where things are located
- Issue ground rules on ordering from room service and other billing issues
- Provide directions on getting from the war room to the courtroom
- Tell everyone what time to meet before court.
- Plan for who will be in court daily (versus occasionally)
- Introduce the Sacred Whiteboard
- Establish the regular time for the daily meeting and reinforce the mandatory nature of the gathering
- Do another systems check to make sure everyone can turn on their laptops, print something, log on to the home office server, and access the Internet

Packing Up Your War Room

In general, your wrap-up team is going to be the same as your advance team. The wrap-up team will need to complete the following tasks:

- Rebuilding and repacking boxes
- Checking that all items on each packing list and the master inventory are returned to the home office
- Shutting down the network and connections
- Making sure that all rented equipment and furniture is returned to vendors in good condition
- Checking that all personal items have been removed from the war room
- Closing out billing with the hotel
- If you are at another firm's offices, thanking the staff and giving a gracious farewell, so that you will be welcomed back next time

Appendix A, CHAPTER 9:
How to Set Up (and Survive) in the Courtroom

Assessing Equipment Needs

Your presentation equipment needs will vary depending on the venue, the audience, and nature of the event, but no matter what, you must consider a series of key questions.

- Where is the event taking place?
  - Federal courtrooms tend to be large and well funded, and they often have most everything you will need for standard presentations
  - State courtrooms vary widely, but they are often small and old and will require you to bring your own equipment
  - Arbitrations usually take place in confined spaces that were not originally designed for adversarial proceedings, so you will need to carefully consider the equipment you bring along
- What kind of event is it?
  - Who the audience is (e.g., one judge versus a judge and 12 jurors)
  - The degree of formality associated with the proceeding (e.g., a formal federal jury trial versus a less formal pre-trial hearing)

- What you are going to be doing during the event

Equipping the Courtroom

Find out what equipment and infrastructure already exist at the venue.

- o Ask the person in charge of your location about both the equipment and technical limitations in the room
- o Do not take everything you are told at face value; have a tech-savvy member of the war room team go and check it out
- o Manners matter:
  - Be flexible
  - Be prepared
  - Be polite
- o Test the equipment
- Will you be allowed to supplement the existing equipment? If you encounter resistance:
- o Be politely diplomatic
- o Be politely persistent
- o When possible, get both parties to make a single request
- o Show the court the advantages of adopting your suggestion
- o Bend over backwards to accommodate the court
- o Ask if your equipment should be taken down at night

Courtroom Equipment Checklist

- 6½ to 8-foot projection screen
- LCD projector, at least 3,000 lumens

- A backup projector and/or a spare bulb
- Portable projector stand
- LCD monitors for key people in the courtroom
- LCD monitors for the jury
- Two powerful laptops—one primary, one backup
- Speakers
- Video kill switch
- Video switcher
- Video distribution amplifier (DA)
- PowerPoint slide advance remote control
- Laser pointer
- Stopwatch or other easy-to-read timer
- Tech table
- Power strips and extension cords
- A document camera
- Annotation screen
- VGA cables
- Gaffer's tape
- Two easels
- A flip chart with a pad of butcher block paper
- Color markers for the flip chart
- A dry-erase whiteboard
- Erasable color markers for the dry-erase whiteboard
- A digital camera
- A signed judicial order

Setting Up Your Equipment

Getting your equipment into the courtroom and set up takes some time—you cannot just show up at the courthouse 30 minutes before your trial starts and assume you can set up your projector and screen. Once you have called or met with the clerk to find out what you are allowed to bring, you need to:

- **Call opposing counsel:** Presentation equipment is almost always shared by both sides at hearings and at trial.

- **Call the court clerk:** Get permission to set up your equipment and to find out when you can get into the courtroom to do so.

- **Get a judicial order allowing you to bring equipment into the court:** All federal courts that we know of require a written order from the judge to bring equipment into the courthouse.

How to Organize Your Material for Trial

Trial Presentation File Formats

Trial material	File Format / Quality / Software
Documents	PDF Adobe Reader for opening files Adobe Acrobat for creating files 300 dpi
Graphics and photos	Maximum-quality JPEG Microsoft Paint Adobe Photoshop At least 150 dpi for graphics At least 300 dpi for photos
Deposition video	MPEG-1 Microsoft Windows Media Player Resolution: 352 x 240
Synchronized transcript	CMS (TrialDirector) MDB (Sanction) PTF & VID (LiveNote)

Non-deposition video	*WMV, MPEG-1, AVI are best* *Microsoft Windows Media Player for playback* *Microsoft Movie Maker or Adobe Premier for editing* *Original resolution*
Animation	*Interactive: SWF (Adobe Flash Player)* *Non-interactive: WMV, MPEG-1, AVI are best (see above for software)*

Two Types of Litigation Databases

- **The pre-trial database** is the larger of the two databases. It is the repository for virtually everything that you gather in discovery that is related to your case.

- **The trial presentation database** contains the crucial subset of material (culled from the pre-trial database) that you will take with you into the courtroom to use as you present your case to the judge/jury.

How to Assemble Your Databases

It's critical that you plan your database. What seems like a simple solution now may cause a lot of difficulty for you in the courtroom later. Take the time to put guidelines in place for you and your support team before you start building your database to avoid embarrassing or difficult situations later.

- Get your documents scanned
  - What constitutes a document?
  - What exactly should be scanned?
  - How should the files be named?
  - Into what file format should they be scanned?

- Prepare your video depositions; syncing options include:
  - o Hire a videographer
  - o Hire a sync specialist
  - o Do it yourself
- Gather your graphics
  - o JPEG file format
  - o At least 150 dpi
  - o Avoid scanned printouts
  - o RGB, not CMYK
- Gather your digital photos
  - o JPEG file format
- Gather your animation files
  - o SWF file format for Flash
  - o Windows Movie File (WMV) or QuickTime (MOV) file formats for non-Flash
  - o Test animation on the computer that is going to be used to present it
- Gather and convert non-deposition audio and video, such as surveillance video, wiretaps, videos of conferences, and site surveys
- Gather and convert materials in out-of-date media formats, such as VHS, Beta, floppy disks, LaserDiscs, MiniDiscs, cassette tapes, and microfiche
- Make a plan for displaying websites
  - o Replication
  - o HTML files
  - o Internet connection in the courtroom
  - o Wireless card

Organizing Your Trial Presentation Database

The first step before adding anything to a database is to create a plan for how to organize and label the incoming material. That plan includes:

- Using consistent naming conventions
- Choosing a date format
- Adding exhibit numbers with leading zeros
- Creating just one document database

Name your documents in a way that allows for easy call-up at trial.

- In your pre-trial database, documents are usually identified by Bates number, but it is better to name your documents in your presentation database by trial exhibit number.
- Rename your documents in one of two ways:
  - The first is to print out the trial exhibits, apply exhibit stickers, scan them and name the resulting files by their exhibit numbers
  - If you want to skip the step of printing and scanning, you can add a trial exhibit field to the documents in your pre-trial database, then export the trial exhibits and have the software name the files by the exhibit number field.
- Branding your exhibits: "Brand" each page of your exhibits with its exhibit and page number to allow attorneys to call up a page in the middle of a document that may not have page numbers

Non-Digital Materials

- **Actual documents.** The logistics team will need to assemble hard copies of certain documents for the courtroom.

- **Physical evidence.** You may have some old-fashioned, non-digital, just plain physical evidence. Arrange with a messenger service to get it into the courtroom. Make sure you can get the evidence past security. That may require a court order.

- **Exhibit boards.** Consider the following when contemplating using a board in court:
  - Image quality
  - Size
  - Material: foam-core or GatorBoard
  - Printing schedule
  - Display easels
  - Transportation of the board to court

Appendix A, CHAPTER 11:
How to Deal With Costs

Types of Spending Plans

No holds barred

Admittedly, these are rare and tend to fall into the patent or corporate grudge-match types of trials. Not too many attorneys come across these types of cases or war rooms, but if you do, keep these two guidelines in mind:

- An unlimited budget does not trump forethought
- Bigger is not always better

Medium, not mediocre

The teams that work these cases go to trial a lot and have developed specific skill sets to keep costs in check and war rooms functioning. What they do that is different than the big budget teams:

- Define things as "need versus want"
- Define roles clearly and early
- Understand the "fast, cheap, or easy . . . pick two" principle
- Plan early
- Understand that some small luxuries are necessary
- Follow through on policies
- Provide catering to their team

Small, but *mighty*

How do you make a small, budget-conscious war room happen? Start with the things that medium-sized teams do (plan early, define roles, use the "need vs. want" principle, etc.) and then add:

- Thinking outside the box
- Working digitally as much as possible
- Keeping people on call, not necessarily onsite
- Considering purchasing rather than renting
- Asking about long-term rental rates

Budget Basics

Things to think about before developing your budget include:

- How many people, ideally, you would have on your team and what roles they will play
- What equipment you will need to accomplish what you want to do, in both the war room and in the courtroom
- What other needs your team will have such as travel, lodging, freight, meals, rental cars, etc.
- Regional variation in prices

Options for reducing your spending plan:

- Alter the structure of your team
- Consolidate equipment where possible
- Go mid-range on the hotel
- Have one person manage all travel
- Use a company credit card
- Pay your invoices on time
- Do not be penny-wise and pound-foolish

Putting Your Budget Into Action

Issues you want to discuss with your Sergeant Major include:

- Does the client have a spending limit or tolerance threshold for updates?
- Are there companies you should or should not patronize due to client contractual obligations?
- What about spending details and invoicing requirements?
- What is the plan for unexpected urgent matters?
- Consider adding a 20 percent "CYA" amount to your estimate

Keep the Client Well Informed

- Document billing practices and requirements early in the relationship
- Keep your client informed of costs periodically; a surprised client is (almost always) an angry client
- Send updates via email

Appendix B:
Golden Binder Sample

Table of Contents

Contacts

Legal Team

Consultants

Expert Witness

IT

Hotel Services

Local Services

Other

War Room Specifics

Network Setup

Access and Passwords

Master Shipping Inventory

Outbound Shipping

Large Format Board Printing

Large Volume Copying

Equipment Vendors

Equipment Rental Agreements

Workspace Rental Contract

Courtroom Information

Courthouse Contacts

Opposing Counsel

Courtroom Layout

Courtroom Schedule

Local Rules

Courtroom Equipment Rental Agreement

Travel Information

Travel Outlines

Local Maps

Travel Guidelines

Expense Guidelines

Hotel Contract

Legal Team Contacts

Name:	**Joseph Atlaw, Esq.**		
Address:	1234 Main Street, Anytown CA 45678		
Home:	(123) 555-7890	Email:	jatlaw@anyfirm.com
Work:	(123) 555-5642	Email:	josephatlaw@anymail.com
Mobile:	(123) 555-1547	Birthdate:	January 1, 1962

Emergency Contact: Elizabeth Atlaw, Wife @ (123) 555-9645, cell

Name:	**Sarah T. Lai, Esq.**		
Address:	5678 Central Street, Anytown CA 45678		
Home:	(123) 555-8974	Email:	slai@anyfirm.com
Work:	(123) 555-6523	Email:	sarah.lai@anymail.com
Mobile:	(123) 555-7631	Birthdate:	August 14, 1971

Emergency Contact: Jonathan Lai, Brother @ (123) 555-2348, home

Name:	**William "Bill" Henderson, Esq.**		
Address:	8956 South Market Street, Anytown CA 45678		
Home:	(123) 555-8961	Email:	whenderson@anyfirm.com
Work:	(123) 555-9824	Email:	wildbillhenderson@anymail.com
Mobile:	(123) 555-3475	Birthdate:	June 23, 1964

Emergency Contact: Michael Johnson, Partner @ (123) 555-5641, cell

Name:	**Ann Smith, Paralegal**		
Address:	754 Elm Way, Anytown CA 45678		
Home:	(123) 555-6428	Email:	asmith@anyfirm.com
Work:	(123) 555-9328	Email:	iheartbooks@anymail.com
Mobile:	(123) 555-8541	Birthdate:	November 20, 1978

Emergency Contact: Thomas Smith, Husband @ (123) 555-4268, cell

Name:	**Marshall Powers, Paralegal**		
Address:	6589 Palmetto Drive, Anytown CA 45678		
Home:	(123) 555-6897	Email:	mpowers@anyfirm.com
Work:	(123) 555-6587	Email:	M_Powers@anymail.com
Mobile:	(123) 555-6389	Birthdate:	September 17, 1975

Emergency Contact: Jennifer Williams, Partner @ (123) 555-1547, cell

Name:	**Marina Nicolas, Paralegal**		
Address:	1289 Surrey Street, Anytown CA 45678		
Home:	(123) 555-2548	Email:	mnicolas@anyfirm.com
Work:	(123) 555-6384	Email:	knitwit@anymail.com
Mobile:	(123) 555-4769	Birthdate:	August 2, 1970

Emergency Contact: Mabel Nicolas, Aunt @ (123) 555-5243, home

Legal Consultants

Trial Strategy/Graphics/Trial Presentation

Name:	**The Focal Point LLC, G. Christopher Ritter – Trial Strategy**		
Address:	501 14th Street Suite 200, Oakland CA 94612		
Main:	(510) 208-1760	Email:	chrisr@thefocalpoint.com
Fax:	(510) 208-1761	Alternate:	info@thefocalpoint.com
Mobile:	(123) 555-6895	Notes:	Partner

Name:	**The Focal Point LLC, Michael Skrzypek – Trial Presentation**		
Address:	501 14th Street Suite 200, Oakland CA 94612		
Main:	(510) 208-1760	Email:	michaels@thefocalpoint.com
Fax:	(510) 208-1761	Alternate:	info@thefocalpoint.com
Mobile:	(123) 555-6895	Notes:	Trial Tech

Name:	**The Focal Point LLC, Amie Bailey – Logistics Support**		
Address:	501 14th Street Suite 200, Oakland CA 94612		
Main:	(510) 208-1760	Email:	amieb@thefocalpoint.com
Fax:	(510) 208-1761	Alternate:	info@thefocalpoint.com
Mobile:	(123) 555-6895	Notes:	Production Supervisor

Jury Consultant

Name:	**Gregory Simpson**		
Address:	9586 Broadway, Anytown TX 89625		
Home:	(123) 555-7523	Email:	gsimpson@deliberations.com
Work:	(123) 555-3274	Email:	2angrymen@anymail.com
Mobile:	(123) 555-9452	Notes:	

Expert Witnesses

Name:	**Dr. Saber Datta, Ph.D.**		
Address:	5684 Willow Ave, Anytown TX 86542		
Home:	(123) 555-6921	Email:	sdatta@fancypantsu.com
Work:	(123) 555-8142	Email:	doctorsaber@anymail.com
Mobile:	(123) 555-6895	Birthdate:	June 12, 1964

Name:	**Dr. Phillipa Smythe**		
Address:	87 Pine Ridge Drive, Anytown PA 89625		
Home:	(123) 555-7523	Email:	psmythe@geneco.com
Work:	(123) 555-3274	Email:	ladyphil@anymail.com
Mobile:	(123) 555-9452	Birthdate:	May 14, 1972

IT

Name:	**Jason Landis, Network Manager**		
Address:	5684 Broadway Apt. 207, Anytown CA 45678		
Home:	(123) 555-6853	Email:	jlandis@anyfirm.com
Work:	(123) 555-2875	Email:	onlineallthetime@anymail.com
Mobile:	(123) 555-3687	Birthdate:	March 12, 1975

Name:	**Laurel Hardy, Onsite IT Specialist**		
Address:	8954 Overlook Terrace, Anytown CA 45678		
Home:	(123) 555-8642	Email:	lhardy@anyfirm.com
Work:	(123) 555-6982	Email:	ladygamer@anymail.com
Mobile:	(123) 555-6451	Birthdate:	February 14, 1982

Hotel Services

Name:	**Mary McFallon**		
Title:	Sales Director, Downtown Executive Hotel		
Direct:	(123) 555-6952	Email:	mmcfallon@dtexecutivehotel.com
Cell:	(123) 555-5684	Notes:	Mon–Fri, 8 A.M.–5 P.M.
Fax:	(123) 555-3457		

Name:	**Stephen Smith**		
Title:	Manager, Catering Services		
Direct:	(123) 555-6427	Email:	ssmith@dtexecutivehotel.com
Cell:	(123) 555-8647	Notes:	24 hours notice required for any
Fax:	(123) 555-3457		menu change

Name:	**Molly Mercer**		
Title:	Concierge		
Direct:	(123) 555-6589	Email:	mmercer@dtexecutivehotel.com
Cell:	(123) 555-6421	Notes:	If Molly isn't available, use
Fax:	(123) 555-3457		concierge@dtexecutivehotel.com

Local Services

Service: **Copy/Shipping**

Address: FedEx/Kinkos, 9086 Maple Drive

Phone:	(123) 555-2547	Notes:	Deadline for FedEx: 5 P.M.
Fax:	(123) 555-5684		In same complex as grocery
Hours:	Mon–Sun, 24 hours		

Service: **Ground Transportation**

Address: Yellow Cab Co., 3457 Lawton Street

Phone:	(123) 555-2585	Notes:	We have an account under
Fax:	(123) 555-5234		"Anyfirm"
Hours:	Mon–Sun, 24 hours		

Service: **Dry Cleaning**

Address: Al's Cleaners, 1254 Main Street

Phone:	(123) 555-2558	Notes:	
Fax:	(123) 555-5663		
Hours:	Mon–Sat 7 A.M.–7 P.M., closed Sunday		

Service: **Pharmacy/General Needs**

Address: Bradford's Pharmacy, 9087 Maple Drive

Phone:	(123) 555-3472	Notes:	
Fax:	(123) 555-3473		
Hours:	Mon–Sat 10 A.M.– 8 P.M., closed Sunday		

Service: **Grocery**

Address: Foodmart, 9088 Maple Drive

Phone:	(123) 555-2541	Notes:	In same complex as pharmacy
Fax:	(123) 555-6541		
Hours:	Mon–Sat 7 A.M.–9 P.M., Sun 8 A.M.–6 P.M.		

Other Important Contacts

Service: **Messenger**

Address: Legal Eagle Messenger Service, 1243 South Main Street

Phone: (123) 555-2547   Notes: After hours deliveries available

Fax: (123) 555-5684   Standard: Pickup w/in 4 hours

Hours: Mon–Fri 5 A.M.–7 P.M., Sat/Sun 8 A.M.–4 P.M.   Expedited: Pickup w/in the hour

Service: **Process Server**

Address: You Got Served!, 8764 North 34th Avenue

Phone: (123) 555-2541   Notes:

Fax: (123) 555-6347

Hours: Mon–Fri 8 A.M.–5 P.M., Closed Sat/Sun

Service: **Large Volume Printing (briefs, case files)**

Address: Legal Copy Services, 8654 Main Street

Phone: (123) 555-3472   Notes: Afterhours service available with

Fax: (123) 555-3473   a couple hours notice

Hours: Mon–Fri 6 A.M.–6 P.M., Sat/Sun 8 A.M.–4 P.M.

Service: **Large Format Printing (exhibit boards)**

Address: 123 Reprographics, 8542 South 37th Street

Phone: (123) 555-3472   Notes: Ask for Dave, our account rep

Fax: (123) 555-3473   Files should be sent as pdfs

Hours: Mon–Sat, 6 A.M.–10 P.M., Closed Sunday   Allow 8 hours turn-around

Network Setup

For questions, call IT contact Jason Landis: (123) 555-2875,
(123) 555-3687 cell

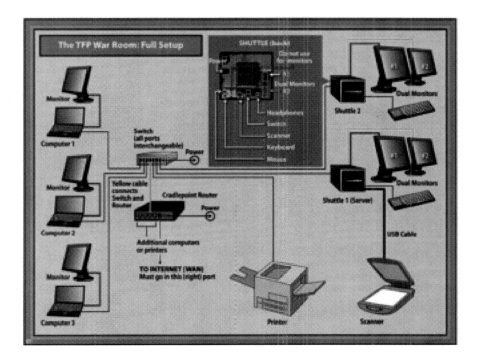

Access and Passwords

Building Access

The war room will be open and available 24/7 through the length of trial. Each participant in the war room will require a security badge to enter the building. Ann Smith will be distributing them to each participant. If you lose your badge, please let her know right away by calling her at (123) 555-8541.

Hotel Access

You will not need anything other than your hotel key to access your room, the fitness center, and the business center at the hotel. If you lose your room key, please see the front desk for a replacement.

Network Access

We will be connected to our home network. Your usual log-in and password will give you full access. If you have any trouble accessing the network, please contact Laurel Hardy at (123) 555-6451.

Courtroom Access

The court is open to the public in this matter, but standard protocols are in place. Please do not bring prohibited items, and keep electronics only to those you absolutely need. Remember: court is a formal environment, and you are representing the firm when you enter the courthouse, so business attire is required.

Master Shipping Inventory

Created By:	Ann Smith	(123) 555-8541	
Box Number	Box Description		Insurance Value
1	Computer hard drives		$2000
2	Monitors		$1500
3	Monitors		$1500
4	Networking equipment		$550
5	Toner		$3500
6	Paper		0
7	Scanner		$550
8	Projector and extra cables		$2500
9	Case files		0
10	Case files		0
11	Case files		0
12	Office Supplies		0

War Room Packing List, Box 12

Box No.	12	Date 06/15	
Created By:	Ann Smith	(123) 555-8541	

Count:	Item Description	Insurance Value	Notes
12	Black Sharpie markers	0	
48	Blue ink pens	0	
48	Black ink pens	0	
36	#2 pencils	0	
12	Black dry-erase markers	0	
36	Yellow highlighters, broad tip	0	
36	Yellow highlighters, fine tip	0	
3	Swingline staplers	0	
2	3-hole punch	0	
5	Clipboards	0	
3	Standard rulers	0	

Outbound Shipping

Shipping Schedule

All packages will be sent via FedEx 2-day.

- Equipment and supplies will ship on Tuesday 06/15 for delivery on Thursday 06/17.
- Please have all items packaged and ready for a shipping label by noon on Tuesday 06/15.

Case-Critical Items and Files

We are happy to ship case-critical or personal items for those traveling to the war room. For budget purposes, we will default to 2-day shipping, unless otherwise instructed.

Outbound Tracking Numbers

- 90890976: Monitors, box no. 2
- 98767302: Network equipment, box no. 4
- 95638290: Office supplies, box no. 12
- 78954632: Toner, box no. 5
- 98763203: Computer hard drives, box no. 1

Inbound Tracking Numbers

Please see Ann Smith for these at the end of the trial if you want to track your package home.

Large Format Printing (Exhibit Boards)

Litigation Print Services
Flat Iron Building
1652 Burgundy Street, Suite 1000
Anytown, CA 12345
Mike Schmidt, General Manager
Tel: (123) 555-4789, Fax: (123) 555-4128
www.litigationprintservices.com
Shop is 24/7 with no additional fee for "after hours" printing

For print:

- Maximum width is 36" by however long
- Can do magnetic boards
- Send either a TIF (preferred) or a high-resolution, sized-to-the-final product PDF with fonts outlined
- Specify ¼" white Gatorboard and dry-erase laminate
- Provide 4 hours advance notice for print and delivery (shop is only a block or two away)
- Send files to both: mschmidt@litprint.com and color@litprint.com

Large Volume Copying

Litigation Print Services
Flat Iron Building
1652 Burgundy Street, Suite 1000
Anytown, CA 12345
Mike Schmidt, General Manager
Tel: (123) 555-4789, Fax: (123) 555-4128
www.litigationprintservices.com
Shop is 24/7 with no additional fee for "after hours" printing

For print:

- Can work with any MS Office file type, as well as Mac, Linux, or Open Office
- Send file formatted to print specs (page break, etc.)
- Specify number of copies you need
- Provide 4 hours advance notice for print and delivery (shop is only a block or two away)
- Send files to both: mschmidt@litprint.com and copy@litprint.com.

Equipment Vendors

Courtroom Equipment

Address: Legal Tech, 2564 Division Street

Phone: (123) 555-2554   Notes: Rep: Henry Stanhope

Fax: (123) 555-5714

Hours: Mon–Sun, 24 hours

War Room Network Equipment

Address: Net/Work, Inc., 5478 Shippley Ave.

Phone: (123) 555-2541   Notes: Rep: Chris Papadopoulos

Fax: (123) 555-6954

Hours: Mon–Sun, 24 hours

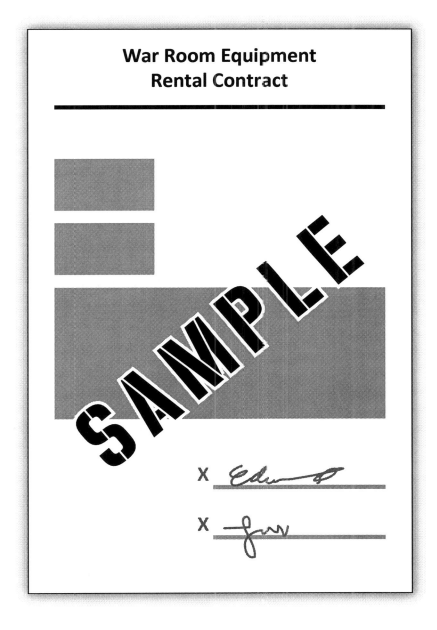

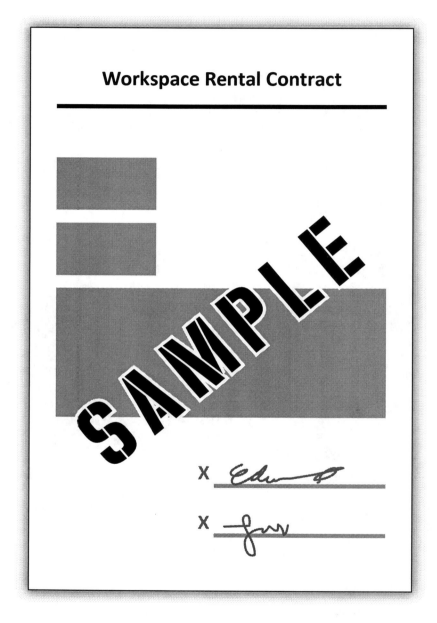

Courthouse Contacts

Courthouse Main Number	(123) 555-0000
Information Desk	(123) 555-0477 ext. 0476
Security (Capitol Police)	(123) 555-0022
Cafeteria	(123) 555-0826 ext. 0827
Law Library	(123) 555-0843
Administrative Office of the Courts	(123) 555-0090
Judicial Information Center	(123) 555-5369
Courts	
Court of Chancery	(123) 555-0515
Court of Common Pleas	(123) 555-0900
Superior Court	(123) 555-0800
State Agencies	
Attorney General	(123) 555-0544
Corrections, Department of	(123) 555-0011
Probation & Parole	(123) 555-0833
Public Defender	(123) 555-0130
Other	
Jury Services	(123) 555-0824
Lost and Found	(123) 555-0022
Prothonotary's Office	(123) 555-0800 ext. 324
Sheriff's Office	(123) 555-0044

Opposing Counsel

Great Big Firm LLP
(123) 555-1254
Lead Counsel: Lawrence Phillips, Esq.
(123) 555-1254   lphillips@opposingcounsel.com
    Assistant: Laurel Mahoney
    (123) 555-5647   lmahoney@opposingcounsel.com

Co-Counsel: Mary Tolliver
(123) 555-6478   mtolliver@opposingcounsel.com
    Assistant: Michael Smith
    (123) 555-5247   msmith@opposingcounsel.com

Co-Counsel: Adam Frith
(123) 555-8794   afrith@opposingcounsel.com
    Assistant: Benjamin Wilkes
    (123) 555-6591   bwilkes@opposingcounsel.com

Co-Counsel: Sandra Bartlett
(123) 555-1237   sbartlett@opposingcounsel.com
    Assistant: Portia Rhyme
    (123) 555-8421   prhyme@opposingcounsel.com

Courtroom Layout

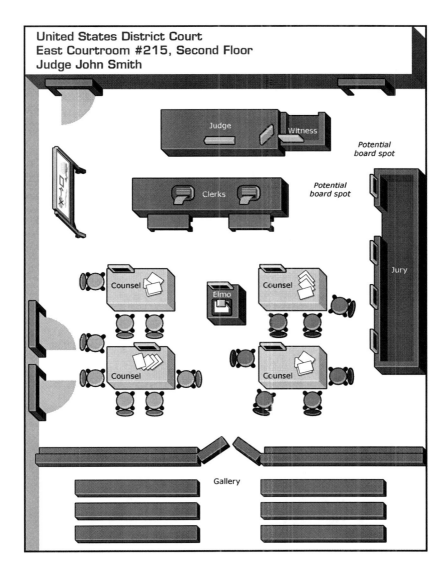

United States District Court
East Courtroom #215, Second Floor
Judge John Smith

Courtroom Schedule

Trial is set to open on 10/18/12, and run for two weeks.

- *Voir dire* will begin on the morning on 10/17/12, and the jury will be empaneled by the end of the day
- Motions will be heard prior to opening statements on the morning of 10/18/12

Court will be in session from 8 A.M. until 3 P.M. Monday through Thursday.

- Court will be dark on Fridays
- There are no holidays that will affect this schedule
- Should trial run long, we can expect to be dark on election day

Local Rules

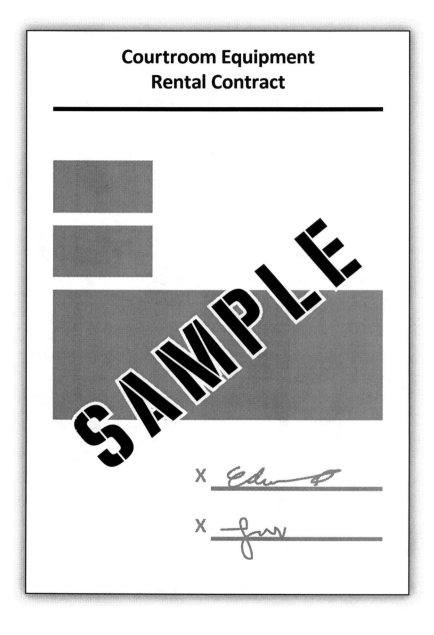

Travel Information: Ann Smith

Personal Information	
Traveler's Name as it Appears on ID	Ann Smith
E-mail	asmith@anyfirm.com
Direct Phone	(123) 555-9328
Mobile Phone	(123) 555-8541
Fax	(123) 555-2355
Shipping address	Any Firm LLP Attn: Ann Smith for Us v. Them 1234 Main Street, Suite 200 Anytown, CA 12345
Credit card used	Any Firm LLP credit card
Case to Bill	Us v. Them
Notes	
Travel Details	
Departure and Destination Airports	LAX to SFO
Departure Date	10/14/12
Return Date	11/7/12
Outbound Flight Info	Virgin America #83, Departing LAX at 5:35 P.M.
Confirmation Number	BH789R
Inbound Flight Info	Virgin America #42, Departing SFO at 10:48 A.M.
Confirmation Number	BH789R
Frequent Flyer Program and Number	Virgin Elevate: 45578
Rental Car Confirmation	Budget, In Terminal: 654879865
Rental Details	Compact car, pick up and drop off same location
Lodging Information	
Hotel Dates	10/14/12-11/7/12
Confirmation Number	TR8976
Notes	Hotel Extended Stay 1248 Main Street Anytown, CA 12345 (123) 555-6427 Main Contact: Trevor Walsh, (123) 555-5472

Directions to Courthouse from Hotel

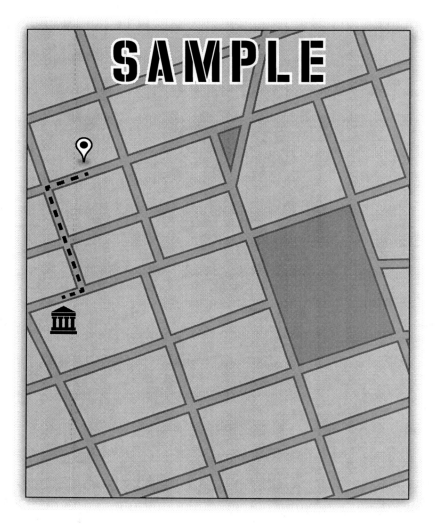

Hotel shuttle will take court team every day at 7:30 A.M. sharp.

Hotel shuttle will pick up the team every day at 3:30 P.M. sharp.

Taxi: (123) 555-2585

Directions to Hospital

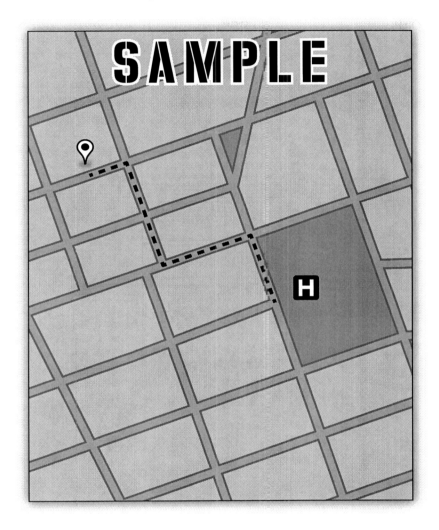

In an emergency, dial 911

Taxi: (123) 555-2585

Directions to Police Station

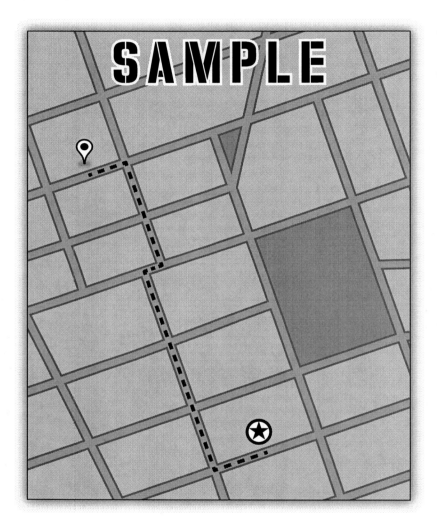

In an emergency, dial 911

Taxi: (123) 555-2585

Travel Guidelines

Ann Smith is to book all travel for Us v. Them.

Airfare

- Ann Smith to book all airfare on Any Firm LLP Visa
- If Ann Smith cannot do, then book your own flight on an Any Firm LLP credit card
- If you do not have an Any Firm LLP credit card, use a personal card and expense the flight

Accounting of Airfare

- All initial bookings will be charged to client/job
- If flight is cancelled and credit is transferrable:
    - First choice—apply refund to credit card if fully refundable
    - Second choice—convert to airline credits
    - Hold credits for future travel on that case
    - If case ends without credits being used, credit reverts to Any Firm LLP travel pool
- If flight is cancelled and credit is non-transferrable:
    - First choice—apply refund to credit card if fully refundable
    - Second choice—convert to airline credits
    - Hold credits for future travel on that case for that employee
    - If case ends without credits being used, continue to hold credit for that employee to travel on another case

- In-flight charges
  - Ann Smith will book seats with extra room (extra leg-room seats or emergency exit rows) when appropriate and available, for example:
    - Coast to coast travel
    - Overnight or "red eye" flights
    - Working flights
  - In-flight meals/snacks are part of your per diem
  - Additional bags required for work and considered extra by the airline are billable, but will have to be paid by the employee at check-in
  - Blankets, pillows, headphones, and baggage are acceptable in-flight expenses
  - All other charges (games, movies, texting, and WiFi) are the responsibility of the employee

Hotel

- Ann Smith to book all hotel rooms on Any Firm LLP credit card
- If Ann Smith cannot do, please book and pay for your own rooms using an Any Firm LLP credit card
- If you do not have an Any Firm LLP credit card, book using your personal card and expense the cost on your next expense report

Rental Cars

- Ann Smith to reserve all car rentals on Any Firm LLP credit card
- Employees will have to use personal credit card to complete transaction upon rental if they do not have an Any Firm LLP credit card

Notes

- Email trail is critical for all initial airfare receipts
- All other travel expenses must be supported by receipts noting who expense was for, purpose, and the case/job

Expense Guidelines

Most expenses incurred while traveling on business are reimbursable. To receive a reimbursement, fill out an expense settlement and submit it—with all receipts attached—to the Accounting Department on the 15th and last day of each month. Receipts for charges on company credit cards must be submitted within one week of purchase. A receipt should be provided for every expense incurred. **You should endeavor to minimize expenses to the extent that this is possible without causing undue inconvenience. If you have questions about whether a cost is appropriate or reimbursable, please ask Accounting.**

Air Travel

- Air travel should be booked by Ann Smith whenever possible
- Our engagement letters outline coach accommodations for air travel; the costs of upgrades to business or first class are not reimbursable
- Any frequent flyer miles or free tickets earned by an employee remain the property of the employee

Hotels

- Hotel reservations should be booked by Ann Smith
- Hotel fitness room fees are not billable to clients, but are reimbursable by Any Firm LLP
- The cost of in-room movies are not billable to clients, but are reimbursable by Any Firm LLP
- Tips to hotel staff are reimbursable and do not require a receipt, but should not exceed what is reasonable and customary
- Any hotel frequent stay points or rewards earned by an employee remain the property of the employee

Ground Transportation

- In the circumstances where a rental car is needed, Ann Smith will reserve
- The gas tank should be refilled before returning the car to avoid excessive fuel charges
- When other ground transport is needed, shuttles or taxis are the preferred method of travel; receipts should include fare, to/from destination and names of passengers
- When parking at an airport for business travel, employees should use a long-term or economy lot

Mileage and Parking

- If an employee uses his or her own vehicle to travel for a business purpose, Any Firm LLP will reimburse at the current federal rate
- Gas, repairs, and maintenance costs cannot be submitted for reimbursement
- Parking charges at work during normal weekday commute are not reimbursable, unless you are traveling that day in your vehicle for client business
- Parking charges at work during weekend case work are billable and reimbursable

Travel and Business Meals

- Business meals are any meals consumed during the course of business, regardless of whether the employee is traveling (this includes late night and weekend working meals)
- A meal can be reimbursed as a business meal only if the majority (>50%) of the time during the meal was spent discussing business issues, or the meal occurred before or after work/meeting

- All meals charged to Administrative, Marketing, and client budgets must be approved in advance (by a Partner)
- When submitting a receipt for any business meal, note the names of the people present during the meal and the business purpose on the the receipt
- For business meals where there are multiple employees of the company present and no partner, an associate should pay the check

Miscellaneous

- If an employee does not have a car to get to the airport, a reasonable method of transportation should be used (shuttle, bus, taxi)
- When travelling in an area where cell phone coverage is not available, employees should plan appropriately by adding temporary coverage to a plan or purchasing a low-cost phone card

Non-Reimbursable Charges

Examples of charges that are not reimbursable include but are not limited to:

- Toiletries for business travel and other personal use
- Dry cleaning/laundry (unless for extended onsite work, more than one week)
- Travel expenses for non-employees, such as family and vendors

Index

Presentation technology support,
54–57
Pretrial databases, 206–207,
Pre-trial hearings, presentation
equipment for, 180–181
Projectors, 188
backup, 190–191
lumens and, 190
Projector stands, 191
Protection times for presentation
materials , planning for, 80
Proxemics, 150

R
Remote support groups, 43, 61
Ritter, G. Christopher, 2

S
Safety, personal, war rooms and,
109–111
Scanning documents, 211–213
Scanning vendors, 211–212
Scheduling, Sergeant Major and,
116–117
Sergeant Majors, 42, 43–45,
115–116
care/feeding of teams and,
117
coordination and, 116–117
daily team meetings and,
118, 126–128
ideal characteristics of,
119–125
protocols/procedures and,
128
scheduling and, 116–117

spending decisions and,
240–241
vendors and, 118
Shipping, considerations for,
162–164
Short-order war rooms, 88–93
Shutting down war rooms,
170–171
Skrzpek, Michael, 2–3
Sleep, 125–126
Slides, defined, 210
Social media, in war rooms, 131
Speakers, 193
Spending plans. *See* Budgets
Staff attorneys, 21–23
Standby people, for war rooms,
40–41
State courtrooms, equipping, 175
Strategic support groups, 43
jury consultants, 60
trial graphics consultants,
61
Strategic teams, 17. *See also*
Logistics teams
coordinating with, 76
determining needs of,
35–36
interviewing, 36–39
Strategy, 10
Support personnel. *See* Courtroom
support personnel; Internal
support teams
Synchronized transcripts, file
formats for, 205–206
Synchronized videos, defined,
211

Trial time frames
  obtaining background
    information, 74–75
  for tasks never too early to
    start, 66–69
  for things to do as soon as
    you know the judge for
    case, 70–75

U

Umbrellas, importance of, 156

V

Vendor contracts, finalizing, 81
Vendors
  scanning, 211–212
  Sergeant Major and, 118
Vendor support groups, 43, 61–62
Venue-level rules, 71–72
VGA cables, 195
Video depositions
  assembling, 213–214
  assembling database of
    potential, 79
Video distribution amplifiers
  (DAs), 194
Video kill switches, 193
Video switchers, 193–194

W

War rooms
  allergies and, 87–88
  communicating in,
    129–133
  communications between
    courtrooms and, 34–35
  confidentiality in, 101–102
  configuring, 165–166
  considerations for, 62–63
  defined, 5, 12–13
  equipment needs and,
    145–147
  ergonomics and, 157
  establishing computer
    networks for, 166–167
  food and sustenance in,
    153–155
  furniture needs for,
    149–151
  green practices and, 106
  guests and, 104
  handling high-pressure
    environment of,
    132–133
  "how" questions for, 15
  items to send to, 139–141
  IT staffing requirements
    for, 53–54
  keeping key personnel in,
    42
  laying out, 83–84
  other key resources and,
    109
  personal distance and, 150
  personal safety and,
    109–111
  planning ahead for, 11
  preliminary questions for
    setting up, 9–10
  running successful, 13–15
  sample layouts for,
    143–144